D1247140

Crossing the Border

Crossing the Border

A FREE BLACK COMMUNITY IN CANADA

SHARON A. ROGER HEPBURN

UNIVERSITY OF ILLINOIS PRESS
Urbana and Chicago

Library of Congress Cataloging-in-Publication Data
Hepburn, Sharon A. Roger, 1966–
Crossing the border : a free Black community in Canada / Sharon A. Roger Hepburn.
p.   cm.
Includes bibliographical references and index.
ISBN-13 978-0-252-03183-0 (cloth : alk. paper)
ISBN-10 0-252-03183-0 (cloth : alk. paper)
1. Blacks—Ontario—North Buxton—History—19th century.
2. Pioneers, Black—Ontario—North Buxton—History—19th century.
3. Free African Americans—Ontario—North Buxton—History—19th century.
4. African Americans—Ontario—North Buxton—History—19th century.
5. Immigrants—Ontario—North Buxton—History—19th century.
6. North Buxton (Ont.)—History—19th century.
7. Community life—Ontario—North Buxton—History—19th century.
8. Blacks—Ontario—North Buxton—Biography.
9. North Buxton (Ont.)—Biography.
I. Title.
F1059.5.N8115H47   2007
971.3'0496—DC22 ·   2007005070

Contents

Acknowledgments

This book has been in progress for many years, more than I sometimes care to admit to. Over those years many people and institutions have assisted me in various ways to bring this project to completion. First of all I wish to acknowledge my sincere gratitude to the Buxton National Historic Site and Museum and most especially to Bryan Prince, who so kindly opened the doors not only to the research materials within the museum but to his own house and private collection, all of which have proven to be tremendously useful over the years. The dedication of the people of Buxton today is truly admirable, and it is their enthusiasm and commitment that makes possible this story of their ancestors. During the initial stages of research, I spend a great amount of time in the Presbyterian Church in Canada Archives and the University of Western Ontario Archives and found both the staff and their collections invaluable to my work. Other institutions whose collections provided vital information were the Chatham-Kent Museum, the National Archives of Canada, the Toronto Metropolitan Reference Library, and the Moorland-Spingarn Research Center at Howard University.

I would further like to express special thanks to several individuals whose assistance proved invaluable in shaping the final product. I owe a profound debt, as well as several evenings of food and drink, to my friend Ellen Goldlust Gingrich, who made time in her busy schedule to read the manuscript in several drafts and offer numerous insightful suggestions. Her careful editing has made this book a much more polished narrative than my own writing skills could have ever created. My sincere gratitude goes to Laurie Matheson, my editor at the University of Illinois Press, for her help and advice in every stage of the publication process. Her patience as I struggled through numerous revisions while fulfilling academic duties and raising a family were much appreciated. I would also like to acknowledge those readers who reviewed various versions of the manuscript and offered their suggestions, often challenging and gently prodding me to broaden my focus and approach. This book is more firmly grounded thanks to their insights. Thanks to Jay Flynn, who worked his technical magic and assisted in the preparation of the maps and illustrations.

Much of the initial research was funded through the Mark Diamond Research Grant from the University of Buffalo, and I am grateful to Radford University for supporting my work through a professional development leave that provided me with the much-needed time to complete a substantial revision of the entire manuscript. I would also like to express my personal appreciation to Ivan Liss, dean of the College of Arts and Sciences at Radford University, for providing a generous subsidy to assist in the completion of this book.

An earlier version of chapter 1 was published as "Following the North Star: Canada as a Haven for Nineteenth-Century American Blacks," in *Michigan Historical Review* 25 (Fall 1999), and is reprinted here with the kind permission of the *Michigan Historical Review.* Some of the material throughout the manuscript was previously published as "Crossing the Border from Slavery to Freedom: The Building of Community at Buxton, Upper Canada," in *American Nineteenth Century History* 3, no. 2 (2002).

Finally, I dedicate this book to my parents, Armand and Meg Roger, for their unfailing support of my education and career, my husband Clarence, whose patience through the years truly cannot be repaid, and especially my two sons, Ryan and Casey, whose lives have spanned the greater part of this project.

Crossing the Border

Introduction

In November 1849, Isaac Riley, his wife, and their two children arrived in Raleigh Township, Ontario, to start their new lives. The Rileys fled Missouri upon learning that Isaac was about to be sold and escaped across the Mississippi River, making their way to Chicago and then to the Canadian border and eventually St. Catharines. There Isaac, who, contrary to the law, had been taught to read by his master's daughter, spied a handbill advertising a proposed all-black settlement in Raleigh Township. Intrigued by the possibilities for cheap land and an education for their children, the Rileys continued to Raleigh Township, camping out in the barn of Rev. William King, the settlement's founder. A few days later, King and fifteen of his former slaves arrived and prepared to take up residence on a 7,000 acre parcel of land purchased from the British Crown and set aside exclusively for sale to blacks.[1]

Together, these men, women, and children formed the nucleus of Buxton, an all-black community roughly twelve miles south of Chatham, close to the shores of Lake Erie in Raleigh Township, Kent County.[2] The community espoused freedom and hope for the future and accepted blacks who were single, married, and widowed; young and old; male and female; freeborn and fugitive. This study chronicles Buxton from its conception and founding through its first decade. A group of individuals, united in their determination to build a haven for those fleeing slavery and repressive legal statutes, formed themselves into a community that offered social and economic opportunity. Overcoming initial opposition from neighboring whites and backed by the Presbyterian Church of Canada and philanthropic Canadians of both races, Buxton grew steadily in population and stature. The settlement became renowned throughout Canada and the United States and even gained some notoriety in Great Britain.

Before the U.S. Civil War, thousands of blacks, both slave and free, crossed the border into Canada, seeking refuge from slavery and racism in the United States.[3] Racial oppression forced blacks—divided by color, class, gender, and background—to unite for protection, companionship, assistance, and development. Blacks could not stem the growth of racial hostility but could survive it by seeking refuge and strength in communities. In response to an increasingly weak position, blacks in Canada and the United States did not exhibit docile passivity but instead built and strengthened their community institutions and community consciousness, protecting themselves from white hostility with tightly knit social and family units. Such communities often resulted from a combination of abolitionist activity and white hostility and existed alongside white society and interacted with it.

African Americans organized settlements in the northern United States and Canada throughout the nineteenth century. Examples are Brooklyn, Illinois, established in 1830 by a group of free and fugitive blacks from St. Louis, Missouri, and central Indiana's Beech and Roberts settlements, founded by free blacks who relocated from Virginia and North Carolina and settled near the fringes of a Quaker settlement, where land was inexpensive and where prospects for good relations with whites were better. Other attempts at organized black settlement were made by Free Frank, a slave who purchased his and eventually sixteen family members' freedom and platted New Philadelphia, Illinois, and John Randolph and Samuel Gist, whose wills manumitted their slaves, and Edward Coles, who in 1819 relocated from Virginia to Ohio, where he freed his slaves and gave each household a small plot of land. U.S. blacks who journeyed to Canada settled primarily in Toronto, London, St. Catharines, and Windsor, where they congregated as communities, and in the rural areas along Lakes Erie and Ontario. Besides Buxton, separate black communities in Upper Canada were established in Wilberforce, first organized by a group of blacks fleeing a hostile racial environment in Cincinnati, and Dawn, which evolved from a manual labor school organized through the efforts of a white abolitionist and an escaped slave. These efforts met with varying degrees of success: Buxton, the Beech and Roberts settlements, and Brooklyn fared well; Edwardsville and New Philadelphia merely survived; and the experiments with the Gist and Randolph slaves, Dawn, and Wilberforce failed.

Although the study of community in African American history has frequently focused on towns and cities, where blacks in greater concentration might find some security, social contacts, and community networks, free blacks often lived in the countryside. Despite the challenges of studying the small minority of blacks who settled in rural areas, they constitute an important area of inquiry. These relatively isolated men and women often felt defenseless against white hostility and had fewer opportunities than their urban counterparts to find marriage partners, to establish families, and to participate in social and religious activities with other blacks. Buxton offered many of the benefits of urban life in a rural setting. Security and solidarity came from residential clustering within the settlement, while the community nature of the settlement, which included religious and educational facilities, provided social contact and interaction. Moreover, Buxton offered blacks the opportunity to own land, which brought at least the prospect of economic independence and perhaps even financial security as a result of independence from external—white—control.

Community, commonly conceived as a site of interaction, revolves around the concepts of locality and social relations; consequently, it requires more than mere numbers. Residents must live in close enough proximity to interact socially and to build core institutions that offer mutual assistance and result in a community consciousness with shared values. Organized black communities may be seen as nascent nineteenth-century expressions of black nationalism and African American complements to midcentury utopian communities. Communal efforts underlying black settlements reflected the humanitarian impulse of that period. A response to the oppressive social and economic conditions that confronted blacks, Buxton was created in part on the philosophy of separation from the dominant white caste.[4]

Throughout American history blacks have turned to migration as a dual means of minimizing racial oppression and increasing control over their destinies. Many blacks settled near the fringes of settlements, where land was often inexpensive, to improve their economic fortunes, and to preserve and maintain threatened ways of life. Founding settlers of the Beech and Roberts communities, for example, came to the Indiana frontier to retain their status as agricultural landholding free blacks. Brooklyn's early settlers were free blacks and fugitive slaves who sought a safe haven from slavery and racial oppression. Wilberforce was the result of increasing racial hostility against blacks in Cincinnati. Similar impulses drove Buxton's founding by free and fugitive blacks—some sought economic or educational opportunities; others were fleeing hostile environments; some wanted to retain their status as property owners; and others desired the chance to become landowners. Seeking to experience freedom, economic opportunity, and a haven from racial tension and discrimination, Buxton residents succeeded in building a separate community through agricultural pursuits based on landholding and by developing churches, schools, and other social institutions.[5]

In the late 1850s, at the height of its success, Buxton had almost seven hundred inhabitants. Although primarily an agricultural community, Buxton featured a lumber mill and brick-making facility that promoted community industry; in addition, the settlement had small artisan ventures such as blacksmith and shoe shops. The town also boasted a two-story hotel, a general store, a bank that held the settlers' modest savings, and a post office. A wilderness had been replaced by a self-sufficient, interwoven, and proud community. Where tall oak, elm, and maple trees once stood, crops of wheat, oat, and corn grew. Log cabins hewn from those trees stood among the fields. All these developments testified to the community's progress. Three schools and four churches served the community's needs. Several graduates from Buxton's school system had entered or would soon enter various colleges to study law, medicine, or theology. Many young Buxton men would go on to serve in the Union Army during the U.S. Civil War, showing their loyalty to and support for both the United States and their brethren in bondage. After the war, many Buxton residents relocated to the United States and contributed to the nation's reconstruction as teachers, lawyers, doctors, and politicians. Despite this population drain, Buxton has survived to this day, although it is no longer an exclusively black town.

Buxton has often been touted as the most successful all-black community established in Canada before the U.S. Civil War. On numerous levels, it deserves such acclaim. Opened in 1849, Buxton remained entirely black until 1860, when its land was officially opened to white purchase; even then, it remained an active black community long after the 1873 dissolution of the Elgin Association, Buxton's support entity. Throughout this period, the community's original mission as a place to improve the spiritual and moral condition of blacks continued, and the settlement experienced social harmony both internally and with the surrounding community.

Buxton's stability and longevity speak for its distinguished success and the firm foundation on which it was established. Buxton stands out not only because it is one of the few antebellum organized black communities that has survived into modern times but also because of its size in both acreage and population. Moreover, Buxton's community consciousness, stable social institutions, and economic independence through landownership gave it status in the broader antislavery movement as evidence that slaves could succeed if they were liberated, educated, and Christianized. Buxton offered a more optimistic picture of black community life than that visible in some of Canada's other organized black communities, including Wilberforce and Dawn, and Buxton life was reminiscent of the life of some rural black communities in the United States.

Buxton's rich history lends itself to the study of several topics vital to the social history of both Canada and the United States, particularly the character of mid-nineteenth-century fugitive and free blacks. Blacks who entered the settlement faced a number of imposing obstacles but rose to meet the challenges. Members of the larger black community generally agreed that the key to the elevation of the black race was self-improvement, an agenda that directly challenged the charge that blacks were innately mentally incapable. Buxton's experience can thus be placed within a larger framework of mid-nineteenth-century reform. The Buxton settlers' story illuminates racial contact between blacks and Canadian whites and as such serves as a window on the immigration and experiences of Canada's pre–Civil War black population. The relationship between the settlers and William King—Buxton's founder, administrator, and spiritual guide—shows the complex nature of white nonslaveholders' attitudes toward blacks. Buxton exemplifies the black community's strength and cohesion, which lay at the heart of Buxton's success.

While most black communities were either the product of black self-activity, as was the case with Brooklyn, or of white philanthropy, as with Gist's former slaves, Buxton's formation and development represented a combination of both phenomena. Buxton's achievements ultimately lie at the feet of those black men and women whose labor transformed roughly nine thousand acres of wilderness into a viable agricultural settlement. Nevertheless, the experiences of Buxton's people cannot be understood without examining the contributions made by whites. Although Buxton was reserved exclusively for black settlement, whites played a significant role in the town's founding, growth, and success. William King, who was largely responsible for the settlement's establishment and who devoted much of his life to it, was white. Most but not all members of the Elgin Association, the business organization that managed the settlement, were white. A majority of the funds raised for the initial purchase of land came from white sources. Moreover, land owned by white farmers and townships inhabited predominantly by whites surrounded Buxton. A white church synod supported Buxton's first church and school. Money from whites in Canada, the United States, and Great Britain helped sustain those and future churches and schools. When the settlers requested substantial loans to support various industrial endeavors, much of the money came from white sources.

Two primary issues concerning Buxton are the degree to which black settlers had autonomy in and control over their lives and how successful they were in exercising whatever autonomy and control they achieved to further their interests. Few mid-nineteenth-century whites perceived blacks as equals, particularly in reason or intellect. Hence, most whites, even those opposed to slavery, assumed that blacks could not be citizens. King did not hold this belief; rather, he desired blacks to take seriously their moral and civic responsibilities as citizens. It is difficult to determine whether King regarded blacks and whites as absolute equals, but he certainly did not view blacks as ineradicably inferior. Many whites believed that blacks could be incorporated into white society only under the most controlled conditions; in Buxton, although there was a certain amount of control over settlers, that control was not absolute.

Blacks at Buxton were not passive objects of King's or other whites' motivations, ideologies, and actions. While the role of whites cannot be ignored, Buxton's accomplishments rest on the hard work and perseverance of the settlers themselves. Despite guidance from King, the Elgin Association, and the Presbyterian Church, black residents formed the community centered on the settlement. Without industrious, responsible, and persistent settlers, Buxton would not have succeeded to the degree it did. It was the settlers who embarked on the community-building foundations that sustained themselves and their families through decades of tribulations. And without the dedication of their descendants, the memory of their lives, struggles, hopes, and achievements might have been forgotten. Buxton's story provides additional evidence in disproving the perception of blacks as powerless victims of white oppression. The actions of Buxtonians attack the assumptions that blacks were passive nonactors on the historical stage.

Racism among Canadian whites has been well documented. Blacks in some regions were denied access to schools and experienced some discrimination in employment, transportation, and public accommodations. But except for segregated education, such actions were not sanctioned by law in Canada, an important difference from the U.S. situation. In Canada, blacks had the basic citizenship rights that U.S. blacks lacked; thus, blacks north of the border encountered less discrimination and prejudice than in the United States and found the freedom they so desperately sought.[6]

Like Canada as a whole, however, Raleigh Township was not devoid of racial hostility. Buxton's settlers faced opposition from local white racists, particularly before the community was established. Yet during the 1850s, Buxton's residents encountered neither extreme nor blatant racial hostility and interacted and cooperated with neighboring whites in a number of important ways, including an integrated educational system and interracial petitions requesting improvements in services from the government. A few blacks eventually held political and government offices, and some served on the Raleigh Town Council and as postmaster. Blacks exercised their voting privileges and affected election outcomes. The local courts were not clogged with interracial disputes, racial disturbances did not break out, and newspapers did not express blatant racial attitudes. This level of racial harmony was uncommon but not unique among black communities and in the broader reform movement.

Kenneth Kusmer recognizes three seminal forces influencing the black experience. *External forces* refer to whites' attitudes, the degree of their hostility toward blacks, and the effect of such attitudes. *Internal forces* refer to blacks' cultural and institutional responses to their circumstances. *Structural forces* refer to things associated with the geographical location of the black community and the wider society in which it was located—the size and proportion of the black community and influence of white culture and community. These forces determined race relations, which in turn influenced other aspects of the black community. At Buxton, these forces worked largely in the settlers' favor. With the not inconsiderable exception of some strong initial opposition to its founding, local white attitudes toward the settlement and its residents were generally benign if not encouraging. Buxtonians developed social and religious institutions that united the community internally. The fact that some of these institutions were integrated worked to develop congenial relations with the local white community. Structurally, Buxton's independence as an all-black settlement in Canada allowed it to evolve into a true community. Buxton, like other all-black communities, offered its residents the fellowship of a majority black population.[7]

This study of Buxton brings to the fore the story of ordinary men and women who struggled to create a community for themselves and their families amid a world dominated by whites. A base on which social history is built is that of historical demography. Family reconstitution through statistical analysis of census enumerations and other vital records allows historians to examine specific families, thus bringing them into the historical narrative. At Buxton, as elsewhere, personal relationships served as the building blocks of community and provided the strength and cohesion of black community life. The story of Buxton is, above all else, the story of those individuals whose sweat and tears were shed making it what it was. It is the story of William Isaac and his wife, Jane Serena Lewis, fugitives who settled in Buxton and raised their family, which grew to include sixteen children. The story of Buxton is that of Henry K. Thomas, who escaped slavery in 1835, living in the northern free states for seventeen years before resettling in Buxton in 1852 with his family. Buxton's story is the story of Solomon King, one of William King's slaves and among the first settlers, who enlisted in the Union Army in 1863. Buxton's story is the story of hundreds of other blacks who, under various circumstances, came seeking new lives.[8]

The historical profession has endeavored to come to a broader understanding of the experiences of American blacks in slavery and in freedom. Early twentieth-century historiography posited slavery as a benevolent institution and blacks as morally and intellectually benefiting from the guidance of their masters. Works by Kenneth Stampp, Stanley Elkins, and others during the 1950s discredited the racial justification of slavery and debunked the stereotypes of slavery as benevolent and of docile slaves who accepted their bonds. The unintended result of that scholarship was a picture of blacks as powerless victims of white oppression. Studies of black communities such as this one challenge earlier scholarship by providing evidence of the collective strength of blacks. Scholarly activity in the history of the African American experience is increasingly exploring the processes through which blacks created and controlled an infrastructure of religious, educational, and social institutions. By analyzing individual parts of the slave and free black experience, scholars strive to explain the whole. Such historical studies stand alone, but they also contribute to the history of blacks in a broader sense. No history is merely of local significance, and all history, no matter how specialized, has meaning within a larger context. This study of Buxton is a small-scale examination of life in freedom in an antebellum community. As such, it focuses on the lives of the free rather than the institution of freedom itself. At the same time, exploring the former reveals much about the latter. In that historical analysis of "the black community" necessitates the study of particular black communities, Buxton can be used to describe the larger free black community. This study is not intended to be a synthesis of U.S. or Canadian emancipation, race relations, or mid-nineteenth-century reform movements, but the work will contribute to the field of emancipation studies and to that of the independent rural black community in Canada.[9]

Chapter 1 will examine the nature of Canada as a haven for American blacks. Chapter 2 turns to William King and his personal journey from slaveowner to founder of an all-black settlement. Chapter 3 looks at how King formulated and carried out his plan to create a community where blacks could improve their moral and social situation. Chapter 4 discusses the complexities of the relationship between blacks and whites at Buxton. The nature of the settlers and the maturing of their community at Buxton will be examined in chapter 5, and chapter 6 discusses the family and community structure at the settlement. The economic lives of Buxtonians is the focus of chapter 7. Strong symbols of the developing community at Buxton can be found in the creation of social institutions, particularly churches and schools, which are the focus of chapters 8 and 9 respectively. Finally, chapter 10 looks at the changes in Buxton during the post–Civil War years and its perseverance over the years

This chronicle of the Buxton settlement from its inception through its first two decades of struggle, hardship, and failure as well as achievement, progress, and triumph re-creates the lives of those blacks who sought refuge in one form or another in the community setting of Buxton. Despite the disabling effects of slavery felt by many of the community's residents, and the sundry obstacles each settler faced, they applied themselves to establishing the social and religious bonds of community. Black Buxtonians formed independent families, carved out an independent living for themselves, built their own businesses, organized schools, and established churches. All these strands of community life had become woven together as blacks in Buxton struggled to achieve the social dignity, economic security, and personal equality that gave full meaning to their freedom. Buxton offered an improvement in economic opportunities, somewhat better race relations, and notably better educational opportunities than free blacks found in most other settings. Buxton served as a training ground for blacks to develop skills that enabled them to succeed in the broader community once they left. Their story illustrates many of the obstacles, tribulations, and adversities facing antebellum blacks. Some such difficulties were overcome; others were not. This is a narrative of struggle, but it is also one of triumph. In an era of slavery, prejudice, social discrimination, and economic hardship, the men and women of Buxton proved their determination—and implicitly that of other blacks—to rise above those adversities and become truly independent and self-reliant.

1

Canada: Canaan or "a Freezing Sort of Hell"

Colonel Samuel Ragland, an Alabama planter, received a rather unusual visitor one day in the early 1850s. The caller was John Rapier Sr., a free black man, and the visit concerned Milton, one of Ragland's slaves. During a recent business trip to Toronto, Rapier had come across some potentially valuable information for Ragland. Milton's brother, Sam, also a slave belonging to Ragland, had escaped some years prior and had made his way to Toronto, where he had acquired a home and several acres of land. A bachelor who had no relations in Canada, Sam had died without leaving a will. The Canadian authorities subsequently put his property, valued at five thousand dollars, in escrow until a legal heir claimed the inheritance.

Colonel Ragland, probably just as Rapier had planned, decided to claim the money, and Ragland, Rapier, and Milton traveled to Buffalo, New York. Fearing that Canadian authorities might not relinquish the property to a slave owner, Ragland remained in Buffalo while Rapier and Milton traveled to Toronto. There, Milton proved kinship to the deceased and acquired the deed to the property, and then he and Rapier returned to Buffalo. Milton and Ragland subsequently went to Toronto to have the property transferred to Ragland, but Milton refused to sign the transfer and declared his freedom by virtue of being on British soil.

Why had Milton not declared his freedom during his first visit to Toronto? The men may have feared that Rapier would be charged with stealing a slave and would consequently lose his freedom and property when he returned to the United States. According to Canadian law, when Ragland, acting on his own free will, took his slave across the Canadian border, he set the slave free. With no legal recourse either to force his slave to return with him or to claim the estate, Ragland returned to the United States minus both his slave and the prospective inheritance. Milton, now a free man, traveled to the all-black settlement of Buxton, where he purchased a hundred acres and married a widow named Agnes.[1]

Milton's story reveals how American blacks viewed Canada as a place where they could live as free men and women. Although the method of Milton's arrival in Canada was unusual, he, like many other blacks, found freedom in Canada. Rapier obviously knew that once on Canadian soil, Milton would be considered a free man, and his freedom would be protected.

This image of Canada as more of a haven than the northern free states may have been more a matter of perception than reality, since by the time of Milton's "escape" most of the northern states offered little hospitality to masters who entered with their slaves. Had Milton declared his freedom in New York, the state's courts would likely have supported him. In 1852 Jonathan Lemmon, his wife, and their eight slaves sailed from Virginia to New York, where the Lemmons planned to secure steamship passage to Texas, their new home. While awaiting passage out of New York, Jonathan Lemmon was served with a writ of habeas corpus to bring before the superior court "the bodies of eight colored persons . . . confined and restrained of their liberty."[2] The slaves were subsequently "discharged" under an 1841 statute that prohibited all slavery within the state. Previous episodes also would seem to have protected Rapier from the charge of theft of another person's property. In 1839 New York governor William H. Seward refused to deliver three free blacks to Virginia to stand trial for helping a slave escape. General theories of comity—courtesy or consideration that one jurisdiction gives by enforcing the laws of another—imply that a free state might recognize a slave's status because the free state valued harmony within the union above its own ideology of freedom. Such was not the case by the mid-1850s, however: most northern states refused to allow even the most minor transit with slaves. The North favored slaves at the expense of their masters and in so doing rejected interstate harmony in favor of antislavery principles. Milton Ragland and James Rapier may or may not have been aware of these precedents, and they may not have wanted to risk Milton's chance of freedom on the whim of the courts. Regardless, they perceived Canada as a safer place of refuge than New York. And Alabama certainly would not have recognized or upheld Milton's freedom on the basis of transience or residency in a free state.[3]

The exact number of U.S. blacks who settled in Canada before the Civil War is unknown. Until recently, the estimate accepted by most scholars was between thirty and forty thousand. A reassessment by Michael Wayne, however, convincingly suggests a more modest figure of around twenty thousand. Contemporary propaganda made the numbers appear much larger, particularly to abolitionists and African Americans. It is significant that historians long accepted—and many still accept—the exaggerated figures. The heavy concentration of blacks in a few localities (such as St. Catharines, Toronto, Chatham, Amherstburg, and

Colchester) contributed to their conviction, although, as Wayne also points out, the 1861 census reveals that the black population was more widely dispersed than is generally believed. More meaningful than the precise number is that blacks left the United States for Canada in large enough numbers to produce in the minds of whites and blacks alike a conception of Canada as a haven for fugitive and oppressed blacks.[4]

The first significant influx of U.S. blacks into Canada occurred during the American Revolution. Slaves throughout the thirteen American colonies saw the conflict with Britain as an opportunity to break the bonds of servitude. Some took advantage of the confusion and lack of authority accompanying the war and escaped, coming to Canada as self-proclaimed free men. Others, also aspiring to achieve freedom, fled to British lines in hopes that the British would grant freedom as a way of hampering the colonial war effort. The escapees' aspirations came to fruition with the Provisional Peace Agreement, signed on November 30, 1782, which provided that refugees who had been behind British lines for twelve months or more were to be allowed to leave U.S. territory. More than ten thousand blacks were among those persons safeguarded by this clause. The majority of them traveled to other British possessions, including Canada.[5]

Canada's function as a haven for blacks was enhanced in 1793 when the Upper Canadian legislature provided for the gradual abolition of slavery by proclaiming that every child born to a slave mother after July 3 of that year would become free on attaining the age of twenty-five. The legislature further declared that no persons who came or were brought into Upper Canada could be subjected to the condition of slavery. The implication—and, indeed, the subsequent interpretation—of this clause, as Milton Ragland's story shows, was that any slave who came into the province, whether brought by a master or fleeing from one, would be considered legally free.[6]

However inaccurately, contemporaries often referred to the subsequent black migration from the United States to Canada as an exodus, suggesting a modern movement similar to that of the Hebrews, who were led out of Egypt into the promised land. Blacks who reached Canada were full of thanksgiving to God for aiding them in their flight and guiding them to freedom. A commonly expressed sentiment was that recorded by one fugitive newly arrived in Canada: "We . . . are out of old massa's reach now. The Lord did help me, and blessed be his holy name!"[7] Such depictions of God's assistance in delivery from bondage played into the creation of an image of Canada as a haven "sanctioned by God" and promoted the exaggeration of the number of blacks who found refuge there.[8]

Slaves incorporated the lore of Canada into their culture, particularly its religious and folklore components. Antebellum black poet Joshua McCarter Sampson expressed such sentiment in his poem-song, "Away to Canada," an antislavery parody of "O Susanna" that concluded with the lines "Farewell, Ohio! I am not safe in thee; I'll travel on to Canada, Where colored men are free."[9] Such a strong association between Canada and the promised land developed that a myth arose equating Canada with the biblical land of Canaan. Many slaves believed that the North Star would lead them to the "promised land" of Canada just as it guided wise men to the infant Jesus. As David Holmes, a Virginia slave who escaped to Canada, testified, "I wanted to go towards Canada. I didn't know much about the way, but I went by the North Star. Heard about that from an old man. . . . He used to point out the North Star to me, and tell me that if any man followed that, it would bring him into the north country, where the people were free: and that if a slave could get there he would be free."[10]

This perception of Canada persisted despite slave owners' best efforts to eradicate it. They disparaged Canada as a "freezing sort of Hell," "so cold that men going mowing had to break the ice with their scythes and with wild geese so numerous and ferocious that they would scratch a man's eyes out."[11] These attempts generally failed; in fact, the harder slaveholders tried to deter their slaves from escaping to Canada, the more the slaves seemed attracted to the idea. According to fugitive slave Samuel Ringgold Ward, the slaves "knew Canada was a good country for us, because master was so anxious that we should not go there."[12] Slaveholders themselves thus inadvertently contributed to blacks' image of Canada as a haven.

Rather few blacks who reached Canadian soil before 1850 came directly from the southern states. Instead, the majority lived in one of the northern states before the search for freedom and economic and social advancement brought them over the border. Despite the abolition of slavery in the northern United States, blacks in the region faced economic, social, and political discrimination from federal, state, and local governments. Using a variety of measures, northern and northwestern states deprived black residents of their legal and civil rights with the dual purpose of discouraging free and fugitive blacks from settlement and of encouraging black residents to leave. These Black Codes included restrictive regulations on immigration, residency, suffrage, military service, education, jury duty, and testimony in court as witnesses. Blacks relocated to Canada in part because of such discriminatory laws, which increased in repressiveness through the 1850s. One of the commonly stated reasons for immigration to Canada was, as fugitive slave John Martin noted, "to avoid the oppressive laws of the States." John Hatfield, another fugitive slave, agreed, stating that he had "come into [Canada] on account of the oppressive laws of the United States."[13]

Among the more restrictive of these laws were the immigration and residency policies of the old Northwest Territory, particularly Ohio, Indiana, and Illinois. Such laws, designed to reserve those states for whites, compelled blacks seeking legal residence to meet onerous requirements, including proof of legal freedom and bonds guaranteeing good behavior. Beginning with Ohio in 1804, the northwestern states mandated that "no black or mulatto person, shall be permitted to settle or reside in this state, unless he or she shall first produce a . . . certificate . . . of his or her actual freedom."[14] Legislation passed in Indiana in 1810 stated that "no black or mulatto person . . . shall be permitted to reside therein, unless bond . . . be given on behalf of such person . . . in the penal sum of five hundred dollars."[15] Regulations in Illinois from 1819 on required all free blacks already residing in the state to present a certificate of freedom to the local county clerk and register themselves and every member of their families. Another direction taken was total exclusion. As early as 1813, Illinois legislated "that it shall not be lawful for any negro or mulatto to migrate in this Territory."[16] Other states followed this example.[17]

The enforcement of these anti-immigration laws varied substantially, but such measures failed to prevent blacks from arriving. Ohio's black population grew from 9,568 in 1830 to 36,673 in 1860. During the same period, Indiana's black population increased from 3,629 to 11,428. Regardless of enforcement or lack thereof, these laws remained on the books, representing a constant threat to the black population and a reminder of the dominance of white society. At any time, local or state governments could mandate compliance with these laws. Such was the case in Cincinnati, Ohio, in 1829 when officials there announced that henceforth they would enforce state laws requiring a bond and proof of freedom. Blacks had thirty days to comply or to leave the state. In the end, this threat of enforcement came to naught, for the government backed down. Nonetheless, a third of Cincinnati's black population decided to leave the United States after this incident, stating that "we . . . must take shelter where we can find it. . . . If we cannot find it in America . . . we must beg it elsewhere."[18] Their decision to leave was reinforced by a rise in racial tension and violence by white mobs. Between three and five hundred of Cincinnati's nearly three thousand blacks subsequently traveled to Canada, some of them establishing Wilberforce, an all-black settlement named for a British abolitionist. Meanwhile, Ohio's Black Codes remained on the books. Blacks living in northwestern states clearly were in a precarious position.[19]

The "free" states limited blacks' lives in other ways. The vast majority of the northern free black population resided in states that either partially or wholly disenfranchised blacks. Many of the older northern states completely denied blacks the vote, while others enacted stiff residency and property requirements, effectively eliminating blacks from the political process. Even as they moved to abolish slavery, New York and New Jersey legislators curtailed black political rights. An 1807 New Jersey law stated that no one could vote "unless such person be a free, white male citizen," thereby closing a loophole in that state's 1787 constitution that permitted blacks and women to vote.[20] In 1821 New York instituted a two hundred fifty dollar bond for voting permits for free blacks. By the end of the decade, fewer than three hundred of the state's nearly thirty thousand blacks were registered to vote. Only in four New England states—Maine, Vermont, Massachusetts, and New Hampshire—did blacks have the same voting privileges as whites. After the admission of Maine in 1819, every state that entered the Union before the Civil War, either in its constitution or by state legislature, confined suffrage to whites. Regardless of the method, African Americans were systematically excluded from the national trend toward more democratic politics and greater popular participation in the political process. Without political rights, blacks' legal status differed little from that of their brothers in chains who lived in southern slave states.[21]

Eligibility for civic duties such as service in the militia was another area in which blacks were deprived of equal rights. As early as 1792, Congress decreed that only white male citizens could enroll in the regular U.S. Army. The northern states followed suit and refused to admit blacks into the state militias. The constitutions of Indiana and Illinois unequivocally forbade the enlistment of "negroes, mulattoes, and Indians" in the militia, reserving it for "able-bodied white male persons."[22] Other state constitutions, like those of Ohio and Michigan, made no distinct reference to race in regard to the militia, thus conceivably allowing for African American enlistment. However, the Ohio and Michigan legislatures subsequently passed statutes that limited the militia to "free, able-bodied, white male citizens," thereby closing the door to the possibility of black service.[23] The Ohio state legislature moved to preserve the whiteness of its militia only a year after its 1802 constitution was enacted. When Ohio revised its constitution in 1850, militia service was restricted to white males.[24]

Blacks faced further discriminatory practices in the area of education. With Massachusetts paving the way, the older northern states set up legal segregation of public school facilities. It is not surprising that the northwestern states also extended their practice of discrimination into education. Ohio officially closed its public schools to blacks in 1829, affirming in all subsequent antebellum laws dealing with education that the schools were "for the instruction of white youth."[25] Separate schools were set up under an 1848 law. Indiana and the other northwestern states did likewise, barring African Americans from common public schools until after the Civil War.[26]

Blacks encountered discrimination in numerous other ways north of the Mason-Dixon line. Black residents in Illinois were prohibited from assembling in groups of three or more and could be whipped for attending assemblies defined as riots. Blacks' legal rights in particular were significantly restricted. In Illinois and elsewhere, blacks were forbidden from bringing suit against white inhabitants. Most free states prohibited blacks from testifying or serving as witnesses in cases involving whites. Of the older northern states, only

Massachusetts allowed blacks to serve as jurors before the Civil War; consequently, blacks in other states could not receive a trial with a jury of their peers and were thus at the mercy of whites. Without the protection of the judicial system, blacks had difficulty defending themselves from criminal accusations or in disputes involving whites. If a white murdered, assaulted, or robbed a black person without a white witness, the victim would be virtually powerless in court. Seemingly at every turn, blacks met with increasingly degrading restrictions and exclusions.[27]

Moreover, racial animosity rose during the 1830s and 1840s. Between 1834 and 1841, a series of major race riots took place in Ohio, New York, and Pennsylvania. Blacks were beaten, and their homes and churches were burned. Cincinnati and Philadelphia were most prone to racial violence, with at least one of those cities experiencing a major race riot every year between 1834 and 1842 except 1837. White racism grew stronger in New York when election disturbances there in 1834 escalated to a riot during which St. Philip's African Episcopal Church, one black school, and at least a dozen black homes were destroyed. John B. Vashon, a respected black leader in Pittsburgh, suffered damage to his residence during a riot in 1839 that was sparked by an interracial fistfight. Four years later, a racial riot in Boston escalated from a verbal and physical attack by white sailors on four black men. Philadelphia was rocked by another riot in October 1849: although the incident lasted only a day and a night, three people died, numerous others were injured, and widespread destruction of property occurred. The northern United States was clearly becoming a less attractive place for blacks to live. The situation became worse during the 1850s, a decade that further disillusioned blacks throughout the North.[28]

Despite their less than ideal—and often less than satisfactory—living conditions, before 1850 blacks living in the northern states generally rejected flight and resettlement as a solution to discrimination and inequality. In debates on the subject, most blacks rejected emigration and colonization as an answer to their problems, adamantly contending that the United States was their home. As a group of blacks living in Columbia, Pennsylvania, stated in August 1831, "Here will we live, here were we born, this is the country for which some of our ancestors fought and bled and conquered."[29]

African Americans particularly reviled the American Colonization Society, which sought to repatriate blacks to Africa and thus, blacks thought, to perpetuate slavery in the United States. According to the abolitionist newspaper the *Liberator,* colonization would "drain the better informed part of the colored people out of the United States so that the chain of slavery could be riveted more tightly."[30] Meeting in 1831, black leaders in New York and New Jersey asserted that "the natural tendency of colonization is to retard emancipation," and two years later another group of blacks announced that they regarded the society "in the same light in which sheep regard wolves."[31] Blacks gathering in Columbia, Pennsylvania, in 1832 saw African colonization as a scheme perpetuated by southern whites to rid themselves of free blacks. And one opponent of colonization argued that if the American Colonization Society's members "would spend half the time and money that they do, in educating the colored population and giving them lands to cultivate here, and secure to them all the rights and immunities of freemen, instead of sending them to Africa, it would be found, in short time, that they made as good citizens as whites."[32]

Opposition to emigration and colonization rested on blacks' complicated conception of their identity as both African and American. The Middle Passage erased national distinctions among Africans, so that the descendants of those who boarded the slave ships as Ashantis and Ghanaians became simply African Americans. Yet they also were never merely Americans, attempting instead to preserve both their racial heritage and their American heritage. W. E. B. Du Bois characterized this identity predicament as a double consciousness that caused African Americans to struggle with "two souls, two thoughts, two unreconciled strivings; two warring ideals in one dark body, whose dogged strength alone keeps it from being torn asunder."[33] Those blacks who ultimately decided to emigrate to Canada or elsewhere found that their identity crisis became more acute.[34]

Blacks also rejected emigration because they did not deem flight from the United States necessary to ensure their safety. Fugitives' primary goal was freedom, and prior to 1850 they could achieve this objective by completing the difficult and dangerous journey to the free states, where lax enforcement of the 1793 Fugitive Slave Law allowed most escaped slaves to live reasonably free of the constant fear of being returned to bondage. Passage of the 1850 Fugitive Slave Law, however, signaled the beginning of a new era for black emigration to Canada.

Designed to strengthen the 1793 law, the 1850 Fugitive Slave Law vastly extended the federal government's police powers by setting up machinery to assist in the return of fugitive slaves. The law allowed no jury trial, no writ of habeas corpus, and no testimony by alleged fugitives on their own behalf. Contrary to a basic premise of the U.S. judicial system, alleged fugitives were guilty until proven innocent and were severely hampered in their ability to prove their innocence. To claim an alleged runaway as their lawful property, slave owners or their agents had merely to present a written or oral affidavit of ownership. The law aided slave owners by rewarding officials with ten dollars if they ruled the accused a fugitive and five dollars if they ruled that he was not. The 1850 law further enhanced slaveholders' power by striking down state efforts to protect the freedom of the accused. As white and black northerners feared, the law essentially deprived fugitive slaves of any safe haven in the northern states and threatened all blacks, fugitives and freeborn, with arbitrary arrest and enslavement.[35]

After passage of the 1850 law, blacks throughout the northern states met to denounce it, declaring, in the words of a Philadelphia assemblage, their sacred duty "to resist this law at any cost and at all hazards."[36] Participants at an 1853 convention of blacks in Rochester, New York, vowed that "that legislative monster of modern times, by whose atrocious provisions the writ of 'habeas corpus,' the 'right of trial by jury,' have been virtually abolished," must be repealed.[37] William Parker undoubtedly expressed the sentiments of many blacks when he defiantly defended his actions in an 1851 riot in Christiana, Pennsylvania, during which he was instrumental in preventing the return of several fugitives to Maryland: "Whether the kidnappers were clothed with legal authority or not, I did not care to inquire as I never had faith in nor respect for the Fugitive Slave Law."[38] Parker; William Johnson, a fellow collaborator at Christiana; and their families would seek refuge on Canadian soil, eventually taking up residence in Buxton.

The passage of this new, more stringent fugitive slave law gave American blacks powerful additional incentive to emigrate to Canada. The *Toronto Globe* reported that within eighteen months of the passage of the new law, three thousand blacks had crossed into Canada. Philadelphia blacks highlighted one of the ironies they perceived in the new law—that is, that "blacks would now be compelled to gain security in the land of a Monarchy which they could not enjoy in this Republic."[39] With good reason, runaways feared that their masters would be more apt to travel north to reclaim their slaves now that the new law mandated government assistance and denied due process. One man who fled to Canada, Nelson Moss, stated, "I did not leave Pennsylvania so much on account of the prejudice, as on that of the fugitive slave bill."[40] Wilson Humbert lived in the northern states for a time after his escape from bondage, but he too "finally left on account of the Fugitive Slave Bill," which he condemned as "a law of tyranny."[41] Frederick Douglass disparaged the Fugitive Slave Law, stating that he saw "the terribly distressing effects of this cruel enactment. Fugitive slaves who had lived for many years safely and securely in western New York and elsewhere were suddenly alarmed and compelled to flee to Canada for safety."[42] While prejudice and discrimination alone had not been enough to drive many of these blacks from American soil, the new legislation was.

In some areas of the free states, the law resulted in what contemporary reports described as a near exodus of black residents. A Harrisburg, Pennsylvania, newspaper reported that that city was "almost deserted of black fellows, since they heard of the new law."[43] More than four hundred fifty black residents of Columbia, Pennsylvania—more than half the city's black population—purportedly left in the months after passage of the 1850 Fugitive Slave Law, heading beyond the reach of the slaveholders' grasp, presumably to Canada. Likewise, Pittsburgh's black population declined considerably, with one observer reporting that "nearly all the waiters in the hotels have fled to Canada . . . and up to this time the number that has left will not fall short of 300."[44] Wendell Phillips, a white abolitionist, estimated that from mid-February to early March 1851 as many as one hundred blacks fled Boston, with most heading for Canada.[45]

Black churches served as a barometer of the law's impact. Black Baptist churches in Rochester and Buffalo, New York, reportedly lost the majority of their members as blacks crossed the nearby Canadian border. Major black churches in New York and New Jersey lost nearly 20 percent of their membership to emigration to Canada. Boston's black churches recorded similar losses: The African Methodist Episcopal Church lost eighty-five members, and the Independent Black Church lost thirty-five parishioners. Construction of a new building for Boston's Twelfth Black Baptist Church came to an abrupt halt when, according to church historian George Williams, news of the Fugitive Slave Law "struck the Church like a thunderbolt."[46]

Many of the refugees relocating in Canada were runaways, yet a considerable percentage—perhaps even a majority, as Michael Wayne contends—were free blacks, many of them fleeing the United States in fear of kidnapping. By denying alleged fugitives the right to a defense or jury trial, the 1850 law increased the danger of abduction. Kidnappers used the new law to their advantage: A person pretending to be a slave catcher could bring a free black into custody as a suspected fugitive slave, have an accomplice appear before a magistrate and claim the suspect as a runaway slave, then take the "slave" south to sell. The possibility of being forced into slavery was enough of a threat to persuade even free blacks that the northern states were no longer a land of freedom. Free black families such as that of Ezekiel Cooper left Massachusetts "to avoid the liability of being seized by the bloodhound man-hunters under the infernal edict of 1850."[47] Cooper and his family traveled to Canada and settled in Buxton.[48]

While contemporary reports described the emigration after the 1850 law as an "exodus," statistical evidence does not indicate such a mass movement. The U.S. free black population as a whole was hardly decimated in the wake of the measure. The U.S. Census recorded the 1850 black population, excluding slaves, as 424,284; a decade later, the number was 476,748. According to the most recent analysis of Canadian census data, fewer than ten thousand blacks relocated from the United States to Canada in the decade before the U.S. Civil War, a considerable number but not enough to warrant the term *exodus*. Nonetheless, the Fugitive Slave Law of 1850 did serve as an impetus for numerous blacks, fugitive or free, to seek refuge in Canada. Even more significant, the legislation clearly underlay the contemporary image of Canada as a safe haven, creating the perception that all the United States was now unsafe for blacks and that true freedom lay farther north, in Canada.[49]

A tangential consequence of the Fugitive Slave Law was its affect on British North Americans. While most British North Americans had previously opposed slavery, most did not actively advocate antislavery sentiments, viewing slavery as an American problem. The plight of vulnerable blacks, accounts of kidnappings and captures, and scenes of blacks being returned to slavery in chains—all highly publicized—worked to create general condemnation of the law and to stir Canadians to action against slavery. Within a few months of the passage of the Fugitive Slave Law, concerned Canadians met in Toronto to discuss American slavery. This meeting resulted in the organization of the Anti-Slavery Society of Canada, in which many of the men who supported the Buxton settlement played instrumental roles.[50]

In addition to the obvious reasons of proximity and a shared language, Canada's image as a haven developed from three fundamental conditions: the absence of slavery, protection from extradition, and the civil rights offered to blacks. Even though historians have commonly concluded that the United States and Canada had few differences in the areas of racial attitudes and discriminatory actions, the evidence supports a more mixed judgment of Canada. Blacks found more freedom and political and legal equality in the provinces than in the United States. Precious rights denied in the United States were available—or were at least perceived to be available—in Canada.

Because many blacks emigrating to Canada were either directly or indirectly fleeing the Fugitive Slave Law, it follows that the most significant explanation for black relocation to Canada was the desire to be secure in freedom. Canadian courts on the whole upheld the principle, established by the 1793 Abolition Act, that regardless of their prior status blacks who entered Canada were thereafter free, and the courts rejected U.S. appeals to extradite such refugees on the principle that accused criminals could be extradited only if the alleged offenses made them subject to arrest in Canada. Because slavery did not exist there, an escaped slave was not guilty of violating any law merely by fleeing from servitude.[51]

In 1819 slaveholders made their first official endeavor to elicit aid in recovering fugitive slaves who found asylum north of the border. During the previous autumn, several Tennessee slaves had escaped to Canada. Discovering where the runaways were, their owners urged U.S. Secretary of State John Quincy Adams to intervene to allow them to go to Canada to regain possession of their property. Adams complied, requesting interposition of the Government of Canada in the matter. Upper Canada's attorney general, John Beverly Robinson, replied that, having taken "the Law of England as the rule of decision, whatever may have been the condition of the Negroes in the [United States], . . . here they are free—For the enjoyment of all civil rights . . . and among them the right to personal freedom." Robinson warned the U.S. government and southern slave owners that in the event of any attempt "to infringe upon [the fugitives'] rights, the courts would be compelled to deal harshly" with the former owners.[52] The Canadian government opposed the extradition of fugitive slaves, a position from which, as southern slave owners were to become painfully aware, it did not bend.[53]

Another avenue whereby slaveholders tried to extradite their runaway slaves was under the pretext that the slaves faced criminal charges before southern courts. This legal stratagem was based on an 1833 Upper Canadian statute that provided for the surrender of fugitive criminals from foreign countries. According to this law, anyone charged by a foreign country with murder, forgery, larceny, or other felonies could be arrested, detained, and ultimately extradited at the government's discretion. This legislation seemed to threaten the freedom of all runaway slaves from the United States first because many slaves had committed such crimes either before or in the process of escaping and second because slave owners might bring false charges to regain their property.

In 1838, however, an Upper Canadian court made a definitive ruling on extraditions arising from the 1833 statute. The case in question involved a fugitive slave named Jesse Happy who stole his master's horse to effect his escape. The court declared that extradition under the 1833 statute was only warranted if the alleged offense was considered a crime under the laws of Canada. The decision implied that any act a slave committed as part of his escape would be considered an act of self-defense rather than a felony. In this particular case, the court ruled that Happy's act was not theft but rather the misuse of a horse. A legal loophole had been opened for fugitive slaves to escape criminal extradition. And, in the end, attempting to extradite fugitives not as slaves per se but as criminals proved little more successful than other attempts to secure the return of runaways.[54]

William Parker's story perhaps best illustrates Canada's position on fugitives. Parker's participation in the Christiana Riot on September 11, 1851, forced him, along with several other resistance leaders, to flee their Pennsylvania homes. Traveling to Toronto via Frederick Douglass's home in Rochester, New York, Parker learned that Pennsylvania Governor William Johnston had officially requested his extradition. Rather than hiding from this danger, Parker appealed in person directly to the governor-general, Sir James Bruce, Earl of Elgin. During the interview, according to Parker, Lord Elgin asked Parker whether he was a fugitive from slavery or from justice. Parker replied that he was a fugitive from slavery, and Elgin sent Parker on his way. As the story has been told through the years, Parker later received a message from Elgin: "You are as free a man as I am."[55] Parker was not extradited. Once again, the Canadian government sustained its pledge to maintain the freedom of those blacks who entered the country's borders. Parker's flight received considerable attention throughout the United States, and his safe passage to and subsequent reception in Canada undoubtedly resonated in the minds of blacks seeking a similar refuge, again bolstering Canada's image as a haven.[56]

Also prominent among blacks' reasons for immigrating to Canada was that, for the most part, the law there recognized blacks as citizens equally with whites. While no law did—or could—erase prejudice, and blacks in Canada certainly experienced discrimination of various kinds, discrimination in the antebellum United States was sanctioned by the laws and the courts, while discrimination in Canada was not. Blacks could attain Canadian citizenship after three years' residency; in contrast, blacks could not become U.S. citizens until after the Civil War.[57]

Antebellum African Americans were aware of the differences between the U.S. and Canadian legal treatment of blacks. Henry Gowens, a former slave from Virginia who settled in Galt, Upper Canada, did so because, "color [was] not recognized in the laws of the land."[58] Another black immigrant, John Moore, admitted that there was prejudice among white Canadians but added that "they have not got the power to carry it out here that they have in the States. The law here is stronger than the mob—it is not so there. If a man insults me here, he is glad to get out of the way for fear of the law; it was not so in the States."[59] Fugitive slave Samuel Ringgold Ward agreed that in Canada, where "prejudice existed it was to be remembered that the law did not sanction it. In any case in which negroes were deprived of their rights on account of the prejudice against them, they had only to go before a court to obtain a just and equitable decision."[60] When a committee in Cincinnati, Ohio, requested information on the condition and treatment of blacks in Canada, a group of blacks responded by noting that "we are compelled to admit that . . . we have to contend with . . . prejudice against color, though it is unlike that which is so formidable in the United States. There it is bolstered up by law—here it has no foundation to stand upon."[61]

Such declarations affirmed the image of Canada as less oppressive than the United States and thus encouraged immigration. The American Society of Free Persons of Colour supported migration to Canada because "under [the Canadian] government no invidious distinction of colour is recognized, but there we shall be entitled to all the rights, privileges, and immunities of other citizens."[62] The *Provincial Freeman,* a Canadian black newspaper, urged blacks to "leave Yankeedom with [its] disenfranchisement and oppression" and settle "in a land of impartial laws and a Constitution having no distinctions of color."[63] In 1863 Samuel Gridley Howe, a white reformer and abolitionist who interviewed one hundred blacks then living in Canada, reported that the standard reply to his inquiry about why they had fled to Canada was the Canadian legal system. Representative of those interviewed was John Shipton of London, Canada, who remarked that "the prejudice here would be a heap worse than in the States, if it were not that the law keeps it down."[64]

Canadian law did not distinguish between blacks and whites in areas such as testifying in court, serving on juries or in the military, access to public accommodations, and voting. Moreover, Canadian law protected blacks against criminal acts, an important difference from the United States. In 1854 the *Provincial Freeman* reported that a white Canadian received the death penalty after being convicted of association with an attempt to kill a black man. "Would this have happened in the United States?" the editors asked. Their answer: "No! No! Even if he had dealt the blows he would have gotten a light prison term."[65] During local militia day in St. Catharines in 1852, a disagreement between two militia groups, one black and the other white, led to a riot that resulted in the injury of several blacks and damage to black-owned property. After peace was restored, many white rioters were arrested, and the property was repaired at their expense. This largely color-blind legal system meant that when faced with prejudice and discrimination, blacks in Canada had recourse to the legal system, a resource that U.S. blacks generally lacked. Citizenship and legal equality reinforced black perceptions that Canada was at least a relative haven.[66]

Furthermore, when confronted with de facto racism, Canadian blacks frequently took vigorous action. In 1854 the drivers of public coaches owned by two hotels in St. Catharines refused to accept black passengers. Local blacks met to protest the discriminatory practice and to develop a strategy to end it. At the meeting, black waiters employed at the two hotels resolved to effect a work stoppage until blacks were allowed to ride in the coaches. The boycott had the desired effect. Within a month, the owner of one of the hotels relented, and the other followed suit shortly thereafter. Similarly, in 1857 in Kent County, Edwin Larwill, a member of the provincial parliament and an avowed racist who, in a reelection campaign, openly called for restrictions on black immigration and for other discriminatory legislation, was defeated. His successful opponent, Archibald McKellar, had clear sympathies toward blacks and owed his victory at least in part to the votes of local blacks, including roughly three hundred Buxton residents.[67]

Participation in the Canadian political process presented blacks with opportunities virtually unknown in the United States. Among the political rights Canadian law protected—and the one blacks most prized not only for itself but as a sign of their legal equality—was the right to vote. The ballot was the enforcement clause of black democracy in Canada, for without the political voice they exerted through the vote, blacks had little protection from racist political officials bent on restricting equality. The ultimate emblem of democratic expression, the franchise was particularly significant for former slaves. Voting symbolized not only freedom but also the rise from the dehumanization of slavery. Canada mandated that black males must attain the age of twenty-one and meet a three-year residency requirement before they could vote, but the same qualifications were required of white males. (Women, of course, did not possess the franchise.)

When whites attempted to deprive blacks of their right to vote, they failed. In 1851 whites in Gosfield, Essex County, forcefully drove black voters from the polls. This temporary disfranchisement, however, lasted only a few hours, until blacks found a local judge who promptly ordered their voting rights restored. The next year, whites in Colchester, Kent County, declared that blacks would no longer be able to vote in that township. Once again, local blacks appealed to the Canadian judicial system. Not only did the court affirm their right to vote, but the chairman of the would-be disfranchisers' meeting received a brief jail term.[68]

Although Canada's legal system was largely color-blind and blacks participated in various aspects of the political and judicial process, equality under the law was imperfect. In one type of case, in fact, the law was frequently used against blacks. Legislative sanctioning for separate schools based on race came in 1850 when the Upper Canadian government passed the Common School Act, which provided for but did not mandate the establishment of separate schools on the basis of race. Even before passage of this act, whites in localities throughout Canada had used a variety of strategies to deny blacks their legal right to attend local public schools, frequently gerrymandering school districts or declaring local common schools private.

Blacks tenaciously tried to protect their right to education, and as in other areas of life in Canada, their record of success was mixed. After their parents protested to Governor-General Charles Metcalfe, black children in Hamilton gained access to the common schools. Meanwhile, in 1846, black citizens of Amherstburg unsuccessfully sought redress when their children were barred from the common school. The Amherstburg school trustees' ruling to forbid blacks access to the public schools was not overturned. Although attempts to protect blacks' educational rights did not always succeed and segregated education was practiced in some localities, no national law sanctioned separate educational facilities in Canada before 1850.[69]

The 1850 Common School Act legislated that any group of twelve black families could request that the local public school trustees establish separate educational facilities for them. Read literally, the 1850 act allowed black parents to choose to send their children to the common schools with white children or to have separate schools for their children maintained from the public school fund. Such wording made it easier for white Canadians to profess a lack of prejudice. It seemed that separate schools would be established only when blacks requested them.

Ostensibly intended to protect the rights of black parents and their children, the 1850 act frequently had the opposite effect. Officials often interpreted it to mean that whites could establish segregated schools without the request and even against the wishes of black families, and then require black children to attend the separate schools. Egerton Ryerson, appointed superintendent of education in 1844, established this principle when he responded to a white school trustee from Malden who explained that the separate black school there had fallen into disuse and local blacks were demanding access to the common school. The trustee inquired what course of action to take. "The Trustees," replied Ryerson, "are not required by law to admit into the public school the children of persons . . . for whom a separate school has been established."[70]

Failing to obtain satisfaction from the superintendent of education, some blacks sought redress through the judicial system. In November 1852 Dennis Hill, a black man who owned three hundred acres of land near Dresden, petitioned the local court that, as a property owner and a taxpayer, he was entitled to have his children educated at a public school. Local whites invoked the Common School Act and refused to admit his children to the common public school. Hill then brought suit against the town but received no relief when the case reached John Beverly Robinson, chief justice of Upper Canada. Robinson's decision in essence sanctioned segregation of educational facilities, asserting that once a separate school had been established in a township, blacks had no choice but to attend the separate school regardless of its quality, its location, or their wishes. Although integrated schooling was accepted in some areas, separate education based on race became the norm throughout Canada, as it was throughout the United States.[71]

White Canadians' racial attitudes constituted another inducement for U.S. blacks to move north. Though they could and did manifest prejudice and practice discrimination, white Canadians on the whole did not evince the same degree of racial animosity toward blacks as did white Americans. Even the discriminatory actions some blacks experienced did not negate U.S. and Canadian blacks' image of Canada as a place where they confronted less racist attitudes and fewer acts of discrimination.

Numerous blacks commented on the free and open society they encountered in Canada. The Reverend Jehu Jones, a black Lutheran clergyman who settled in Toronto in 1839, was struck by the apparent lack of prejudice there, stating that Upper Canada "seems to invite colored men to settle down among the people, and enjoy equal laws. . . . Here [blacks] can mingle in the mass of society without feeling of inferiority; here every social and domestic comforts can be enjoyed irrespective of complexion."[72] Thomas H. Jones, who was born a slave in North Carolina but gained his freedom in 1849 by stowing away on a ship headed for New York City, later settled in Canada, where he found "a home of refuge, full of true, warm, generous, Christians, whose hearts abounding with the love of God are full of sympathy."[73]

The liberality of Canadian laws and various individuals' favorable appraisal of racial attitudes notwithstanding, black people resident in Canada did experience prejudice and discrimination from Canadians. Black and white contemporaries described numerous scenes in which blacks were denied seating on trains, steamers, and carriages as well as rooms at inns and service at eating establishments. Francis Henderson, who escaped slavery in 1841, wrote a narrative in which he described several instances in which he suffered discrimination at hotels. Similarly, according to Ward, "in many cases a black person travelling, whatever may be his style and however respectable his appearance, will be denied a table at a [hotel], at a country inn, or on a steamer."[74] Ward himself had been the victim of such discrimination. Nevertheless, Ward believed that the prejudice in Canada was not as pervasive as that in the United States.[75]

Canada's reputation as a land of freedom and opportunity emerged from antislavery legislation such as the 1793 Abolition Act of Upper Canada, from the reluctance of Canadian courts to extradite fugitive slaves, and from Canada's political and legal system, which generally made little distinction between black and white. In practice, not all American blacks who resettled in Canada found the personal freedom they sought, and they did experience racial intolerance, not all of which was satisfactorily redressed through legal means. Although Canada's image as the promised land had some substance, it was not a utopia for blacks. And yet if the promised land did not fulfill all expectations, it satisfied enough for thousands of blacks—fugitive and free, young and old, single and married—to flee the United States and make their way north.

Past scholarly works have portrayed the emigration from Canada after the Civil War as a mass movement and as evidence that Canada was far from the haven that blacks desired. In reality, as Michael Wayne has skillfully demonstrated, not even a majority of Canada's blacks left for the United States after the war. The Canadian census counted approximately 13,500 blacks in 1871.[76] Projecting a probable 1861 black population of around 20,000, the black population of Canada decreased by just under 33 percent from 1861 to 1871, a substantial but not overwhelming decline. Furthermore, those who left Canada may not have done so because of an intolerable situation in Canada but rather because they desired to return to their homeland, to the place they had once fled but now where much of the intolerable circumstances of slavery, including the Fugitive Slave Law, had been removed.[77]

Blacks who considered leaving the United States during the first half of the nineteenth century faced a formidable decision. The difficulty of weighing various characteristics of the northern United States versus those of Canada or other places, and making such an enormous life decision, shows the power of blacks' determination to be self-sufficient. At some point in their lives, every black man and woman, slave or free, faced the need to weigh the choices, select a course of action, and act on that decision. Many blacks reached the same conclusion as Williamson Pease, an escaped slave from Maryland who made his way to Canada: "There is some prejudice here ... but it has not the effect that it has in the States, because here the colored man is regarded as a man, while in the States he is looked upon as more a brute." For the roughly twenty thousand blacks who traveled to Canada and for countless others who remained in the United States, Canada, despite its limitations, was the promised land. Whether they followed it to Canada or just gazed at it in the night sky, the North Star held the image of Canada and freedom.[78]

2

The Reverend William King

Though once a slave owner, William King grew to deplore the institution of slavery and sought to reverse what he believed to be its harmful effects on blacks' social and moral condition. While contemporary and historical opinions of King and his involvement with the Buxton settlement vary, a consensus has arisen that without King's seemingly boundless energy and support for the settlement, Buxton would not have achieved the success and renown that it did. Truth be told, without King it would not have existed at all. He conceived the idea, visualized the concept and mission of the community, obtained government and public support, raised the necessary funds and arranged for the purchase of the land, directed the settlers' early religious and educational instruction, and managed the settlement's business. Throughout its existence, King was a vital part of Buxton.

The youngest of seven children, William King was born on November 11, 1812, on his family's farm near Newton-Limavady in Londonderry, Ireland. Five generations earlier, the family patriarch had settled in Northern Ireland after leaving England during the reign of the Prince of Orange. William's mother, Elizabeth Torrence, was of Scottish ancestry. Her family had emigrated from Scotland during the persecution under Charles II. Both families were of modest Presbyterian farming stock.[1]

King's education greatly influenced his adult life, especially the ideology behind Buxton's creation and his relations with its residents. Between the ages of six and thirteen, William attended a public school run by a Roman Catholic described by King as "a good classical scholar but of a hasty and violent temper [who] would sometimes beat the scholars unmercifully for the most trifling offence."[2] From this tyrannical disciplinarian, King claimed to have learned the fine points of authoritarian education. King later became known as an extreme enforcer of his own moral code, which apparently derived largely from this early example. In 1826 King enrolled in the Presbyterian academy at Colraine, near his family's country home, to study the classics in preparation for college. During his second year there, while under the guidance of Rev. James Bryce, William made an open profession of faith in Christ and formally joined the Presbyterian Church. On this occasion, King later wrote, he vowed to become a minister.[3]

With this goal in mind, King finished his studies at Colraine Academy, journeyed to Scotland, and in the fall of 1830 entered the University of Glasgow, graduating with honors in 1833. His plans to enter divinity school directly from the university were cut short when his family decided to emigrate to the United States, persuaded in part by propaganda promising abundant cheap and rich land. The timing could hardly have been better for the family. The Kings' potato crop that year was plentiful and of high quality, while the American crop was poor. Sent as the family emissary to prepare the way for settlement in the new land, William boarded the ship *Dorothy* in May 1833 and, with the ship's cargo hold filled with the family's potatoes, journeyed to Philadelphia.[4]

After selling the potatoes for a substantial sum, King traveled to New York, where he waited for the rest of his family, which arrived in September. While the new immigrants remained in New York, William was again sent ahead, this time as point man to find a suitable site for settlement. William spent the winter of 1833–1834 in Northfield, Ohio, about twenty miles southeast of Cleveland, visiting Bryce Hunter, an acquaintance from the University of Glasgow. King was impressed by the area's agricultural prospects and recommended the site to his family. Relying on his assessment, the Kings established residence in the farmlands southwest of Cleveland.[5]

In fall 1835, after seeing his family established in Ohio, King headed south to pursue a teaching career. He spent the next several years in Natchez, Mississippi, tutoring local planters' sons on the plantation of Colonel Solomon M. Brian. Here King first earned his reputation as a strict disciplinarian. In January 1836, barely two months after taking up his new duties, one of the seven boys under his tutelage quarreled with a schoolmate, striking him on the head and nearly breaking his skull. King announced that the offender was to be thrashed, sending a clear message that such conduct would not be tolerated. Enraged that King was going to "treat his boy as he was in the habit of treating his slaves," the boy's father removed his children from the school.[6] Rather than discrediting King or removing him from his position, Colonel Brian backed the tutor. In an outcome surprising to King, the school grew after the incident, reaching forty scholars by the end of the first year. According to King, the episode enhanced his reputation: "My name was getting up as an excellent teacher, and for governing bad boys, several boys that the teachers could do nothing with at the College came to me and I had no trouble with them."⁷ This reputation as a strict disciplinarian would follow King for the rest of his life.

In 1840 King left Natchez and headed to Jackson, Louisiana, to serve as rector of Mathews Academy. Situated in the parish of East Feliciana, twelve miles from the Mississippi River, Mathews Academy catered to male children of affluent local planters. More than two hundred pupils studied Latin, Greek, French, and other subjects meant to prepare them for either a collegiate course or for the gentlemanly planter life. The following year, Mathews Academy was united with the nearby preparatory school for Louisiana College and King became superintendent of this combined institution.⁸

During his tenure at Mathews Academy, King transformed the school on the monastic model of his childhood educational experiences. He instilled an exhausting regimen of highly structured time for prayers, classes, study, food, and sleep that left precious few moments for the rambunctious activities to which southern males were accustomed. In a society that often equated manliness, chivalry, and honor with military machismo, King took away his students' "toys": an assortment of pistols, shotguns, rifles, bowie knives, daggers, and stilettos. Violators of his weapons ban received automatic dismissal. King clearly believed in order, respect, and discipline.⁹

On January 10, 1842, William King married Mary M. Phares, the daughter of a local planter. King's marriage connected him personally with slavery, an institution he claimed to disdain. According to Louisiana law, a wife's dowry became her husband's property upon marriage, and Mary's dowry included two female slaves, Amelia, Mary's mammy, and Eliza, her childhood companion. Although he at first resolved to have nothing further to do with slavery, King entered the ranks of slave owners in his own right on February 1, purchasing a slave named Talbot to assist in the domestic duties associated with the running of the academy. Shortly thereafter, King acquired two additional slaves for the same purpose.¹⁰

An extremely religious man, King opposed in principle the idea of human bondage. He saw Christianity and slavery as incompatible, remarking that "the morals connected with the system were such that it [could] not exist with Christianity[;] it would destroy Christianity or Christianity would destroy it."¹¹ Before emigrating to the United States, King had been a theoretical abolitionist. In his childhood and young adulthood, he had come into contact with the growing British abolitionist crusade, reaching the personal conclusion that the enslavement of other human beings was morally and ideologically wrong. While attending Glasgow University, King had participated in a winter 1831 series of antislavery lectures and debates that King later credited with persuading him that "the evils of the system . . . bore as heavily on the white families as on the black."¹² Although he departed Glasgow in 1833, King may have been active in the initial movement that led to the establishment that year of the Glasgow Emancipation Society, part of the British movement to abolish slavery in the United States. Moreover, King's tenure at the University of Glasgow coincided with that of James McCune Smith, a black American studying medicine. Although King did not mention Smith in his autobiography or other writings, it seems unlikely that King would not have at least have heard of Smith, and his presence may have influenced King's enlightened views on racial equality.[13]

King subsequently became especially concerned with the moral evils associated with slavery, which, he insisted, subverted the morality of white southerners in their private lives. He saw slavery corrupting the white population: "There was the sin of Sodom—fullness of bread and plenty of idleness in the sunny south human passions were strong and lust reigned there, without restraint," and whites lived "under such corrupting influence [that it] was almost sure to corrupt their moral principles and ruin them both for the life that now is and that which is to come."[14] To King, white southerners openly loved pleasure more than they loved God. He noted with contempt their drinking, gambling, and dancing on the Sabbath. He further criticized their theaters and brothels. Moral degradation seemed to pervade all southern white society, and King believed slavery to be the cause.

King was certainly not the only white American to ponder slavery's moral and social effects on white society. King's predecessor at Mathews Academy and superintendent of the Sabbath school at the nearby Presbyterian Church, Dr. Bullen, was equally concerned with the moral degradation of southern white society. In his farewell address, Bullen dwelled "on the nature of the soul, and the danger of losing it by a person's being entangled with the riches and pleasures of this world."[15] His warning against pursuing worldly pleasures at the expense of an eternal home in heaven evidently made King aware of the dangers in his situation with "the prospect of wealth and a gay and fashionable world with all its pleasures spread out before me," which could induce him to forget preparation for the next world.[16] A man who desired to be trained in the ministry found extremely frustrating this dilemma of living in the real world while preparing for the next, of living in a sinful society of slave owners and enjoying the benefits of that society while professing faith in God.

King seems to have accepted the argument put forth by southern ecclesiastical apologists for slavery that the institution performed a missionary function. Those who advanced this argument, including many southern churchmen, perceived American slavery as a divinely inspired means of indoctrinating Africans in Christianity. This in many ways represented the only thesis in favor of slavery that King could accept. If King were to become a minister, his concern, therefore, would be the salvation of souls rather than bodies, of Christianizing rather than liberating slaves.[17]

King thus compromised with his religious conscience, convincing himself that his purchase of Talbot and other slaves was justifiable because of the difficulty of obtaining and retaining reliable servants in an area where slave labor dominated. Like others then and since, King insisted that the institution of slavery eroded the South's free labor system, so distorting southerners' work ethic that free laborers, both white and black, not only were hard to find but were often of the most undesirable moral sort. King's experience with free laborers had been neither pleasant nor successful. When he became superintendent of the preparatory school for Louisiana College, King hired a full domestic staff of free servants, including a cook, a gardener, dining room attendants, and laundry women. Some were white, others were black. Shortly thereafter, a white male dining room servant was caught stealing from the academy and was subsequently sent to state prison for petty thievery. King hired another white man for the position but soon dismissed him for drinking. Meanwhile, his cook, a free black woman, died from drunkenness: according to King's autobiography, most of his other servants were addicted to the same vice, undesirable and unreliable. In a letter to his friend, Dr. James Cunningham, King wrote disparagingly of his hired help: "I found myself without a Cook, with drunken and disobedient servants and fifty boarders to provide for."[18] King thereafter ceased employing free wage laborers. He next experimented with hired slaves but also found this class of laborers unacceptable because they "soon became demoralized and you could not trust them."[19] King consequently concluded that "one could not get faithful and trustworthy servants unless you bought them."[20] So he did.

King further rationalized his slave purchases by adopting the principle that he should do to others, as he would that they in similar circumstances should do to him. He bought a cook and drawing room servant with the view of treating them kindly and setting them free as soon as circumstances would permit. King believed that being a benevolent and generous master would mitigate the wrongness of owning slaves. King assumed that because he was aware of slavery's ill effects on whites' morals, he could avert such damage to his own character. King saw himself as saving his slaves from worse fates at the hands of unkind masters and from the degrading effects of southern slavery. In his mind, these men and women were better off as his slaves than as free blacks in the South. With each additional purchase, King's conscience seems to have bothered him less. More than five years passed before he freed his slaves, and by then he owned more than a dozen.[21]

William King thus found himself in the position of enjoying the southern way of life yet professing to disdain the system that made that life possible. King's stumbling block was an inability to hate either the land of slavery or the holders of slaves. King was not the only person to struggle with this dilemma. Like others, he was entranced by the secluded Big House yet expressed horror at the slave quarters and the effect of slavery on southern whites. A look into the life of William's brother, James, reveals an alternative way of handling this paradox. Like William, James settled in Louisiana, obtaining a position under his brother at Mathews Academy. Again like William, James married the daughter of a southern planter and slave owner, Martha Sims-Douglas, a landed widow who brought to the marriage a prosperous plantation and seventeen slaves. Unlike his brother, however, James refused to accept the southern tradition that the existence of slavery inevitably predestined men of substance to own slaves. His wife's slaves, who became his when the couple married, were subsequently manumitted and sent to Liberia. James King would spend the rest of his life in the South without the benefit of slaves. He later became the mayor of Jackson and governor of the lunatic asylum there. While both brothers voiced concerns about slavery, one embraced the establishment with excuses, while the other denounced the institution in both words and deeds.[22]

Although seemingly settled both professionally and personally, William King had not given up his desire to enter the ministry, and in late 1843 he sailed to Edinburgh, Scotland, to begin theological studies at New College (also known as the Free Church College), the Free Church of Scotland's divinity school.[23] Ironically, as he embarked on the life path that would eventually propel him to end his slaveholding status, he added to his holdings. Before leaving Louisiana, King purchased a two-hundred-forty-acre plantation to serve as a home for his wife and their son during at least some portion of his absence. Included in the purchase of the land were two female slaves, Fanny and Mollie, and two eight-year-old children, Sarah and Peter, whose parentage is unclear. In a separate purchase, King acquired a slave named Jacob to help farm the land.[24]

According to his autobiography, King agonized over being unable to free his slaves. His concern was not strong enough to prevent him from adding to his human holdings. King would later claim that legal difficulties stood in the way of his freeing his slaves before his departure for Scotland. And indeed, although they were not insurmountable, Louisiana presented legal obstacles to manumitting slaves. According to state law, slaves under the age of thirty could not be set free without a special act of the Louisiana legislature unless they had saved the life of their master or a member of the master's family. A 1830 law mandated that any manumitted slave leave the state and required the posting of a one thousand dollar bond to ensure the departure of the freed slave. Such legislation may have deterred but did not eliminate manumissions, as can be seen in the case of James King, who took over his brother's position as the superintendent of Mathews Academy. While William claimed to need slaves to effectively run the school, James saw to it that the same duties were performed without their assistance. He evidently hired reliable, effective servants or at least laborers he found acceptable.[25]

During his ministerial training, calamity struck William King's family. In 1844, at the end of his first school term, William returned to the United States intent on bringing his wife and son, Theophilus, to Scotland. Before heading abroad, the trio traveled to Ohio to visit William's family. Along the way, Theophilus contracted a fever and died. After burying him in the family plot in Ohio, William and Mary continued their journey to Scotland. There Mary gave birth to a daughter, whom they named Johanna Elizabeth. In January 1846 William and Mary received word of her father's death. Already weak with a fever and a cough, Mary took the loss with particular difficulty. She seemed to lose her will to live and within four weeks was dead. Three months later, William's daughter also succumbed to a fever, and William was left alone. In less than a year and a half, William had lost four close family members.[26]

This series of tragic events altered King's personal circumstances and set the stage for his founding of the Buxton settlement. As a result of inheritances, King now owned several additional slaves. John Phares's will listed his daughter, Mary, as inheriting Ben, Emeline, Robin, Ise (Isaiah), and Old Stephen as well as a share in the estate's other slaves, which eventually brought King another slave, Harriet. Now the owner of fourteen slaves valued at an estimated nine thousand dollars, King nevertheless continued his studies at divinity school. His studies exposed King to further antislavery views, not only through the church but from other community institutions, including the Edinburgh Emancipation Society.[27]

Although few individuals knew the extent of his involvement with the institution of slavery, King's ownership of slaves did cause him some difficulties during his divinity training. While he was in Edinburgh, a group of visiting American abolitionists, Frederick Douglass among them, gave several antislavery lectures.[28] The abolitionists apparently discovered that King owned slaves and, without specifically mentioning his name, repeatedly lashed out at what they viewed as the hypocrisy of someone who would preach the gospel while owning slaves. At the time, King confided his secret to James Cunningham, the principal of New College, and offered to respond to the accusations by explaining to the delegation that legal difficulties stood in the way of freeing his slaves. Seeking to protect King and the church by not confirming the accusation that a slaveholder was enrolled in the school, Cunningham advised King to say nothing. Probably because only a few members were aware that the abolitionists were referring to King, the Free Church did not censure him or force him to leave divinity school.[29]

Several church rulings supported King's position. In 1845 the Free Church asserted its position on slavery: Although the slave-master relationship encouraged abuses that were clearly sinful, the institution itself was not a sin. Being a slaveholder in itself was not considered a sin and did not warrant exclusion from church membership. Conveniently for King, the church thus distinguished between the system of slavery and the actions of slaveholders: Slaveholders were acceptable if they treated their slaves humanely and looked after their moral and religious improvement. The church's willingness to cover for King during Douglass's attacks suggests that King convinced those leaders who knew of his involvement with slavery that he fit that description. A further argument, put forth at the church's 1846 general assembly, aided King as well. The Free Church general assembly again held firm against critics, including members of the Glasgow Emancipation Society, by distinguishing between "holding" and "having" slaves. In the first category, masters voluntarily chose to hold slaves; in the second, masters had slaves because the law prevented their release or because manumission might place the slaves in the hands of cruel masters. Church leader Robert Candlish wrote, "We are prepared to consider the circumstances in which [slave owners] are placed and to make allowances for the difficulties of their position."[30] King and presumably the Free Church believed that his ownership of slaves fell into the second, acceptable category. Nevertheless, his ongoing association with slavery posed a difficult and embarrassing threat.[31]

After King completed divinity school, the Free Church assigned him to a missionary post with the Toronto Synod of the Free Presbyterian Church of Canada. Before assuming his new position, King visited his late wife's family in Louisiana for both personal and official business. King was the executor of his father-in-law's will and needed to settle the estate. He also needed to divest himself of his personal property in Louisiana, and he presumably desired to free his slaves. His farm had not prospered as he had hoped during his absence, incurring a debt of one thousand dollars in part because armyworm had ravaged the cotton crops for two consecutive years. To free himself of this debt, King sold his farm and household furniture, placing his slaves on the Phares plantation. The failure of King's slaves to prosper on the farm without closer supervision may have influenced his decision about their future in freedom. Comments in his writings revealed, perhaps unconsciously, his reservations about whether blacks had adequate facilities to take care of themselves without (white) direction and guidance. He might then have resolved that for his slaves to succeed in freedom, he needed to remove them from the South and substantially involve himself in their future.[32]

Yet another problem confronted King in Louisiana. He found himself enmeshed in the legal intricacies surrounding his wife's and father-in-law's estates. In particular, challenges to his rights under John Phares's will delayed King's formal inheritance of the slaves left to Mary Phares by her father. The other heirs questioned King's right to inherit through his daughter since she had been born outside of the United States. While he had hoped to liberate his slaves at this time, this difficulty and other legalities prevented him from doing so. When

King arrived in Toronto on November 16, 1846, to take up his missionary work, he still owned slaves. He took up his duties without revealing his secret.[33]

Not until the spring of 1847 did King finally reveal to the church his true association with slavery. In his "confession" letter, King claimed that his long delay had resulted out of fear that word of his intention to set his slaves free would reach Louisiana. Such a revelation, King asserted, would have made his goal more difficult to achieve. He feared that those who opposed his inheritance would use the prospect of their freedom to thwart his efforts. King now found it necessary to request a few months' leave from his work in Canada to return to Louisiana to deal with the growing legal problems in executing John Phares's will. Such a request required a full explanation to his superiors, which prompted his revelations. When King informed his superiors of his situation, "the news fell like a bomb shell on the members of the Presbytery."[34] The church leadership, having by this time moved toward a more antislavery and antislaveholder stance, took a narrow view of King's admission, ruling that as long as he owned slaves, he could not remain in the ministry. Church leaders felt that King had misled them about his circumstances to receive his appointment and forced him to resign his appointment until he emancipated his slaves. Candlish and Cunningham, who had been aware of King's situation while he was attending divinity school and had supported him, were in Scotland and could not come to his aid.[35]

The Free Church played a leadership role in the Canadian antislavery movement. Roughly 30 percent of the leaders of the Canadian abolitionist movement whose denominational affiliations are known were members of the Free Church. Two men were particularly influential in the church's decision to force King to resign: Michael Willis, who had recently accepted a position as professor of theology at Knox College, the Presbyterian Church of Canada's higher educational institution and theological school, and Robert Burns, a minister and teacher at the college. Both men had earlier taken strong antislavery stances and were much less tolerant of slaveholders than either Candlish or Cunningham. Willis had relocated to Canada after publicly breaking with the Free Church in Scotland over its association with slavery and its fellowship with slaveholding churches. In 1846 he had helped form the Free Church Anti-Slavery Society, promoting immediate emancipation and seeking to convince Free Churchmen to end the church's fellowship with southern slaveholding churches. Willis attacked the assertion that people might be slaveholders against their will and argued that slaveholders refused to liberate their slaves because they were "so completely under the domination of selfishness, that [they could] not help keeping [their] fellow-man in bondage."[36] Burns had initially supported the church's association with southern slaveholding congregations but later changed his mind and became a staunch critic of any association with slavery.[37]

William King's delayed and tortured decision-making process over manumission has parallels in the experiences of other prominent holders who freed their slaves, including Edward Coles, Samuel Gist, and John Randolph. All four men possessed both slaves and the ideal that slavery was wrong, and all four cultivated their antislavery sentiments throughout their adult lives. Some differences also existed among the circumstances of these men: Coles and Randolph were born into wealth, property, and slave holdings, whereas Gist and King became slaveholders only in adulthood. Unlike Coles and King, Gist and Randolph freed their slaves only posthumously, thereby avoiding personal economic loss as a result of manumission. Coles and King, in contrast, compromised their financial standing in putting their abolitionist sentiment into action.

Coles and King also had similar experiences that influenced their antislavery views. Both men had had their antislavery sentiments first aroused while in school. In fact, a course taught by James Madison initially brought Coles's attention to the inherent contradiction between the ideology of the nation's founding and slaveholding. Coles later wrote that the class and private conversations with Madison had convinced him that he "could not consent to hold as property what I had no right to, & which was not, and could not be property, according to my understanding of the rights & duties of man—and therefore determined that I would not and could not hold my fellowman as a Slave."[38] Years would pass from the time Coles came to this realization and the manumission of his slaves. While King put off freeing his slaves to pursue his theological degree, events similarly delayed Coles's freeing of his slaves. From 1809 to 1815, Coles served as Madison's presidential secretary. After resigning from that position, Coles scouted land in Illinois and began to plan to relocate with his slaves, but his plans were interrupted by his appointment as the president's special envoy to Russia and then a grand tour of Europe. In 1819 Coles finally began the journey to Illinois with his slaves. Coles and King thus shared a similar dilemma—they were intent on not disrupting the accustomed way of life for their family and friends, but they also were not comfortable in keeping property in other humans as the price of that life.[39]

Both men owned fewer than twenty-five slaves and kept silent about their intentions prior to manumission. Coles did not initially divulge his antislavery convictions or his emancipation plans out of fear that his father would not bequeath the slaves to him. When his father died in 1807, Edward made his plans known. As expected, he encountered strong opposition from family and friends, who argued that under Virginia law, emancipation and subsequent relocation would cause great distress and family separation among the people he was trying to help. Neither Coles nor King accepted this contention, rationalizing that the end result—freedom—would outweigh the pain of separation. In both cases, slaves apparently were not told in advance of their impending manumission, perhaps to avoid raising false hopes or to prevent the spread of ideas of freedom that might foment discontent among other slaves and subsequently prove detrimental to the abolitionist cause.[40]

Gist and Randolph possessed close to four hundred slaves each, and the process involved in freeing their slaves in their wills was lengthy and tortuous. Gist was an absentee landowner living in England from before the American Revolution who had owned slaves for decades. Gist's first will, dated June 1808, included a manumission clause, but several codicils were added later to meet various contingencies. Gist's first codicil, dated March 4, 1811, addressed his fear that the Virginia legislature might not allow the manumission. He ordered that in the event that the legislature deemed it "impolitic and perhaps improper" to liberate so many slaves, his slaves were to be kept together for the joint benefit of his two daughters.[41] Several years later, Gist apparently became more confident that Virginia would uphold his desire to manumit his slaves, and he subsequently fashioned convoluted contingency scenarios designed to free his slaves and provide for his daughters, both of whom were married but had no children and were beyond childbearing age.[42]

John Randolph's first will, written in 1819, freed his slaves and provided them with a trust fund, while his second will provided for the purchase of land for their resettlement. Yet a third will, written in 1832, specified that his slaves should be sold rather than manumitted, but this will was invalidated by reason of insanity. Randolph too was largely an absentee landowner, since his life in politics meant that he was often absent from his home plantation. A complicated man, John Randolph supported private manumission even as he publicly defended slavery. Randolph was not an advocate of emancipation, especially national emancipation, which he viewed as an assault to property. His conservative position was that public evils could be cured only through private actions. The remedy for slavery was not general emancipation but individual manumission.[43]

William King held more egalitarian views than Gist, Randolph, or even Coles. He was also the most outspoken abolitionist—the one to take his antislavery sentiment to the level of advocating general emancipation and engaging in abolitionist activity. Determined to liberate his slaves and rejoin the church, King once again traveled to Louisiana, where, after almost a year of legal difficulties, he reported that he had concluded his affairs and was returning to Canada "with fifteen servants that I have manumitted."[44] Because manumitting slaves in Louisiana involved many technicalities and because any evidence documenting this manumission is lacking, it is likely that despite his declaration, King never legally freed his slaves. Rather, it seems that he left Louisiana with his slaves without securing any official free papers. In fact, King asked for and received a bill of sale for those slaves coming to him by inheritance, presumably to thwart any attempt to challenge his ownership. In his mind they were free, but according to Louisiana law and thus the law of the United States, they were not. Ironically, King added to his slaveholdings even as he maneuvered to set his slaves free. A young boy named Solomon had recently come into his possession. King later wrote that Solomon's mother, one of King's slaves, had come to him "with tears and asked if I would not buy her child that she might take it with her."[45] The heir who had inherited Solomon was apparently agreeable to the sale at the price of one hundred fifty dollars, but King at first told the mother that he "did not see it [his] duty to buy children and set them free."[46] His abolitionist commitment seemed to have limits. Only after further pleading from mother and child did King agree to purchase the boy.[47]

Several weeks before beginning the long journey, King gathered his slaves together to inform them that they would soon be leaving for Canada with him. King's recollection of this moment was that "they seemed not to understand what was meant by going to Canada," some apparently thinking "it was some new plantation that I had purchased and I was going to take them to it." King says he then explained that Canada was a free country and that when they reached it he would give them their freedom. This news "seemed to have little effect on them." They considered "that slavery was their normal condition." Not knowing what freedom meant, they "thought that to be free was to be like their master, to go idle and have a good time." Such recollections reveal much about King's beliefs regarding blacks' intellectual capacities—or at least his naïveté. It is unlikely that his slaves had not heard of Canada, and they undoubtedly understood at least the concept of freedom. Either they were pleading ignorance to avoid jeopardizing themselves or his recall of the event was skewed.[48]

Edward Coles took a similar approach to informing his slaves of their impending freedom and his plans for their future. During their journey to Illinois, Coles gathered his slaves together on the barge upon which they were traveling and made known to them "the glad tidings of their freedom." He proclaimed that they were "no longer Slaves, but free—free as I was, & were at liberty to proceed with me, or to go ashore at their pleasure." Unlike King's slaves, the effect of the news on Coles's slaves "was electrical." After a few seconds of shock, during which "they stared at me, & at each other, as if doubting the accuracy or reality of what they had heard . . . unable to utter a word," the slaves broke out in a "kind of hysterical giggling laugh" and then "gave vent to the gratitude, & implored the blessings of God on me."[49]

King and his slaves headed north aboard a steamboat along the Mississippi and Ohio Rivers to Cincinnati. The journey caused quite a sensation. At Bayou Sara, where the steamboat took on its soon-to-be-well-known passengers, a crowd of spectators gathered to see the party start off for Canada. Southern planters traveling on the same steamboat as King, presumably unaware of the

true situation, noted with astonishment the amount of freedom that King allowed his slaves. A southern minister who knew of King's plans called King
"foolish" and attempted to convince him to place his slaves "on a plantation
and preach to them."[50] There, according to this minister, King's slaves "would
minister" to him "in carnal things" and he "would sanctify the institution of
slavery by administering to them in Spiritual things."[51] A number of abolitionists
along the way conversed with King's slaves; not believing that King was taking
his slaves to freedom, the abolitionists tried to convince the blacks that King
was planning to sell them and that they should escape before it was too late. In
a sign of somewhat blind faith, none of King's slaves deserted him.

Arriving in Cincinnati five days later, King had to wait several days before
he could get a boat to carry the group to Toledo because the regular packet
boat along the Miami and Erie canal refused to take his slaves with the other
passengers. Unwilling to be separated from his slaves, King booked passage on
a freight boat, aboard which blacks could travel unhampered. Because of the
slowness of the boat, King's slaves would often walk on the towpath along the
canal, and "in passing the villages on the canal the people would come out and
gaze on the negroes supposing them to be runaways from the south making
their way to Canada."[52]

When the travelers reached his family's Ohio farm, King informed his fifteen
slaves that they were now free. Again, their true freedom was subject to interpretation. An 1846 Louisiana law stated that slaves were not to be considered free
simply because they had been in free territory with or without their owner's
consent. King's slaves were unlikely to have been aware of the letter of the law.
The state of Ohio, however, likely considered them free by virtue of their removal
to the state. By the 1830s abolitionist lawyers had weakened slaveholders' ability to control enslaved blacks in Ohio. According to abolitionist doctrine, any
slave who entered the state with the knowledge and consent of his or her master
became automatically free. King's slaves met that legal condition. Many cases
in the northwestern states show that slaves were freed in precisely this manner,
with no formal registration of manumission. Others, including Coles, secured
free papers for those slaves they emancipated. Of course, this became a moot
point when King's former slaves crossed the border into Canada, which recognized their freedom regardless of prior circumstances, simply because they
had set foot on Canadian soil.[53]

King further explained to his slaves that, if they so desired, they could stay on
the King farm for the winter and then join him in Canada. In the meantime, King
would return to Canada. King's slaves accepted the offer and remained in Ohio,
learning farming techniques and other necessary skills, while he prepared the
way for their emigration to Canada. Also living on the King homestead were at
least two dozen members of the King clan, some of whom instructed the blacks

in reading and writing. By the time King returned to take them to Canada, all except five-year-old Solomon had learned the rudiments of reading, and most were learning to write.

William King now entered the third stage of his life. At first a righteous critic of slavery, he had become a slaveholder. Then, as he extricated himself from that morally untenable position, he began the transition from master to working with blacks for their welfare. During the first phase, King was concerned primarily about the immoral effects of slavery on whites rather than its oppressive effects on the slaves. In his second stage, King enjoyed the prerogatives of the master, a situation that suggests that King's conscience may not have troubled him as much as his protestations about slavery and its effects would suggest, particularly in light of his brother's contrasting actions. In the third phase, he freed his slaves. Exactly what accounted for this metamorphosis is unknown. In some respects, it appears that King gave up his slaves because the church insisted that he do so. Another probable explanation is that the series of family tragedies and his training for the ministry altered his thinking about slavery, so that when the church ordered him to end his relationship with the institution, he was prepared to comply. His ideological commitment had led to an act of personal sacrifice, relinquishing the wealth and status that accrued to a southern gentleman slaveholder. He was also intent on doing more than merely manumitting his slaves. King felt it his duty to look after his former slaves, to educate them, and to make them into useful citizens. He further believed that the same could and should be done for other blacks. This conviction ultimately led to the creation of Buxton. King did not merely divest himself of his slaves and end his association with slavery and blacks. He did not simply extricate himself from the web of slavery. Rather, he immersed himself in the cause of improving the condition of African Americans and committed his life to their uplift.

3

An Idea Becomes Reality

By the time William King reached Ohio, he had formulated a plan to establish an all-black settlement in Canada and provide an environment in which blacks could improve themselves morally and socially. After temporarily settling his slaves on the King family homestead, King returned to Canada to set his plan into action. He oversaw the purchase of approximately seven thousand acres of land in the Western District of Upper Canada, setting aside that land for settlement exclusively by blacks. King founded a corporation, the Elgin Association, to raise capital to purchase the land and subsequently to oversee its sale and management. The Presbyterian Church approved the endeavor, promising to establish and maintain a mission in the settlement. The Buxton Mission was soon formed to supervise the settlement's chapel, schools, and missionary work. Buxton thus had institutional structure and support that other black communities lacked.[1]

King no longer considered the black men, women, and children he had left in Ohio his slaves but continued to feel a degree of responsibility for them. Edward Coles felt a similar duty. In April 1819, Coles came to Edwardsville, Illinois, with his slaves: an extended family consisting of Ralph Crawford, his wife, and their three children; Robert Crawford and his sister, Polly, both younger relatives of Ralph; and an unrelated single man and young woman. The following July 4, Coles gave these men, women, and children their freedom papers at the local courthouse. In return for their years of service, Coles gave each male head of household a quarter section of land in nearby Pin Oak Township, Madison County. Other free blacks later joined Coles's former slaves in Madison County—according to one local history, the number of blacks in the community reached as high as three hundred. Unlike King, however, Coles did not create an organized settlement nor did he take an active role in the lives of his former slaves; he apparently believed manumission and a grant of land fulfilled his responsibility to them.[2]

King believed that he had to do more: In his eyes, mere emancipation was a lofty act without substance. Blacks needed not only freedom and economic resources but also self-emancipation from what King referred to as the "Slavery of Ignorance."[3] King believed that blacks' degraded and oppressed condition was a consequence not of innate inferiority but of slavery, and that removal from slavery alone would not automatically elevate the race. Blacks' social and moral condition required improvement through Christian education. Part of King's philosophy may be attributable to the fact that he lacked the wealth of John Randolph, Samuel Gist, or even Coles. King's former slaves would have to rely more on themselves than on their former master. That King's approach was necessary is illustrated by the fate of some of Coles's former slaves: at least two—Ralph Crawford and Thomas Cobb—lost their land when they were unable to repay money they had borrowed to buy farm tools and provisions.

King differed from Coles and others who freed slaves in that he had a real vision for what they would do after being emancipated: They would live on land that they "could own, could buy, and not merely receive as a gift" and would have institutional support and personal assistance in their endeavors that would enable them to establish themselves as independent and self-reliant settlers.[4] He also hoped that their success would serve as a model for others.

King was certainly not the first or only person to have such a vision. Much like King, Gist had a utopian plan that included providing his former slaves with land, instruction "in the Christian Religion according to the Protestant Doctrine," and for "schools for the education of the children."[5] Frances Wright had a similar philosophy and followed through on her beliefs by establishing Nashoba along the Memphis River in Tennessee during the mid-1820s. With the additional goal of future colonization outside the United States, she focused more on the training of blacks in manual labor and academic study than on the development of a cohesive community. Nashoba's original blacks lived communally and did not own land individually. Within a year of the settlement's establishment, whites were admitted, leading to a decline in the status of black residents. Nashoba ultimately became just another early-nineteenth-century utopian community, and it failed at that as well.[6]

King drew on his personal experience with community work and lessons learned from other areas of black settlement in carrying out his self-appointed mission. While attending divinity school in Edinburgh, he had been involved in a missionary project under the direction of the Reverend Dr. Thomas Chalmers, principal and professor of divinity at New College from 1843 to 1847. Chalmers, a social theoretician, had worked and written extensively on the problem of churching the urban poor. Chalmers's experiment in poor relief was designed to improve the condition and religious nature of poor people in an area of the city called West Port. The plan involved an intensive program of door-to-door visiting, closely acquainting its missionaries with detailed knowledge of each household in their section. The primary focus was to conduct religious and moral education and provide assistance in finding work. Financial aid was shunned and dispensed only in extreme cases, while temperance and piety were stressed.[7]

King served as one of Chalmers's missionaries and served as superintendent of the West Port Sabbath School. He immediately became concerned about the physical appearance of the area's children, who were "in a state of filth and rags."[8] Under King's direction, the children were washed, barbered, and otherwise attended to, and he later noted that their clean appearance had a positive moral influence on their parents. He also opened a night school for those who could not attend the day school. During King's tenure at the West Port Mission, Sabbath school attendance rose from twenty-five to three hundred, and church attendance rose from eighty to two hundred fifty. According to King, this success at West Port was the result of the moral influence brought to bear on the people under his guidance.[9]

In creating Buxton, King drew on his West Port experiences and on what he had learned from Chalmers, emphasizing appearance and morality. One of Buxton's cornerstones was the belief that Christianity and education were interchangeable and necessary for the social and moral improvement of "neglected and degraded people."[10] King made few distinctions between "degraded" whites and "degraded" blacks, believing that members of either group could be uplifted through education, example, and guidance.

King also learned from mistakes made in several other efforts to organize black settlements. One such attempt had been the Wilberforce community in Canada, founded in 1829 by blacks forced to leave Cincinnati when city officials began requiring black residents to provide a certificate of freedom and post a five-hundred-dollar bond. Black residents were given thirty days to comply or leave. Facing this choice, many Cincinnati blacks decided to leave and seek shelter from such discrimination in a community of their own.[11] With financial assistance from Quakers in Ohio and Indiana, eight hundred acres were purchased a few miles northwest of London, Upper Canada, and the plan for an all-black community proceeded. Named Wilberforce after the leading British abolitionist, the settlement struggled from its inception. Wilberforce's black population never topped two hundred, and the numbers declined steadily to about one hundred in 1840 and to fifty-two ten years later. Most historians have deemed the experiment a failure. The settlement lacked a single strong leader, those in charge engaged in numerous clashes, and apparently managerial corruption and incompetence further undermined efforts to create a community.

With such problems at the top, adequate financial support could not be found, a situation that in turn caused further difficulties. Moreover, neither the black college nor the theological seminary that had originally been planned became a reality, and settlers never had access to more than a rudimentary education. On top of everything, Wilberforce failed to attract enough new settlers to provide an adequate population base and it was unable to establish a real sense of community and stability among its residents.[12]

King also drew ideas from the fate of the Dawn settlement, an all-black community founded near Dresden in Upper Canada in 1842. Hiram Wilson, a white American with an antislavery background from Lane Seminary and Oberlin College, and Josiah Henson, an escaped slave who had settled in Canada, organized a school, the British-American Institute, around which the community grew. The institute came to own approximately three hundred acres of land, and individual black settlers owned another fifteen hundred acres. The Dawn settlement came to be home to almost five hundred blacks and boasted Baptist and Methodist churches and several schools. Some of its industrial endeavors were a sawmill, brickyard, and rope factory. Despite these superficial accomplishments, however, both the institute and the larger community lacked stability. Beset by bad management and inept leaders, the institute incurred debts between four and five thousand dollars. Leaders began to squabble, and in 1868 the institute was abandoned and its land sold. Without the institute, the settlement deteriorated. There simply was not a strong enough sense of community to survive alone without the institute. As in the case of Wilberforce, the failure to build a stable community of residents caused Dawn's ultimate downfall. Neither settlement was successful in developing a true community that could withstand such difficulties.[13]

King visited both Wilberforce and Dawn to examine and learn from what they had done right and from what they had done wrong. According to King, these settlements had failed in part because they "depended upon individual effort and voluntary contributions," which were irregular and often failed to materialize when they were most needed.[14] Consequently, King decided that his settlement would need to be managed like a business. In addition, King believed that lack of community development had constituted another contributing factor in the failure of earlier black settlements. King specifically deplored the migratory nature of blacks. Very often, he observed, black settlers were squatters on land that they did not own and to which they had no real ties. Rather than creating a stable community, blacks typically formed a floating element of the population—uneducated, landless, without permanent homes, ignorant, and without moral development.

King's assessment rang true. Propertyless free blacks tended to move frequently. Free black landowners, however, were generally less transient. Throughout Canada and the United States, frontier farmers often staked out a claim on public lands, grew crops for a season or so and then decided whether to stay. Such practices tended to hinder community development and stability. This was true of the Beech and Roberts settlements, where many of the settlers at first squatted on the land. In fact, three-quarters of the landless Beech families in 1840 were not in the area a decade later. Samuel Gist's lack of foresight, commitment, and assistance doomed his intended community of freedpeople. The final terms of his will directed that his slaves be freed and provided for from the proceeds of the plantation, but unfortunately he made no provisions for the enactment of his vision. Four years after his death, his executors completed the process of manumission and Gist's former slaves were transported to Brown County, Ohio, where proceeds from the sale of the plantation was supposed to purchase a two-thousand-acre tract of land for their settlement. A devastating complication arose, however, when most of the money from the estate went to satisfy creditors. The former slaves, having no land, resources, guidance, or assistance, were simply dumped in Brown County. The community they were to develop fell apart, as some squatted in the area as farmers while others sought employment as laborers. Despite the brief existence of a school and temperance society, the community structure deteriorated and the blacks either left the area or were absorbed into the general population.[15]

In this light, King argued, people had to be settled permanently in one spot "before we can realise the hope of improving their religious condition."[16] Such permanence rested on a foundation of landownership. Then, after a permanent home had been established, "the hope of supplying the parents efficiently with the means of grace and their children with a Christian education" could be realized.[17] He embraced the contemporary mind-set associating independence and manhood with landownership. The possession of property, moreover, was, and is, a middle-class virtue, cultivating the virtues of responsibility and reliability, characteristics King wished to instill in the settlers. Land would give Buxton residents a stake in society and in their community and would encourage the development of habits of social integrity. Buxton was designed with an indelible middle-class orientation.[18]

From the nation's inception, Americans defined themselves legally, politically, and socially on the basis of property ownership. Abolitionist Gerrit Smith believed that the only way blacks could become truly free was to avoid positions of servility by leaving the cities and "scatter[ing] themselves over the country," becoming independent farmers and craftsmen—in short, by owning land.[19] Blacks understood that the ownership of land constituted the essential prerequisite of true independence. Often, former slaves and freeborn blacks were dependent on whites; such dependence generally stemmed from an economic dependence. Land was the means by which blacks escaped dependency on whites. In addition to economic independence and autonomy, property ownership provided a sense of well-being, assertiveness, and self-confidence. It provided a means, albeit limited, of circumventing racial oppression and discrimination as well as protection resulting from the legal identity and standing American society places on property holders. Free black landowners were more than merely free blacks, they were free people of substance and standing in society. At Buxton and at a New York black settlement that Smith founded at around the same time, land would provide settlers with power and control that was unavailable to most blacks.[20]

Blacks, too, perceived "free labor" to mean farming their own land. Coles recalled that when he revealed to his slaves his intention to free them, one man, Ralph, "appeared to feel less than any of the others the value" of the freedom being bestowed. Then, when Coles announced that the former slaves would receive land, Ralph became "more pleased," understanding that in some respects, freedom without land was not true freedom.[21] By working small plots of land, blacks could both earn their subsistence and resist white authority. Landowners stood at the top of the rural black social structure.

The primacy of land further connected Smith, King, and others to a romantic ideology that the frontier provided an escape from servile city life and to the Jeffersonian yeoman ideal. Romantics ascribed regenerative powers to the wilderness. Smith, for example, urged all poor blacks to quit "their city life, their servile life, their self-indulgent life" for land in the wilderness where they could begin a new life, braving the rigors of the wild and making "a hardy and honorable character" for themselves.[22] Similarly, Augustus Wattles, a Connecticut-born abolitionist, believed that northern freedpeople had merely substituted city temptations and discrimination for the degradations of slavery. In 1835 Wattles purchased almost two hundred acres of land in Mercer County, Ohio, and built a manual school, around which a black community grew. Wattles intended this community as a place where Cincinnati blacks could become farmers and thereby "cure the vices and problems that city life had brought to them."[23] Some black leaders joined white leaders in advocating rural life. Frederick Douglass saw Smith's settlement as an opportunity for blacks to combine physical vigor with spirituality, thereby becoming self-sufficient and advancing the black race. An 1843 convention of the American Moral Reform Society, an African American group, issued a report urging blacks to pursue agriculture, because farmers were independent and could acquire both economic independence and respectability.[24]

With these principles, King embarked on his venture. To avoid the weaknesses he observed elsewhere, King proposed purchasing a large tract of land in the Western District of Upper Canada, where land was available at moderate prices, and then resold to black settlers on terms they could afford. His plan included a school, a church, and a missionary dwelling house from whose core a community based on agriculture and industrial pursuits would evolve.

To help establish this proposed settlement on a firm foundation, he turned to the Presbyterian Church of Canada (part of the Free Church of Scotland) for advice, support, and financial assistance. At King's request, the Presbytery of Toronto presented the synod of the Presbyterian Church of Canada with a memorial outlining King's plan for a mission for blacks. Although acknowledging a deep interest in the concept, the synod initially withheld formal approval out of concern that the church lacked the prerogative as a religious body to undertake a mission with such extensive temporal implications. Perhaps the synod felt that the fine line between religious and secular administration would be crossed. Or maybe it was simply concerned about the financial obligations that such a settlement would incur.

After further consideration and presumably with some assurances from King about these concerns, the synod decided to participate in King's plan and appointed a committee to assist King in bringing the subject before the church laity. This advisory committee included Robert Burns and Alexander Gale, ministers who had supported King when he revealed his slaveholding status to the church, along with Michael Willis, who had recently arrived in Toronto as theology professor at Knox College, and the Reverend Henry Esson, also a professor at Knox. All four men possessed strong abolitionist sentiments, as presumably did the rest of the committee. The committee was instructed to assist King in forming an association for the financial advancement of his proposal and to communicate with the commissioner of Crown lands on the purchase of a tract. Perhaps as a means of further connecting the proposed settlement and spiritual matters, thereby assuaging the synod's unease, King was appointed missionary to the black population of Upper Canada, a post he held until his retirement in 1883. In his capacity as missionary to the Buxton settlement, King bore responsibility for the settlers' spiritual and educational enlightenment and guidance.[25]

Seeking governmental approval next, King, accompanied by two influential church members, the Reverend William Rinstead and John Redpath, visited Lord Elgin, Canada's governor-general. Elgin expressed interest in the proposal and promised government aid in obtaining land for the settlement. With Elgin's approval and promise of support, King and the other proponents of the settlement formed an association to raise private financing for the purchase of the land. In January 1848 King began to solicit investors, selling stock in the association at ten pounds per share. By March 16, 335 stockholders had underwritten the necessary funds for the land purchase. Many subscribers were Canadian and U.S. abolitionists, while others were antislavery advocates from Ireland, Scotland, and England. The stockholders included landlords, manufacturers, and unskilled laborers, but the largest numbers were in commercial trade, the professions, and skilled labor. Although the stockholders of the Elgin Association (named in honor of Lord Elgin) belonged to a number of religious denominations, they understandably included a substantial percentage of Free Church members (40 percent of those whose denominational affiliation is known). Approximately 13 percent of the stockholders were affiliated with the Anglican Church. Of the 193 Elgin Association stockholders whose race has been identified, 44 were black.[26]

The Elgin Association boasted an impressive group of officers. Its first president was Skeffinton Connor, professor of law at the University of Toronto. The association's two vice presidents were Michael Willis and Robert Burns, both of whom were leading Presbyterian clergymen. J. S. Howard, treasurer of the united counties of Peel and York, held the same role in the association. Little is known about Nathan Gatchel, the association secretary, but he too was likely a community leader. The twenty-four directors included, among others, John Fisher, a prominent Hamilton iron manufacturer and that city's mayor; Peter Brown, the father of George Brown, owner and editor of the *Toronto Globe*; Peter Freeland, a wealthy manufacturer; Wilson R. Abbott, a wealthy black Toronto businessman; Andrew Hamilton, a leading Toronto merchant; and Archibald McKellar, a successful farmer, sawmill owner, and politician. Such a notable group of men embracing King's idea indicates his success in creating a strong support base, which in turn facilitated the plan's success, particularly in the face of the strong criticism that was soon to come.[27]

King's design incorporated a division between civil and religious matters, formalized by the establishment of two distinct spheres of activity. This division constituted a major difference between Buxton and other attempts at antebellum black settlements and was motivated by two primary factors. The first was what King perceived as the detrimental effect that the lack of separation between church and state had on the development of Wilberforce and Dawn in particular. The second was the Presbyterian Church synod's concern about the mixture of secular and religious interests. In the end, these two realms were represented by the Elgin Association and the Buxton Mission, respectively. White community leadership, as King envisaged it, had two facets: the missionary, providing religious training and education, and the civil, overseeing the settlers' secular needs. The distinction between the two bodies' roles in the settlement was clearly delineated in both the association's and the synod's reports: "the object of the [Buxton] Mission is to supply those coloured families with the means of grace[;] the Synod as such, has no connection with the Elgin Association."[28]

The Elgin Association attended to Buxton's secular business, seeking to "provide the colored families with homes, and improve their social condition."[29] The association's board of directors ran the settlement's financial, social, and legal affairs, raised capital to buy land, oversaw public relations (both locally and internationally), and devised property and home-building regulations. In these roles, the association had a certain degree of control over the development of the settlement and influence over its residents. As the association's representative, King handled the settlement's day-to-day affairs, worked closely with Buxton residents, and supervised the collection of the annual loan installments. King conceived the association as having a somewhat confined scope: "As the object of the Society is one of pure benevolence . . . it is not contemplated that it shall continue longer than the time necessary to settle the lands. At the end of ten years the affairs of the Society would be wound up."[30]

King's creation of and reliance on an administrative organization was not unique. The British-American Institute was managed by a board of tuition that oversaw internal affairs and an executive committee that handled external matters. The land purchased for the Randolph slaves was held in trust for them, and Gist had likewise set up a trusteeship for his freed slaves. Gist set up a convoluted legal method of controlling his slaves long after both his death and their manumission. Control of the slaves was placed with William Wickham as the trustee in Virginia, but he did not take an active, day-to-day role. Rather, local Quakers took a more active role with the settlements, aiding the needy and regularly visiting the settlements, much like the Elgin Association and, in a way, the Presbyterian synod. Unfortunately, the results were not nearly as beneficial as those at Buxton.

Whereas the Elgin Association was responsible for administrative duties, the religious and educational functions of the settlement fell under the umbrella of the Buxton Mission, established and sponsored by the Presbyterian Church of Canada. Although the Free Church assisted in the initial approval and planning, it retained no formal connection to the Elgin Association, although the mission provided the church with a forceful presence in Buxton through its supervision of the settlement's chapel, school, and missionary work. To support these services, the Presbyterian synod set up the Buxton Mission Fund, for which a collection was taken annually by all Canadian Presbyterian churches. All money contributed to this fund was allocated to the settlement's spiritual and educational needs. St. Andrew's Church and the Buxton Mission School would subsequently be funded in part from these resources and be overseen by the Presbyterian Church of Canada. King was subsequently appointed to represent the interests of the Presbyterian Church of Canada in the settlement and to supervise the Buxton Mission. Considering the racial makeup of the Presbyterian Church of Canada and its synod, blacks were overshadowed by white rule in this as well as in the secular arena.[31]

Although two distinct entities formally handled Buxton's administration, they were more closely aligned than might at first appear to be the case. Considerable overlap existed between both the membership and the leadership of the Elgin Association and the Canadian Presbyterian Church. Almost 40 percent of the Elgin stockholders can be documented as members of the Presbyterian Church, and the percentage may well have been higher. Several influential members of the Presbyterian Church played roles in the association, including Michael Willis. Willis, a prominent minister and leader of the Presbyterian Church of Canada, owned three shares of Elgin stock (whereas most stockholders held single shares) and served as a vice president of the Elgin Association throughout its existence. Willis further provided leadership to the Buxton Mission, regularly serving as a member and occasionally as the mission committee's chair.[32]

King's simultaneous leadership positions in both the Elgin Association and the Buxton Mission obviously weakened to some extent the intended separation between civic and religious matters. Nonetheless, the anticipated effect of a division was largely maintained. King, the main proponent of the separation, professed his constant awareness of its importance, and his actions backed up his words. When soliciting contributions, King distinguished between the interests of the association in the purchase and settlement of the land and the arrangements made by the mission for the spiritual benefit of the settlers.

With the essential particulars of the settlement's management having been determined, the association needed to acquire official recognition and sanction from the Canadian government and to purchase land, and the community had to be initiated. More than a year after the Elgin Association's organization in June 1849, the Canadian government officially incorporated the body in September 1850. The association's work had already begun by that time. In October 1849 it purchased 4,300 acres of land. By 1853, it would purchase an additional 3,000 acres. As managing director of the Elgin Association, King selected the land.

During the summer of 1849 King, accompanied by James H. Price, commissioner of Crown lands, visited prospective areas in the Western District of Upper Canada before selecting a block of land in the township of Raleigh, Kent County. King had sought land that would be well suited to agriculture, the settlement's primary economic foundation. Such land had not only to be fertile but also to have ready access to transportation and sufficient markets. Situated in southern Canada, Raleigh Township met those requirements. Buxton's tract lies in the center of the township, between Lake Erie on the south and the Thames River on the north. It is also close to Lake Huron, which borders the northern section of Kent County. A military road had already been cut through the tract, and strong indications showed that a railroad would soon pass through it as well. The township possessed several potential market areas for Buxton residents and their crops, including Chatham, located within twenty miles of the settlement. The land was also touted for its agricultural capabilities. When describing the selected land, King noted that "the soil is fertile and well calculated to produce those crops which [blacks] have been accustomed to cultivate."[33]

After choosing the land, King played a leading role in gaining possession of it. Initially, King sought to have the Canadian government put the selected land aside for the explicit sale to blacks, and he desired financial assistance, perhaps in the way of a discounted price. King further requested that one lot of the land be given to the Presbyterian Church of Canada for the explicit purpose "of erecting a Church, an industrial school and other necessary buildings in connection with the mission."[34] The Canadian government agreed with King that the condition of blacks in Canada was deplorable and approved of the proposed settlement in principle. But the government was wary of giving preferential treatment to blacks, at least partially as a result of fear of criticism and political backlash from those who viewed such governmental action with alarm. Such critics argued that offering favorable treatment would lead to an influx of U.S. blacks into Canada. In the end, Elgin and the legislative council declared only that the land would be specifically set apart for black inhabitants. No other special considerations were to be received. The Elgin Association purchased the land at the going local rate and then advanced the land to the settlers. The Presbyterian Church did not receive any land but was not prohibited from purchasing it. In the end, it was probably to Buxton's advantage that the government evidenced little favoritism: Any glory for the community's successes thus could not be preempted by the government but would accrue to those whose hard work and persistence molded Buxton. And, King's most important request had been granted: The land was reserved for black settlement.[35]

In choosing a location for Buxton, King again learned from the experiences of his predecessors in establishing black settlements. He understood the importance of race relations in determining the success or failure of black community development. Hostility from local whites could seriously impair the success of a black community, as in the case of Randolph's Mercer County, Ohio, settlement. With Wattles's school already established there, Randolph's executor, William Leigh, apparently assumed that race relations were at least relatively good in the area. Wattles himself contributed to this misconception, assuring Leigh that the Randolph freedmen would be welcomed, reporting that the white neighbors of the black community were tolerant of free blacks and "pleased at the prospect of an increase in the local labor supply."[36] Unfortunately, such was not the reality. The Wattles community faced white hostility, including physical harassment, that grew over time, and local whites so vehemently opposed the concentrated settlement of blacks that they effectively prevented the Randolph blacks from settling on the land that Leigh had purchased for them. Randolph's slaves subsequently scattered throughout several counties in Ohio, marking the failure of Randolph's plan to effect the continuation of his former slaves as a single community. Also affected by the increase in white hostility was the Wattles community, which, citing prejudice and isolated location, relocated to Bucks County, Pennsylvania, in the mid-1850s.[37]

In contrast, the Gist slaves settled in regions of Ohio that featured substantial Quaker populations. The Quakers sympathized with the plight of blacks and greatly assisted the Gist freedmen over the years, offsetting local white hostility, which never reached the levels of violence encountered by the Randolph and Wattles freedpeople. The Gist settlers thus experienced a reasonable degree of tolerance on the part of local whites, and, as time passed, the former slaves became less outsiders and more accepted within the larger community. Similarly, the presence of local Quakers greatly benefited the Beech and Roberts settlements.[38]

So, in choosing a location for Buxton, King looked to Canada, where relations between whites and blacks were often less hostile than in the United States. Nevertheless, Buxton had its opponents. The first indication that critics of King's proposal were attempting to sabotage his plans came during the incorporation of the Elgin Association. William Notman, a member of Parliament, warned King that criticism of his proposal had surfaced and that the incorporation of the association might meet with formidable legislative opposition. Critics of the Elgin Association began to voice their opinions in April 1850, when the Raleigh Township Council sent a unanimous remonstrance to the Legislative House of Assembly (part of the Canadian Parliament) urging that incorporation of the association be denied because such a right should not be accorded to "foreigners by birth, and [people] of a different race."[39] Such aversion to the proposed settlement was thus based on both nativist and racist sentiment. This resistance never gained momentum, and the incorporation of the Elgin Association eventually occurred, although the process was lengthy: Official incorporation of the Elgin Association did not take place until September 1850, almost a year after the first black families had established themselves in Buxton.[40]

Perhaps more crucial were local critics of the proposed all-black settlement. On March 8, 1849, months before any blacks settled on the land, the Western District Council petitioned the Legislative Assembly, asserting that such a settlement as was proposed "would be highly deleterious to the morals and social condition of the present and future inhabitants of this District."[41] Opposition to King and his proposed settlement rapidly solidified in the Western District. Edwin Larwill, the opposition's unofficial spokesman, was a resident and local official of Chatham in Raleigh Township and a member of Kent County's elected delegation to the Canadian legislature. English-born and a tinner by trade, Larwill had a reputation as an agitator. He was vocally antiblack. Larwill's name appeared at the head of more than three hundred signatures to a blatantly racist and nativist petition sent by the "Inhabitants of the Township of Raleigh and its Vicinity" to the Presbyterian synod in Toronto in June 1849. The memorialists avowed that they did not question the "pure and philanthropic motives" that prompted King and the synod to assist in ameliorating the condition of blacks.[42] The signers also claimed to harbor no ill will toward blacks. Indeed, the petitioners asserted that the black race in general deserved every right to rise in life and to develop fully: "we have no objection to [blacks] enjoying every privilege and right[,] religious, moral, political, and social."[43] The signers simply did not want blacks to accomplish these aims in Canada, especially not in Raleigh Township.

The memorialists who petitioned the Presbyterian synod expressed further concerns. In particular, the petitioners were apprehensive about what they foresaw as the settlement's negative effects on their neighborhood. The Raleigh group was convinced that the proposed settlement would severely depress local land values and that scores of the region's most respected citizens would leave. Citing the fact that Raleigh was an old and well-settled township and claiming that its inhabitants were "moral, industrious, and intelligent," the petition insisted that establishing a colony of the type proposed would be detrimental to the advancement of the present residents. Those who signed the petition asked, "would true benevolence be consulted, where one class [was] injured [so] that another less deserving may be benefitted?"[44]

In an apparent contradiction, the signers of this memorial did not argue that the settlement was doomed to failure because of the supposed inherent weaknesses of blacks. Rather, the petitioners evidently assumed and feared that the settlement would prosper and that such success would lead to problems for white settlers. Success was more alarming than failure. The petition argued that "if such a colony should flourish . . . other religious and philanthropic societies would adopt a similar course and, other townships and other districts, would be crowded with negroes." The petitioners asked the synod to "imagine our Legislative Halls studded and our principle [sic] departments managed by these Ebony men." In addition to these racial objections, the memorialists denounced blacks because they "are from the United States and [are] Republicans" rather than royalists. In these ways the petitioners revealed that both nativist and racist sentiments were at work.[45]

Popular opposition to the Buxton settlement reached its climax on August 18, 1849, when more than three hundred people assembled at the Royal Exchange Hotel in Chatham, the town nearest to the proposed settlement site. As one local newspaper reported, they gathered "for the purpose of adopting such measures as might be deemed advisable to prevent the . . . colonizing of Colored people in the settled townships of this district."[46] Specifically, the meeting sought to prevent blacks from purchasing land in Raleigh Township. The meeting's leaders included Larwill, Thomas Williams, George Young, and George Duck. Although uninvited, William King was present, obviously to rebut whatever charges might be leveled at his proposed community and with the hope of allaying some of the local whites' fears. After the meeting had been called to order by Sheriff John Waddell, King rose and inquired about the gathering's purpose. Young, the chairman, candidly replied that it was to stop blacks from purchasing Raleigh land. King responded by alleging that the meeting had been called for unlawful purposes since it was illegal to prevent blacks from buying property. This comment aroused immense animosity, which in turn engendered a considerable fracas and threw the meeting into great confusion. The meeting then moved to the front of the hotel, perhaps to better accommodate the large and growing crowd. There, despite objections from Larwill and others, King again addressed the group and, amid boos and hisses, expounded on his assertion that blacks were legally entitled to the land. Not intimidated by the unfriendly crowd, he declared that the Buxton settlement would not introduce "coloured riff-raff" into the area. He sought to assuage opponents' fears by explaining that prospective settlers would have to provide evidence of good character before being allowed to reside in the settlement. King explained the object of the Elgin Association and tried to impress on the crowd "the effect a colony of sober industrious coloured men would have on developing the natural resources of the Township."[47] King contended that "by improving the wild lands and, making them valuable," the settlement would "increase the taxes and add to the wealth of the Township," thus benefiting all.[48]

After heated discussion and despite King's impassioned argument, the crowd passed a series of resolutions. First, in a manner similar to the Raleigh inhabitants' petition to the Presbyterian synod, those assembled stated that they abhorred slavery and wished to see blacks enjoy their political and civil rights. Nevertheless, the assembly asserted, such enjoyment must not be pursued in any settled area of the province. The petitioners noted their belief that it was the government's duty to prevent an incursion on what they considered to be their rights as established citizens of the vicinity. They professed that true philanthropy would be better served through the settlement of blacks on a large tract of land in some previously unsettled area. There, the petitioners believed, the former slaves would be free from white interference and prejudice. Walter McCrae, a local leader, delivered a keynote address that articulated the attendees' general sense when he stated that "the slaves of the United States [should] be free, but let it be in their own country, let us not countenance their further introduction amongst us; in a word, let the people of the United States bear the burden of their own sins."[49] Larwill and the other petitioners had at least something in common with King in that they all believed that blacks would benefit most from settlement separate from white intrusion. The opponents differed from King in that he did not desire this separation to be permanent or so all-encompassing that blacks and whites would have no contact or interaction.

Larwill and his followers also disingenuously argued that they had blacks' best interest in mind. Despite Larwill's comments on black inferiority, which the crowd members presumably shared, the resolution insisted that the petitioners did not dispute "the equal intellectual abilities of the black man, and would be glad to see him in the enjoyment of every political and moral privilege."[50] Those present at the meeting further attempted to neutralize allegations of negative racial feeling by resolving that the government also should not sell large tracts of land to any foreigners.

Printed versions of McCrae's address, along with copies of the resolutions passed at the meeting, were later sent to the governor-general, the commissioner of Crown lands, Parliament, the Canada land agent, and the president of the Elgin Association. This wide dissemination of the resolutions was intended to propagate what those who had met in Chatham believed and presumably wanted others to believe—that is, that general and widespread dissatisfaction and alarm has arisen at the prospect of an all-black community in Raleigh Township. King noted that further actions taken by the Chatham meeting included appointing a "committee of vigilance" to follow the proceedings of the Elgin Association, prepare petitions for presentation to Parliament, and to "watch [King's] movement."[51]

Despite outward appearances, not all participants or observers of the meeting at the Royal Exchange agreed with the resolutions passed there. One citizen opposed to both the sentiment expressed at the assembly and the lack of decorum in the meeting itself wrote an anonymous scathing letter in which he deplored the manner in which the assembly had acted. He particularly took issue with "the gross partiality displayed by the Chairman [toward opponents of King's plan], the intemperance of the speakers, and the behavior of the crowd."[52] Among the participants, "drunkenness abounded and obscene language, and shocking oaths were bandied about from mouth to mouth."[53] This concerned citizen not only objected to what had occurred at the meeting but also tried to undermine King's opponents by portraying them as a group of base, ignoble, and disgraceful men who were undeserving of serious attention. The *Examiner,* a Toronto newspaper, decidedly opposed the resolutions, directing editorial criticism against the memorialists' adversity to both colonization and interracial association. The editor censured Larwill and his supporters for expressing alarm at the possibility of blacks establishing a settlement in "their" community. Complete and permanent segregation was not desirable, according to this journalist, who was probably white. The editor argued that a "coloured individual . . . may be infinitely preferable [as a neighbor] to a White; and he may also be a better citizen and christian. Why then should his colour, or his origin, or his previous suffering and degradation, while in bondage to white tyrants, be urged as any reason for perpetuating his debasement?"[54]

One indirect result of the August 18 meeting and its resolutions was that it aroused Wilson Abbott, Adolphus Judah, and other black stockholders in the Elgin Association to action. These men collectively wrote to Malcolm Cameron, one of Kent County's elected representatives in the Legislative Assembly, to express concern about blacks' civil rights. In particular, they wanted to know how Cameron felt about the settling of blacks in Raleigh Township and elsewhere. They also inquired about whether he would assist in protecting the legal rights and privileges of blacks who chose to settle in the vicinity. The response to this inquiry was favorable. Cameron unequivocally defended blacks' rights throughout Canada and pledged his support for their civil and religious rights. Cameron further reported that the Canadian government took the position that blacks could buy land and settle wherever they wanted, either singly or in groups. If Cameron accurately represented the government's position, Larwill and his supporters obviously faced an uphill battle against King and the proposed settlement.[55]

The Chatham meeting spurred other voices to support King and the Elgin Association. "Quid," an anonymous letter writer in the *Toronto Globe*, defended King and his proposal while condemning King's critics, especially those at the meeting. A further response to the meeting was a public letter signed by one hundred six residents of the Chatham area and published in the *Globe* that declared that "a large and respectable portion of the inhabitants of the District, offer no opposition" to the proposed black settlement.[56] The letter carried substantial potency in that it was signed by Archibald McKellar—a member of the Elgin Association's board of directors—Thomas Williams, and George Jacobs, all of whom were justices of the peace and prominent local leaders. Weighing in on this debate over the purchase of land for black settlement, the *Church*, the official voice of the Anglican denomination, asked, with "Scots, Irish, French, and German settlements why may we not have an African settlement?"[57]

Some of those who opposed King's proposal considered doing so with more than mere words. King believed that his enemies were determined to prevent him from settling blacks on the tract of land he had purchased and that "what they could not do legally they determined to do by mob violence."[58] After purchasing the land, King appointed a local surveyor to accompany King and a government agent to the tract to begin dividing it. A local vigilance committee apparently planned to come out "with a number of Roughs" to drive them off the land.[59] Fortunately for King, the government agent became ill, necessitating a postponement of the trip. Unaware of the delay, the committee and the "roughs" went out to the land and "spent the day in drinking and threatening what they would do to [King] should he appear on the land."[60] Some black residents in Chatham heard about the threat to King and went out armed, "determined to fight if [King] should be attacked."[61] King was convinced that if he had appeared that day there would have been bloodshed, violence that "would in all probability have proved fatal to our cause."[62] King's trepidation that violence could have spelled the end of the plan was not unwarranted. After all, such mob violence had prevented the Randolph slaves from settling as a group in Mercer County in Ohio. The delay worked to calm emotions on both sides, and the surveying expedition later took place without incident.

The opposition to King's plan did not simply fade away. Larwill and his supporters persuaded the Western District Council to send an official protest to the Canadian Parliament. On October 8, 1849, the council appointed a committee to draft an address to the governor-general on the issue of black immigration. The address argued that previous petitions in favor of the proposed settlement had been "principally if not wholly, signed by Colored People in order to mislead the Government" and as such did not "embody the sentiments or feelings of the respectable, intelligent, and industrious yeomanry of the Western District."[63] The document concluded by reasserting that "that there is but one feeling, and that is of disgust and hatred," that blacks "should be allowed to settle in any Township where there is a white settlement."[64] Those opposed to King's ideas no longer pretended to be concerned about black rights.

Apparently without the council's knowledge, Larwill added several recommendations of his own to the committee's address after it was approved by the council but before its delivery to the governor-general. Larwill suggested that blacks be barred from public schools and public office, that a poll tax be imposed on them, and that the practice of allowing blacks to vote be examined. Even more radical was Larwill's request, reminiscent of the black laws of the northern United States, that all blacks be required to post bonds if they wished to stay in Canada. In the end, this independent action destroyed Larwill's influence. Many of his supporters concluded that he was an extremist and withdrew from his campaign, unwilling to go that far to restrict black liberties and rights. In the end, the Canadian government did not seriously consider any of Larwill's recommendations or the address from the Western District Council.[65]

Opposition to King's proposed black settlement extended beyond Raleigh Township. In September 1849, a citizen from Montreal, Lower Canada, wrote to Lord Elgin expressing concern arising from reports of the public meeting at the Royal Exchange Hotel. He referred to King's proposal as an "impolitic, unpatriotic, demoralizing and dangerous" undertaking.[66] The writer contended that black settlers were hampering and would continue to hamper the settlement of "more desirable" British emigrants and that blacks were compelling whites to leave Canada. This citizen insisted that if unchecked, this state of affairs "may prove highly detrimental to not only the advancement of the Western District, but to the future of the whole province."[67] This "concerned citizen's" letter closed with an appeal to Lord Elgin to persuade the government to cooperate with the leading members of society and enforce a policy that would give preference to British emigrants and discourage the further introduction of black settlers. This appeal, like others before it, failed. Lord Elgin gave his support to King and the association bearing the Elgin name, and the plan proceeded.

King responded to his critics in a letter published in the *Chronicle*, a Chatham newspaper. He explained that the Presbyterian Church was not, as some believed, sponsoring the settlement to the exclusion of other denominations. He further sought to mollify critics who feared an influx of undesirable residents by reiterating that the settlement was to be open only to the moral and industrious. Ironically, this reassurance itself attracted criticism. At least one antagonist of the proposed settlement rejoined that if the settlement was in fact to be open only to those blacks who had shown their moral and industrious nature, those blacks most needing assistance would be neglected.[68]

King's settlement ultimately benefited from Larwill and other critics' attacks. The conflict resulted in much press attention, and the plan for the Buxton settlement consequently became well known throughout Canada and the northern United States. As is often the case, with propaganda came exaggeration. Various rumors circulated about the settlement. One such rumor reported that King had chartered a vessel and was planning to bring a whole shipload of blacks to form a colony in Canada. Such publicity helped Buxton in that it made blacks more aware of the community, thereby creating a sort of boom situation in which the settlement at Buxton grew much more quickly than had at first been anticipated. Moreover, additional white advocates of King's proposal became attracted to his cause as a result of the increased circulation of news about the settlement.

Aversion to King and his proposed settlement demonstrated the distrust and dislike that greeted the Buxton experiment in some quarters. This aversion further showed that Canada was not devoid of prejudice and that, presented with an opportunity, some of its white citizens could prove themselves just as antiblack as some U.S. residents. At the same time, the controversy showed the Canadian government's support for its black residents. Despite the pressure brought to bear on his administration, Lord Elgin did not disavow either King or his plan to improve the situation of blacks. King and his proponents succeeded, and establishment of the settlement proceeded.

4

A Settlement Takes Shape

The history of the Buxton settlement is best examined from the dual perspective of white control and black empowerment. The Buxton settlers, like those of other black communities, defined their history by their actions. White influence, however, also defined the settlement. The Buxton community exemplifies the complexities of the relationship between blacks and whites. At the same time, it typifies the active roles played by blacks functioning both alone and in concert with white reformers.

To guide Buxton's growth and development, the Elgin Association set certain standards and prescribed numerous regulations. The lack of focused administration and direction of that kind, King believed, had been a primary stumbling block at other black community organizing attempts. Both contemporaries and historians have viewed these regulations as overly paternalistic and unnecessarily rigid and harsh. In particular, critics have faulted King for being dictatorial. King cannot, though, be held solely accountable either for these regulating principles or for the exclusive governing of the settlement. King's initial prospectus had called for the settlement's administration to remain in the hands of the association's executive, presumably the president. This directive was never implemented as intended. Instead, the terms of settlement were placed in the hands of the stockholders and their appointees—a board of directors. In accordance with the association's constitution, the directors were empowered to "make and subscribe all such rules and regulations touching the purchase, management and disposition of lands . . . of the said Association, and the settlement and improvement of the said lands."[1] When first proposing his plan to create an all-black settlement, King had laid out the duties of the settlement's supervisor, presumably thinking of himself for the position: "The person . . . would act as agent for the company, attend to the settling of the land, and collecting the annual payments as they fell due."[2] As he planned, the directors appointed men to superintend the affairs of the settlement. During the early years, William King was the sole superintendent, but by 1859 Archibald McKellar and Alexander Knapp were recorded, along with King, as managing the settlement's affairs.

Although King had a great deal of influence with the association and no doubt advised the board of directors to enact many of the regulations, the final decision technically rested with the board, which had sole authority to mandate conditions of settlement. The settlement's official rules and regulations came, in theory, from the association board, while implementation and enforcement rested with King. Unfortunately, no extant evidence clarifies exactly where the power over the association's affairs resided in practice. It is unknown whether the board simply rubber-stamped King's directives or whether it acted independently on occasion. The fact that McKellar and Knapp joined King as superintendents of the affairs of the settlement suggests, however, that a rift may have developed between the board of directors and King over his management of the settlement.

This system of oversight, or at least the concept of retaining some white control of the black settlers and community, was implemented in similar experiments. The British-American Institute likewise had managerial control, albeit limited, over the Dawn community. Through the creation of a trust, Samuel Gist legally arranged to control his former slaves long after their manumission. Like King and the association board, the Gist slaves' trustees were armed with the conviction that they knew what was best. King, Gist, and other white reformers attempted to protect formerly subject people whom they perceived as dependent by confining them to a trust relationship.

Black responses to the oversight varied. Extant evidence does not suggest that Buxton settlers opposed the control of the Elgin Association or King personally. A different outcome emerged between the former Gist slaves and both their trustee, William Wickham, and the Quaker agents. In the late 1840s the Gist freedpeople began to request that Wickham replace the Quakers, whom the blacks deemed negligent. In one such appeal, the settlers contended that the Quakers dealt "very unkindley with us they give us nothing."[3] The primary complaint seems to have been that the Quakers lived far off and only rarely involved themselves with the settlements. The distinction between King and Wickham seems to have been that King's relationship with the Buxton community was principally to Buxton's advantage, while that between Wickham, the Quakers, and the Gist community was to the former slaves' detriment. In the cases of John Randolph's former slaves and those of Gist, the trustees carried out the wishes of the former master and lacked King's personal interest in and concern for the former slaves. Significantly, Randolph, Gist, and Edward Coles were far less intimately connected with the lives of their former slaves than was King. Further, none of these men seemed interested or involved in the larger reform movement, as King did.[4]

Although approximately a quarter of the Elgin Association's stockholders were black and the settlement was established for the benefit of blacks, only a single black man, Wilson R. Abbott, was elected to serve on the first board of directors. Furthermore, the settlers had no active role in Buxton's general management. In this respect, the association took a protectionist if not paternalist approach to its task. The majority of the board members subscribed, to some degree at least, to contemporary white society's belief that blacks could not sustain themselves and their families without white guidance and support. Having contributed the monetary means for the beginnings of the settlement, the association's stockholders were undoubtedly anxious that the money not be squandered or otherwise abused. The association members thought the way to prevent waste was to retain control of the purse strings. The Buxton stockholders knew of the financial ruin of both Wilberforce and Dawn, knowledge that surely influenced the Elgin Association's leadership and decisions.

The association's constitution specifically mandated that the land encompassing the Buxton settlement, known as the Elgin tract, be exclusively reserved for settlement by blacks and that the land be sold to them at the lowest terms that would remunerate the stockholders for their initial expenditure. The directors devised additional regulations. As a protection against white intrusion, black purchasers could not resell the land to whites for ten years. King and other leaders of the Elgin Association feared that white encroachment would harm the black settlers and the community's independence. When King first broached the idea of creating the association, he stated that its purpose would be "to protect the land for coloured settlers."[5] The association leaders were worried that unscrupulous whites would take advantage of black settlers' vulnerability, as had occurred at Gerrit Smith's settlement, where whites cheated many settlers of their land.

According to King, any plan to ameliorate the condition of blacks must be adapted to "their peculiar circumstances," by which he meant that when "mixed with the white population they do not improve; Prejudice excludes them in a great measure from the common schools and operates against their advancement."[6] King argued that prejudice also prevented blacks from experiencing the advantageous social mixing that assisted immigrants in adopting the customs of, forming connections with, and becoming absorbed in the general population. Blacks were often excluded from these advantages and thereby remained "in the community the same degraded being that slavery has left him."[7] Segregation on their own land, protected from white intrusion, would provide black settlers at Buxton with opportunities unavailable to other blacks. One aspect of community, common space, was thus already established in Buxton, whereas other black communities often had to carve out that common space amid the presence and competition of whites.

The land composing the Elgin tract was sold in fifty-acre plots for two dollars and fifty cents per acre on an annual installment plan of 10 percent down with the balance, plus 6 percent interest, to be paid within ten years.[8] The association adopted the fifty-acre minimum based on King's recommendation that fifty acres was the smallest amount of land that would allow a black family to support itself. One contributing factor to the failure of most manumission settlements was that, planned as agricultural communities, they usually consisted of farms too small to sustain even self-sufficiency. Blacks in most such settlements subsisted in a limited economic environment, with minimal planning, and little community structure. King tried to avoid the pitfalls that had occurred in other settlements by making land available in tracts that would provide adequate subsistence for families. Nothing prevented a person or family from acquiring more than fifty acres. A number of families, including those of Isaac Riley, George Hatter, Hampton Bailey, Levi Anderson, Walter Toyer, and Joseph Elliss, purchased one-hundred-acre plots.

The Elgin Association's financial arrangements may seem prohibitively expensive for the intended settlers and even contrary to the stated intent of the settlement as a refuge for fugitives. Fugitive slaves and even many free blacks would have been unlikely to have much in the way of start-up resources whether in the form of seed and livestock or rudimentary household and farming implements, let alone cash for the down payment of twelve dollars and fifty cents. Why the Elgin Association decided to impose this financial arrangement is unclear. Their commitment to creating a settlement based on independence and self-reliance is well documented. Despite the apparent unreasonableness of their financial requirements, this goal may have been foremost in their minds when composing the regulations. The board may further have considered recent local white criticism of the proposed settlement, particularly the remonstrances of the Chatham meeting. Mindful of such fears, the association's directives may have been intended in part to create a perception that only responsible, upstanding settlers who could afford the financial obligations would enter Buxton.[9]

In practice, the required down payment may not have been collected prior to or immediately upon settlement. Incoming settlers may have received grace periods before the required funds came due. Some sources allude to a payment plan consisting of ten annual installments, implying that the initial payment was not actually a down payment due on arrival but rather just another annual payment. Settlers could then acquire the money, presumably by hiring out their labor. Various employment opportunities existed, from day laboring on local farms to work on the nearby railroad. Of course, any such outside employment hindered settlers' progress in clearing their land, building their homes, and planting their crops. Given the nature of the settlement, it is also reasonable to assume that needy settlers would have received assistance from other community members. More established residents or those families who came to the settlement with more resources, including Wilson R. Abbott, George Hatter, and Milton Ragland, may have made funds available to newly arrived families. Perhaps King or other sympathetic whites loaned money to arriving settlers. Furthermore, Buxtonians apparently did not lose their land if they failed to make one installment, perhaps more. In an 1857 article on Buxton, the *New York Tribune* referred to a man, previously a slave, who had been at Buxton six years and had in that time paid four installments on his farm. Whether this case was typical remains unknown, but the final report of the Elgin Association, filed in 1873, showed only two lots with unpaid balances. Despite any apparent prohibitive nature of the financial arrangement, in the end the Elgin Association provided blacks access to a homestead for a relatively small sum and with the prospect of receiving title. Lacking capital, most blacks elsewhere must have felt that their chances of becoming independent farmers were dismal. Buxton made that goal possible.[10]

The availability of an installment payment plan at Buxton contrasted sharply with the procedure for acquiring land on the U.S. frontier. Much of that land was available at a minimum price of a dollar twenty-five an acre, meaning that settlers could receive clear title to half a quarter-section of public land (eighty acres) for one hundred dollars, payable in cash. According to one estimate, "to buy and fully open a farm" in Illinois during the early nineteenth century, "a man did best to bring about five hundred dollars in cash with him."[11] Many settlers lacked access to such financial resources and therefore became squatters on the land. An estimated two-thirds of Illinois's farmers in 1828 were squatters on public domain. Without the availability of Buxton's installment plan, settlers would not have been able to purchase land in their own right.

The titles to all the lots were held by the association until the land had been completely paid off. Only then did the settlers have full right to use the land as they saw fit. Until that time, the Elgin Association and its representatives implemented certain mandates for the use of the land. Settlers had to buy the land, not rent it or live on it as sharecroppers. And, as previously stated, if the land was resold during the first ten years, the new buyers must be black. King sought to exercise "a wholesome vigilance . . . over the whole settlement that would stimulate the idle, encourage the industrious, and promote the social improvement of all," implying the settler's incapacity to accomplish such goals on their own or at least the unlikelihood of their doing so.[12] The rules were intended not to be detrimental but to protect and assist the settlers. The Gist slaves, who could never hold full title to their land, perceived similar restrictions as hindrances to their activities, although Wickham intended these measures to protect the settlers from being swindled out of their land by outsiders. William Wickham was proud of this condition: "[T]hey could live on the land, they could work it, and taxes would still be due on it, but they neither owned it nor could sell it. They were free, but their land was not."[13] This encumbrance proved a dead weight to the settlers. Because they lacked legal titles to the land, the Gist freedpeople had no encouragement to make any improvements on them, and the lack of legal boundaries dividing their plots caused strife among the settlers. Perhaps most significant, lack of title meant that many in the settlements did not own any property at all, meaning that they could not use that property as collateral against loans for tools, seeds, and farm implements. Few of the former Gist slaves succeeded at farming, and most turned to selling their labor to others: By 1860, twice as many heads of household were laborers as were farmers. Without landownership among the settlers, the settlement failed. For all their apparent similarity in intentions, King's and Wickham's settlements created different results.[14]

In many respects, the guidelines mandated by the Elgin Association provided for outright segregation as well as a form of indenture, albeit of a voluntary nature. All settlers were to be black and subject to oversight, although they could, of course, choose to move out of the settlement. These regulations were meant to protect the settlers in two ways: by separating them from hostile whites and by preventing white opportunists from swindling the settlers out of their land. King believed that previous experiments to establish black communities had failed in large part because blacks relatively quickly became a foreign element in what were intended to be their own communities as white settlers purchased land and moved in. In King's mind, such unsympathetic white settlers then interfered with improvements to blacks' religious and moral condition, and he believed that a minimum of ten years was needed to accomplish the education and degree of self-sufficiency that would allow blacks to maintain themselves. Reformers in general confronted a paradox: They sought to promote independent behavior yet at the same time to protect blacks from exploitation by whites, a form of paternalism toward those who were believed incapable of protecting themselves. One approach to this dilemma, an approach taken by King, Wickham, and others, was to institute a form of segregation. It is not clear whether Buxton's blacks approved of these arrangements, but they certainly had no say in the matter, since the decisions were made before the arrival of the first settlers.[15]

Just as blacks disagreed about the efficacy of emigration from the United States, they debated the positive and negative aspects of segregation and integration. This controversy reflected a fundamental dilemma facing black activists. Should blacks strive for acceptance in white America or struggle to achieve a distinctive culture and separate society? Should segregated facilities be viewed as an end in themselves or as a transition device and so be shaped to bridge white and black communities? Questions such as these were prominent in the thoughts of nineteenth-century U.S. and Canadian blacks. Some black spokespeople objected to the separatist tendencies that many all-black settlements encouraged. Samuel Cornish advanced the position that blacks should participate with whites in the joint development of new agricultural communities. Conversely, the Reverend Lewis Woodson advocated that free blacks establish separate settlements like Buxton rather than disperse themselves among white pioneers. He openly called for blacks to establish their own separate communities, separate businesses, and separate churches. Buxton fell somewhere between the extremes. Although Buxton was an all-black settlement, it was not exclusively black, nor completely separate from the white community.[16]

King and the Elgin Association served as a semi-protectorate, attempting to shield black Buxtonians from the threat posed by white society. Most of the organized black communities of the antebellum era were likewise founded by whites who acted in a supervisory capacity. Wickham assumed a distinctly paternalistic attitude toward Gist's former slaves whom he thought of as "children who needed to be protected from themselves" and who were "incapable of acting for themselves."[17] Such an attitude was not always welcomed by blacks, who often begrudged the moral guardianship, yet they could hardly afford to risk alienating their allies by expressing this sentiment.

Buxton's imposed segregation was never intended to be permanent. Whites could and did purchase Elgin land after the expiration of the ten-year ban. Even during the initial ten-year period, residential segregation was not complete. In addition to King, a small number of other white families lived on the tract, including the Roes (Rowes) and Broadbents, who had settled on the land before the Elgin Association purchased the bloc. These families were not forced off their land and did not choose to leave when blacks began to move in. Instead, these whites lived and worked as neighbors to the black settlers. Buxton's segregation also did not extend beyond landownership and settlement. White settlers lived on plots of land bordering the Elgin tract, thereby inviting contact between whites and blacks. There were also black families who settled on land near, but not officially part of, the Elgin tract. Buxton's schools and churches were integrated, as were social and business concerns. Such cooperative living shows that Edwin Larwill's influence was neither widespread nor effective. Those white settlers who would have the most personal contact with the black settlers were not so concerned about the consequences of the black settlement that they relocated.[18]

The Elgin Association's 1850 annual report stated that "more than one year has elapsed since the society was formed; and during that time nothing has occurred to mar the harmony of its proceedings."[19] Reported disturbances between local whites and black settlers were few. King's writings, however, imply that some disagreements existed between black Buxtonians and their white neighbors. King noted his concern that when a school was started, "the mob would break it up and . . . so anoy [*sic*] the settlers, as to cause them to leave."[20] When disputes arose, King acted as a kind of arbitrator, noting proudly that such disputes were "generally settled . . . amicably without going to law."[21] In his typical manner, King actively oversaw the relations between Buxton settlers and local whites. He "kept a strict watch over the affairs of the settlement" and counseled the settlers to refer any difficulties directly to him; he would "see that justice was done them."[22] King cautioned black residents to bear with patience their trials and to give no offense to their white neighbors. King's intention to maintain peace in the community through personal intervention could be interpreted as the desire to ensure that black settlers not offend whites or as the desire to prevent whites from taking advantage of or otherwise abusing black settlers.[23]

King specifically referred to only one incident, amicably settled, between black and white settlers. This dispute concerned land and had little, if anything, to do with race. The standard subdivision of Crown land was two-hundred-acre lots. The white families already in the Elgin tract believed that they owned an entire lot but had deeds to only one hundred acres. The so-called back hundred was unsettled at the time of Elgin Association's land purchase, and the association bought the land from the government and in turn deeded it to Buxton settlers. The resulting uncertainty in ownership caused some difficulty during the first winter of settlement.

One such confrontation involved John Rowe (white) and Robert Harris (black). During the winter of 1849, Harris took up residence on one of the rear lots in the eleventh concession and set about erecting a log cabin. The owner of the acreage adjoining Harris's lot, Rowe, believed that he was the land's rightful owner and ordered Harris off the lot. Harris produced a location ticket as proof of his claim to the land, but Rowe disregarded the ticket and threatened to drive Harris off by force. To avoid an altercation, Harris departed.

King was on a business trip to Toronto at the time but heard about the incident when he returned. According to King, he called a meeting between the two men at which Rowe reported that a Chatham man had said that Rowe could purchase the back hundred of his lot. Rowe gave the man the money and consequently believed himself to be the legal owner of the disputed land. King then requested Rowe's deed to the land to substantiate his claim. Rowe was unable to provide this proof, and King brought forth the Elgin Association's title to the land. With such verification of Harris's claim, Rowe apparently gave in.

There is no evidence that either party took further action, and Harris's name appears on that lot on future Buxton maps.[24]

Other disagreements undoubtedly arose between black Buxtonians and their white neighbors. Such disputes seem to have been handled congenially and did not result in deep divisions between black and white settlers. There are periodic references to a Buxton settlement court, presided over by King, to handle disputes both among Buxtonians and between them and their neighbors. Unfortunately, no extant records provide details of any specific cases brought before the court. The Elgin Association's Third Annual Report stated that the court of arbitration had amicably resolved five cases during the year but gave no further details. This rather cordial relationship undeniably played a role in the success of Buxton. Local whites might not have been as sympathetic and supportive as were the Quakers in the area of the Beech and Roberts settlements, but they were not overtly hostile. Meanwhile, Gist's former slaves probably experienced more tension than did Buxton if only in that the most racist counties in Ohio were in the southern part of the state, the very area in which the Gist freedpeople settled. Pike County, where New Philadelphia was located, was not free from racial hostility either. Free Frank initially found support among Pike County white settlers, but his early success seemed threatening to some whites, and Free Frank's later activities in promoting New Philadelphia were carried out in an atmosphere of antagonism and racial conflict that kept the settlers in a state of tension.[25]

Another regulation imposed by the Elgin Association was that the settlement accepted only people of approved moral character. After visiting Buxton in 1852, white abolitionist Samuel May noted that "none were admitted into the Association unless they brought certificates of good moral character."[26] According to May, King insisted that such a high standard was indispensable to the settlement's success, arguing that "if all should be admitted who might come, whether they were temperate or intemperate, industrious or indolent, honest or dishonest," the community might be so seriously impeded that it could not succeed.[27] This regulation was not necessarily meant to be permanent. May reported King's contention that when the foundation of the community was securely laid and a strong conservative moral influence established, the association could become less particular in its examination and acceptance of prospective settlers. Indeed, at some point, Buxton "may be even willing to admit persons known to be bad, in the hope of reforming them."[28] Despite King's best intentions, this regulation may well not have been strictly or even loosely enforced. After all, many settlers were fugitive slaves who could hardly be expected to produce certificates of good moral character. Free blacks may have had difficulties complying as well. King may instead have spoken with prospective settlers to personally determine their moral fiber. No extant evidence suggests that settlers were either turned away or asked to leave Buxton because of unacceptable character or behavior. The leaders of the Buxton settlement expected residents to live respected, restrained, moral lives. In this vein, when Coles freed his slaves, he also gave them some unsolicited advice, his fervent wish that they "behave themselves and so well, not only for their own sakes, but for the sake of the black race held in bondage."[29] They "should so conduct themselves, as to show by their example, that the descendants of Africa were competent to take care of & govern themselves."[30] Blacks elsewhere were similarly admonished to make choices that would advance their acceptability to whites and convince them of black suitability for citizenship and equality.[31]

Regardless of the regulation and its enforcement or lack thereof, it is not surprising that the moral stature of its residents was of such value at Buxton. Such moral concerns were analogous to that of black society elsewhere. In response to racism, some blacks increased their efforts to prove themselves respectable, and black leaders promoted moral reform and self-improvement, featuring it prominently in speeches and writings published in newspapers, pamphlets, articles, and books. James McCune Smith, a black activist, "preached adherence to the traditional values of thrift, punctuality, hard work, and moral rectitude," believing that moral virtue and a strong work ethic instilled hope and created self-esteem.[32] Moral improvement was viewed as an essential tool with which to effect a change in both the condition of blacks and white attitudes toward them. Black leadership yearned for the larger black community to make themselves "respectable" in their eyes as well as in the eyes of whites. As such, they strove to inculcate the proper moral attitudes and encourage blacks to behave in a respectable manner, stressing the importance of "propriety of conduct, industry and economy."[33] Flamboyant dress, drunkenness, gambling, frolicking, and raucous behavior were seen as signs of degeneracy and as harmful to the cause of black society. John Rapier counseled his son in Buxton to "keep out of bad company" and save his "money and lay it out for land in place of liquor and cigars."[34] Black and white leaders lectured blacks on the necessity of living conservative lives above reproach. Reformers frowned on any action that might be used to bolster racists' argument that blacks were inherently immoral and hence inferior and fit only for slavery.

This idea of moral reform figured prominently in the context of the dominant strategy of black leaders; namely, self-improvement. Through self-improvement, the black community desired to challenge, on two major points, the charge that blacks were innately inferior. First, by demonstrating their potential for achievement and advancement, blacks countered claims that they were mentally incapable. Second, by demonstrating their capacity for moral transformation, they countered claims that they were immoral. Blacks believed that self-improvement would elevate the race and eradicate prejudice. Of course, this was dependent on prejudice being caused by the deficiencies of blacks—deficiencies that would be eradicated through education and moral reform—rather than as a result of deeply ingrained prejudicial attitudes. A central link was made between inequality and degradation—that the black race experienced inequality not because of the ingrained prejudicial attitudes of whites but rather because of the degradation of blacks. Unfortunately, the failure of such logic was its lack of recognition that whites "might hate an educated black as well as an ignorant one, that whites might not want to live and work with proper, abstemious blacks any more than with black drunkards."[35] Self-improvement was, therefore, more useful as a strategy to raise the conditions of blacks than one to end discriminatory treatment.[36]

The core aspects of this self-improvement agenda were education and moral reform, both of which figured prominently in King's vision for Buxton. King agreed with the logic inherent in the idea of self-improvement—that is, that prejudice was the result rather than the cause of the debased condition of free blacks. He believed that prejudice "operated powerfully" against the moral improvement of blacks and contended that "this prejudice will remain as long as they continue in ignorance," implying that an improvement in moral and social conditions would result in a corresponding decline in prejudice.[37] At the same time, King showed what may be interpreted as racist tendencies when he commented that "if permitted to live in the degraded state in which slavery has left them" blacks would "become a dangerous and troublesome society."[38] After the 1840s, strategies for advancement focused more intently on practical self-help and economic achievement than on moral uplift. Buxton's focus involved a combination of both strategies.

The Elgin Association further influenced the community's development and appearance. From its inception, Buxton was intended to be a community based on self-reliance and independence rather than on individuality. Substantial planning was involved in the settlement's design. King's "blueprint," with a clear pattern of streets and houses, attests to this focus on community. The Crown land that had been purchased was already laid out in a gridlike pattern, and the settlement's design followed through on that plan. Each fifty-acre plot bordered a concession line along which a road was to be built. Houses were to be built facing the proposed road. Even in its early development, Buxton was to be structured as an interlocking community. The ultimate objective here was a true community rather than a settlement composed merely of individuals and families. King's initial plan included a school, a church, and a missionary house in the belief that a community would evolve around these institutions. Joined by a post office, store, hotel, and various other businesses—a steam sawmill, a brickyard, a pearl-ash factory, with blacksmith, carpenter, shoe shop, and a country store—these structures would eventually compose Buxton's center square.

Buxton thus benefited from the fact that the Elgin tract was purchased as a bloc relatively uninhabited by white settlers and made available only to blacks, thereby assuring Buxton residents the advantage of common space, which, in the words of the trustees for Gerrit Smith's land, was important to enable settlers "by mutual aid" to overcome difficulties and create an independent black community.[39]

At Buxton, according to association directives, houses had to be set back no less than thirty-three feet from the road. Each homestead was required to have a picket fence and a front garden that included flowers. The cabin itself had to meet minimum standards. A front "gallery" or porch was required, extending across the side facing the road. The houses were to be no less than twenty-four feet wide and eighteen feet deep and the roofs no less than twelve feet high at their peaks. Each house was to be divided into at least four rooms. As with the fifty-acre requirement, these conditions were minima. By 1861, eleven frame houses had been built alongside the more typical log homes. Two of these frame houses had more than one story, and a twelfth house was a two-story brick building. As in other areas, part of the motivation for such housing regulations came from perceived failings at Wilberforce and Dawn. The Reverend William Proudfoot, a white minister, had visited Wilberforce in 1833 and reported that "the dwellings of the Negroes [are] wretched, badly built and very small."[40] King and the Elgin Association board desired to avoid such problems in Buxton.[41]

In still other areas, King assisted or arguably controlled the settlers' decision making. Early in Buxton's development, King organized the settlers into work crews to clear land and raise cabins. Robin Phares, one of King's former slaves, described those early days: "We were just like wild deer in the woods and didn't know how to take care of ourselves. Mr. King had to teach us and do everything for us."[42] Phares may have overstated the helplessness of the early settlers, but every new community benefits from sound leadership, and King filled that role. Later, King strongly suggested that the settlement be based on temperance principles and that it not resort to the practice of begging or accepting aid from outsiders. After community meetings to discuss the issue, the settlers adopted both these suggestions. Though these practices noticeably benefited the community and were accepted by the majority, King continued to control the decision making, at least to some degree. Nonetheless, Buxton residents were not necessarily merely following King's lead in this matter. As their actions show, they agreed with the idea of moral respectability as a path to acceptance by white society. The Buxton settlers' embrace of moral uplift had as much to do with their beliefs and actions as with King's ideology.

These rules and regulations provide insight into the mind-set of King and other white reformers active in Buxton's founding and development. King's writings, both private and public, demonstrate clearly that he viewed blacks as socially and morally subordinate to whites—the social and moral improvement of blacks was the primary objective for the settlement's establishment. Like Gerrit Smith, King distinguished between moral and material progress. What mattered most to men such as Smith and King was obedience to God and the moral state of blacks, not accruing wealth.

King repeatedly described those blacks living in Canada as existing in a "low state of moral degradation" and as "living in that degraded condition in which slavery has left them."[43] He believed that blacks' inferior position had been caused by the debasement of slavery rather than by any biological inadequacy, thus opening the possibility of redemption. King unquestionably believed blacks were capable of rising above the ill effects of slavery and of improving themselves socially, economically, and intellectually. Otherwise, there would have been no point to his establishment of Buxton. King stated that he "held to the theory that, from the same chances, the southern negro would succeed in self-sustaining enterprise. Why not? In slavery he supported both his master and himself. In freedom, as I believed . . . his capabilities would not desert him."[44] The conviction of the majority of whites in the nineteenth century was that blacks were innately inferior. Seen from this perspective, King seems enlightened. All the same, King's views were not entirely altruistic. King viewed it as essential that all be done to assure that slaves, upon achieving freedom, be raised up from their degraded state, for, if they were to receive "the full privileges of free citizens and at the same time allow them to remain in ignorance[,] . . . we shall bring calamity upon ourselves; for they will become a dangerous and troublesome element."[45] As his views toward slave ownership once centered on the institution's negative effect on whites, so now did his concerns about freedom. King's opinion was qualified: blacks could overcome the ill effects of slavery only if provided with the right opportunities and supervision. This qualification provides insight about the limits of King's racial egalitarianism. King maintained that to rise above slavery, blacks needed guidance from whites. The settlement's prospectus, written by King, made it clear that the residents of the community were to be "placed under a careful and judicious supervision."[46] Other whites echoed King's sentiments in this matter, although blacks often denounced such opinions.

Buxton represented the work of a collaborative effort between whites and blacks. This characterization may not be unique to Buxton, but it was one of the most successful examples of the phenomenon. Brooklyn and both the Beech and Roberts settlements resulted from independent black activity. New Philadelphia, although it became a biracial town, was established by a black man. Wilberforce and Dawn were the products of efforts of white and black leaders, neither of whom, however, worked especially effectively. Gerrit Smith's settlement, which he called North Elba but residents referred to as Timbucto, was the project of a white philanthropist, albeit one who worked well with black leadership. The manumission efforts of Gist, Randolph, and Coles were predominantly orchestrated by whites. Whereas most antebellum efforts by blacks and whites failed to pay off, a working relationship seems to have arisen at Buxton.

The prevailing mid-nineteenth-century racial ideology greatly influenced relations among King, the Elgin Association, and Buxton residents. A range of differences in approaches and objectives divided antebellum white and black reformers, and one crucial distinction lay in the fact that white abolitionists tended to concentrate primarily on emancipating slaves while free black leaders stressed achieving full civil rights for blacks as much as ending slavery. Black leaders often pursued their goals both in conjunction with whites and separately. Black and white abolitionists' perceptions of the meaning of racial equality differed. The day-to-day realities of blacks' lives included acts of discrimination, economic difficulties, and lack of educational opportunities that whites did not experience.[47]

King took a fairly radical stance toward abolition. Like Gerrit Smith and his colleagues, King stressed equality, although he did not quite agree with the view that blacks should be treated as full equal members of society. King and most white abolitionists held that the black masses had to improve themselves before they could qualify for equal treatment and that guidance and education were needed to stimulate this improvement. In the culture of white Protestantism, reformers, including King, saw themselves as missionaries seeking to uplift blacks to the levels of white civilization. Despite their efforts, few whites ever completely overcame their racial and cultural biases. Perhaps King did so better than most white abolitionists. Whereas most white abolitionists tended to associate only with "respectable" blacks, King purposely worked with lower-class blacks to raise their social, moral, religious, and economic condition.

The relationships among King, the Elgin Association, and Buxton residents were complex. At one level existed a mutual reciprocity of duty and responsibility. King provided Buxtonians with what he defined as spiritual, moral, and educational advancement as well as protection from both slave masters (or their agents) and white encroachments on black rights and liberties. In return, the settlers adhered to the various regulations set up by King and the Elgin Association. At least a loose analogy can be made between the regulations, control, and interference in the lives of Buxtonians and the various constraints adults place on children. Children, it is generally believed, should not make significant decisions for themselves or chart their own course in life. Parents or guardians make such decisions until the children become adults. In King's paternalistic eyes, Buxtonians reached adult status only when their spiritual knowledge, education, and morality had improved and eradicated the effects of slavery. King undoubtedly looked on his former slaves and other blacks who would settle at Buxton in a fatherly fashion, and he may have perceived them as a surrogate family, replacing his dead wife and children. The available evidence indicates that Buxton's residents reciprocated this view, seeing King as a patriarchal figure, the undisputed leader of the community.

Others similarly perceived the relationship between King and Buxton residents. In a brief description of the Buxton Mission, the *Provincial Freeman* depicted King as "a philanthropist—for he has undertaken to look over, officiate as Minister, and act the part of a father to a colony of coloured persons."[48] Samuel May referred to King as "a sort of Patriarch among" the Buxton settlers. May continued, "All of them know how much he has thitherto done, and is now sacrificing for their improvement and elevation. This, of course, binds them to him by ties of gratitude."[49] Thomas Henning, a white journalist for the *Toronto Globe*, went even further in his portrayal of King: "the Rev. Mr. King . . . is regarded throughout the settlement as the King whom all are bound to obey, and to judge from what I witnessed, the obedience of the settlers was no less implicit than their confidence and respect were sincere and profound."[50] This description of King, reprinted in the *Provincial Freeman*, was followed by an editorial highly critical of Henning's wording, particularly the reference to King as king. The *Provincial Freeman* implored its readers and the Buxton settlers to "regard Bro. King, hereafter, as a *father*, and not 'as the King.'"[51] The editors further noted that if by the expression "all are bound to obey" Henning meant that "men and women are to yield their *conscience* and give up their *private* judgment in obedience to 'the King,' then . . . the Elgin Settlement . . . never can develop an *independent and self respecting people*."[52] These editors, then, had no qualms about referring to King in paternal terms but drew the line at calling him a monarch or dictator. Moreover, the journalists did not view Buxton residents as unquestioningly following King like a flock of docile sheep. There is no record of Buxtonians' reaction to Henning's words.

Whether King's actions appear interfering, as they do at times, or seem merely influencing, as they do at other times, Buxton's settlers consented to those acts. Furthermore, despite the continuing influence of King and the legal authority of the Elgin Association, blacks in Buxton exerted a greater degree of autonomy over their own lives than had been the case under slavery. Any conception we form of King's stewardship or protectorship necessitates a determination of the degree to which the Buxton settlers' decision making was restricted. Nineteenth-century blacks faced formidable challenges in gaining control over their destinies. The Elgin Association's regulations and King's oversight probably did not appreciably hinder black settlers' efforts in this regard. Despite the apparent authoritarianism in some matters, neither King nor the Elgin Association dictated the entire scope of the settlers' lives. Notwithstanding King's emphasis on religion and education as the means to improve blacks' condition, residents were not compelled to attend either church or school. No communal regulations existed other than those adopted voluntarily by the settlers themselves. No police regulations existed other than those pertaining to all of Kent County. And the inhabitants had free choice about what to grow in their fields and what livelihood to follow. In a general way, the various regulations pertaining to housing established by King and the Elgin Association resemble modern zoning laws.

Adherence to the regulations varied. The regulation most strictly enforced was that excluding white settlement during the initial ten-year period. Both the Presbyterian Church and the Canadian government had insisted on this exclusion as a condition for supporting the venture, and this regulation had been incorporated into the Elgin Association's constitution. King strongly believed that the settlement's success depended on this principle, so he would presumably have rigorously enforced it. According to the 1861 census, the first year for which reports for the Township of Raleigh are extant, twelve white families were living on the Elgin tract. Most of them had settled on the land prior to its designation as the Buxton settlement, although at least two—the families of George Thompson and Peter Straith—had not. Thompson became a teacher at the Buxton Mission School, and King had solicited Straith to assist with the management of the local sawmill, leading to the conclusion that the settlement's prohibition against white settlers was overlooked in cases of whites deemed essential to the community.[53]

The association and King made concerted efforts to rigorously enforce those ordinances pertaining to housing. An association committee, composed of stockholders or their representatives, annually visited the settlement to gather vital statistics for the association's annual report. One of the committee's duties was to inspect the settlers' homes and report any violations. Contemporary descriptions of the settlement confirm that the homes met the standard requirements. The majority were of the same dimensions and had identical basic structures and designs, with white fences, flower gardens, and verandas running the length of the houses. Further evidence suggesting that the settlers conscientiously and consistently followed the housing regulations comes from concerns one family expressed about possible penalties if the regulations were not followed. In conferring with each other over their landholdings in Buxton, members of the Rapier family discussed the need to build a house that met the specifications. James Rapier, who was living in the settlement, expressed a degree of anxiety about the status of the family land. He noted that if King could show that the Rapiers had not complied with the conditions of the deed, the family might lose the land. His concern was well warranted, he stressed, as another family had recently lost its holdings for just such a violation. In at least one instance then, a settler's land was sold off for failure to comply with association rules.[54]

Several descriptions survive of Buxton residents' homes during the 1850s. After his 1852 visit to Buxton, May commented that "all who have been there six months, have good, substantial log houses. . . . Around most of their houses are lots of land . . . cleared and fenced and planted."[55] May further described the houses as "really picturesque. Around their doors and windows were rose and other bushes, and various vines, and their doorways were smooth grass plats."[56] After visiting Buxton in the fall of 1855, Henning reported that "the houses are all erected on a uniform plan, after a certain model," and that "while none may build houses inferior to the model, all may surpass it as far as they please. Several have availed themselves of this license, and have constructed larger and more commodious dwellings."[57]

Other evidence suggests that the housing standards were not universally followed. When a correspondent from the *New York Tribune* toured Buxton in 1857, he visited the cabin of a resident who had immigrated from Kentucky only two years earlier. The cabin in question "was smaller than the model." Nevertheless, the owner had "an eye at some future time of adding to it [and had] built the chimney double and a large brick fire place."[58] With this exception, however, the *Tribune* account confirms adherence to the architectural requirements. According to this newspaperman, the houses were "set back the prescribed number of feet from the road and each one surrounded by its kitchen garden. . . . [O]ver the wide porch in front of the cabin creepers were frequently trained. . . . Some of the gardens boasted flower beds and bright coloured phloxes, and poppies and corn flowers."[59]

Evidence suggests that the stipulation regarding the minimum acreage was more laxly enforced. Building lots in the "Village of East Buxton" were advertised in the *Provincial Freeman* as available in one-, three-, and five-acre lots. An advertisement that the Elgin Association placed in 1857 indicated that Buxton town lots were to be sold on the terms of half an acre each, substantially less than the fifty-acre minimum. According to the 1859 tax assessment for Raleigh Township, at least fifty-eight heads of households in Buxton possessed less than the prescribed fifty acres. Approximately twenty-one other Buxton settlers had houses with less than one acre of accompanying land. There is no evidence that the regulation of fifty acres minimum was rescinded, suggesting that it was merely ignored. Nor does it seem plausible that King would have so blatantly disregarded the rule without at least the implicit sanction of the association. The often destitute circumstances of incoming settlers may well have led King or the association's directors to reevaluate their position on the required acreage, and they may have decided that the best interests of the settlement and of their investments necessitated that they make exceptions rather than deny admittance to settlers who could not afford to purchase or maintain fifty acres. If this were the case, the question then arises why this criterion was not officially changed. Perhaps the association believed that publicly lowering the standards of the settlement would result in an influx of undesirable settlers as well as open the settlement to criticism from local whites. The founders may have been concerned that lowering the standards would be interpreted as a failure of the settlers, and perhaps even blacks in general, to live up to the expectations of freedom and true independence.[60]

The public often seems less inclined to engage in close moral scrutiny of acts that proceed from benevolent motives or those aimed at promoting good or preventing harm. Many people prefer a society where others are inclined to intervene in their lives with the aim of promoting their own good. Those free blacks and fugitive slaves who settled in Buxton showed such a preference. The settlers chose to allow other persons a certain amount of control over their lives rather than live in a hostile society such as the U.S. South or the ambivalent and sometimes hostile North. While neither of the latter alternatives may have been particularly viable or appealing, Buxton's inhabitants could conceivably just as well have migrated to other areas of Canada or to such places as Haiti, Mexico, or Africa.[61]

5

A Community Arises

On a bright, warm September afternoon in 1856, more than eight hundred people from the Buxton settlement and its vicinity gathered under a large wooden arbor. Dinner, prepared by a head cook and baker with the assistance of community members, was served by waiters appointed from among the residents. There was venison and wild turkey from the woods; beef, lamb, and chicken from the farm; and vegetables of every description, accompanied by coffee, ice water, and lemonade. Homemade pies and pastries finished off the meal. Music from a brass band completed the dining experience. The honored guests included a delegation appointed by the directors of the Elgin Association to observe the settlement and report back to them. After dinner, guests were further entertained by the band, and the afternoon was rounded out with speeches from members of the delegation. In addition to the association delegates, there were two honored guests: Lord Althorp, eldest son of Earl Spencer, and John Probyn, a member of Parliament. The whole community had joined in the preparations for the dinner celebration. Trees had been felled and carried to the local sawmill. The finished lumber was then brought to William King's property, where the hundred-twenty-foot-long, twelve-foot-high arbor with latticed sides and a boarded roof had been constructed. A temporary kitchen with storeroom and cooking stove was added, and a platform was erected at the other end of the arbor. The day represented more than a social gathering. It was a sign of accomplishment and pride. It was the culmination of community feelings that had developed over the preceding seven years and bound the residents together into a community.[1]

After the incorporation of the Elgin Association and its purchase of land in Raleigh Township, the time for proposals and debate had passed. The work at hand was that of developing a community—ideally, a stable and prosperous community. That community was built from a block of wilderness, regulations and bylaws, proposed maps, diverse ideologies, and, perhaps most important, human toil. The settlers made Buxton what it was. The collective history of any new settlement (characteristics, achievements, failures), regardless of its location, reflects the people who arrive, build, and live there. A successful community begins with a common identification among the people who compose it. In Buxton's case, the residents had much in common: They were of African heritage; individually and collectively they had experienced prejudice and discrimination; many of them were fugitives; and they desired land, education, and economic opportunity. The collective story of Buxton's settlers illustrates their ingenuity and strength.

Because of Buxton's experimental nature, friends and foes alike in Canada and the United States either excitedly or apprehensively awaited the settlement's success or failure. Abolitionists eagerly yearned for its prosperity, which would provide further ammunition for the contention that after being released from bondage and given a chance to prove themselves, blacks could provide for themselves and their families. Critics desired Buxton's downfall so that they could point to it as an example of how blacks were incapable of living outside slavery. Historian Philip Schwarz has called the scrutiny to which Buxton and other black settlements were subjected the "fishbowl factor," with free blacks under close observation.[2] Both abolitionists and slavery's proponents viewed such communities as test cases.

Buxton's first settlers arrived on the land before William King did. After completing the necessary arrangements for the settlement's establishment, King returned to Ohio to rendezvous with his former slaves. When he left his family home in Ohio and headed back to Canada, he assumed that the fifteen blacks who traveled with him would be the first black settlers on the Elgin tract. But camped in his barn, waiting for him on the Elgin reserve, were Isaac Riley, Riley's wife, and their two children.[3]

The Buxtonians encountered numerous obstacles—some endemic to new communities in general and some specific to Buxton as an all-black antebellum community. Put into a larger perspective, Buxton settlers did not have as harsh a life as frontier settlers elsewhere, in that they did not have to contend with hostile natives, a government had been established, a town lay reasonably close by, and the Elgin tract was not a complete wilderness. For many blacks, nevertheless, particularly those just emerging from slavery, securing financial independence for themselves and providing for their families tested the limits of their endurance. The Rileys and other early settlers encountered an almost unbroken forest. Initially, the only buildings in the settlement were those on King's homestead. So, the first order of business for blacks arriving at Buxton, as for any pioneers, was to provide housing for themselves and their families. Until shelters were erected, King probably housed the first settlers in his barn and other outbuildings. Even in these earliest stages, Buxton's settlers showed considerable community togetherness, perhaps because external factors such as racism placed high premiums on internal cooperation and harmony. The tasks of clearing land and raising cabins were organized community events. Here the men who had once legally belonged to King showed the worth of their Ohio experience, forming the core of a crew that built Buxton's first houses. King noted that within a short time, a group of twelve men had become experienced enough to put up a log cabin in one day. In a blatant overstatement, King gave himself full credit, as their teacher, for the settlers' building achievements. Of course, it is likely that, as former slaves, many of Buxton's male settlers were acquainted with house raisings, since slaves built their own quarters in the U.S. South.[4]

Comfortable homes were soon established, as numerous visitors to Buxton attested during the 1850s. Despite the pioneer conditions, comfort and plain homemade furniture abounded. Buxtonians lived in small but sturdy cabins with large fireplaces and well-used porches. Visitors described household furniture and implements, including beds and bedding, chairs and tables, rocking chairs, glassware, and tableware. One family's home was equipped with "chairs, a table, a large chest, a cooking-stove, and its utensils." Another contained a bed and the accompanying bedding as well as "chairs, tables . . . a rocking chair and a large sew safe."[5] Yet another had prints on the walls, a carpet, a sofa, and a large cooking stove in addition to the "usual articles of furniture."[6] Despite the regulations stipulating dimensions, porches, galleries, and whatnot, the homes in Buxton were not uniform. One unnamed visitor, in describing some of the homes he visited, provided evidence of variation. One cabin, though small, had a double chimney in anticipation of a future addition. Another was larger than the model and had a hall in the center with a room on either side.

After building shelter, the next priority was to prepare land for planting. The settlement opened in late fall, leaving the initial settlers with only a short time to clear enough acreage to provide their families with food and seed crops for the next season. Neighbors assisted each other in the race against nature in what was arduous and sometimes dangerous work. Neither gender nor age mattered in this endeavor: Women and children helped by burning timber and stumps to prepare land for planting.

The settlement's communal nature continued as Buxton grew. By the end of the year, a number of other families joined those of King, his former slaves, and Isaac Riley; paid initial installments; and took up lots. The early arrivals were Jerome Boome, William Jackson, William Garle (Garrel), George Chase, Peter Grey, William Fields, Isaac Harden, Henry Phelps, and Green Doo (Due). These men settled with their families on lots in the eighth, ninth, tenth, and eleventh concessions, in the northern section of the Elgin tract, mostly bordering the Centre Road.[7]

Green and Abigail Doo arrived at the Elgin tract in December 1849, roughly a month after the settlement's official opening. Both Doos were in their thirties when they came to Buxton, bringing with them at least five children, who ranged in age from four to twelve. The family grew to include thirteen children in 1861. The Doos took up land on the ninth concession and came to own one hundred fifty acres of land in the Elgin tract worth ten thousand dollars by 1880. Green Doo would become a community leader, serving as a trustee for both the British Methodist Episcopal Church and one of the Buxton schools. Abigail and Green's son, Elijah, would serve in the 102d U.S. Colored Troops during the Civil War.

Like Isaac Riley, William Jackson had been a slave, as presumably had his wife, Martha. The Jacksons settled on the eighth concession, not far from the Doo family. According to the 1861 census, the Jacksons had no resident children. Their young ages—they were in their early thirties when they settled in Buxton—leads to speculation that the couple had children but had been separated from them during their years as slaves or had been forced to leave them behind when they escaped. Little is known about the other early settlers.[8]

Throughout the life of the Buxton settlement, cooperative labor built cabins and cleared newcomers' acreage. A. R. Abbott, a black man well acquainted with the community although not a settler, wrote, "Whenever a settler took up a lot the neighbors . . . came and assisted him to build his house and barn and make a clearing."[9] Before newcomers' houses were raised, they were probably made welcome in more established settlers' homes. A cohesive sense of community arose through close residence with and dependence on one another. Buxton's early pioneers played critical roles in guiding later emigrants, providing much-needed assistance to new arrivals. It is difficult to determine how many of Buxton's settlers brought with them or had the resources to purchase the material possessions—household goods, farm implements, livestock—necessary to set up their households and agricultural pursuits. It is likely that relatively few of the new arrivals—and certainly not those who were fugitive slaves—possessed such materials, which made their resettlement harder and community assistance more vital.

As the number of residents increased, they assisted each other in clearing and improving the roads, which were at first only marked out by a surveyor. With the few roads in existence merely rough-cut dirt roads through the wilderness, the early settlers cleared their own trails. Their early ties to one another grew along footpaths worn through the forest, which in time became stump-filled dirt roads. As late as the mid-1850s the main road was described as "merely a wide cut lane cut straight through the forest, with the roots of trees everywhere."[10] Provincial laws required that landowners maintain the road bordering their property and perform statute labor to maintain roads through public tracts. In Buxton's case this meant Centre Road, running in a north-south direction through the heart of the Elgin Tract. The road was not complete when Buxton opened, and the settlers agreed to pool their required labor to complete the ten-mile road, partly because the land running along the proposed road in the most northerly and southerly sections of the Elgin Tract had not yet been taken up by families, so no one was legally required to maintain any roads there yet. Additional efforts were undertaken communally throughout the 1850s and 1860s as Buxton settlers labored to build a system of ditches in a seemingly never-ending struggle to solve the water problems that plagued their crops. These activities, while certainly not unique to Buxton, helped to lay a strong foundation for future community development.

Buxton's community spirit went beyond working bees, as group decisions formed the basis of many of the town's guiding principles. Shortly after the settlement's opening, residents adopted a policy of refusing individual charitable aid, and with the exception of contributions and loans for the benefit of Buxton's schools, churches, and industry, the community as a whole accepted no outside aid. When the American Anti-Slavery Society of Boston learned of the new settlement, they sent several boxes of clothing to Buxton. This gift presented a dilemma: Accepting it would encourage future charity, but rejecting the gift might offend the givers and inadvertently harm Buxton's cause. At a community meeting, the settlers voted to accept the gift rather than risk insulting well-intentioned friends. At the same time, Buxtonians resolved to make clear to the public that they were determined to support themselves. They agreed with King's philosophy that true independence meant no charity, viewed the soliciting of charity as having soiled the reputations of earlier black communities in British North America, and were determined that this calamity be avoided in Buxton. "We do not think it right that . . . colored persons, who are supporting themselves by their own industry, should lie under the disgrace of being called public beggars, when they receive nothing, and don't want anything."[11] A committee of Buxton residents consisting of Samuel Wickham, Robert Harris, and Edward Gants subsequently issued a public antibegging statement in which Buxton asked philanthropists to "send neither petticoats nor pantaloons. . . . The few cases of real want which arise . . . can with trifling effort be relieved here, without making a pretext for a system of wholesale begging in the United States."[12] This strategy of not relying on charity apparently worked for the majority of Buxtonians. After an 1854 visit, Benjamin Drew commented that Buxton's settlers carried themselves with a "manly, independent air and manner." Their lack of outside assistance clearly struck him: "Most of them came into the Province stripped of everything but life. They have . . . erected their own buildings and supported their own families by their own industry; receiving no aid whatsoever from any benevolent society but carefully excluding donations of any kind from coming into the settlement."[13]

The community also vowed to adhere to the tenet of temperance. As the first year of settlement came to a close, an Englishman named Woods purchased a farm owned by a white family in the Elgin tract. Woods opened a general store and procured a license to sell whiskey. This development caused immediate alarm among the numerous Buxton residents concerned with possible harmful effects on the settlement's moral character. King too viewed this development with consternation, believing that if the sale of liquor were permitted, "it would do more to demoralise the settlers, than I could do by the Gospel and education to elevate them."[14] Since the residents had no legal power to prevent Woods from selling liquor, a public meeting was called to discuss a community response. Buxtonians resolved not to buy their groceries at Woods's store until he agreed to stop selling liquor, a strategy that apparently worked. King later noted with obvious approval that the only difference between the clearing and raising events staged by whites elsewhere and those staged by blacks at Buxton was that "the coloured people had their chopping bees; and their logging and raising bees all without liquor."[15] This effort to keep liquor and its negative effect from Buxton did not meet with complete success. At least one settler, James Rapier, wrote to family members in the United States about "drinking intoxicating beverages, heavily at times."[16] Nevertheless, the Buxton community stood on temperance principles.

The championing of temperance reflected Buxton's emphasis on moral improvement. It also mirrored the commitment among black leaders (and white reformers) to temperance as an issue in the crusade for moral reform. Temperance societies flourished in black communities throughout the northern states; black newspapers devoted substantial space to articles discussing the evils of alcohol; and national and state conventions invariably discussed the issue and passed resolutions urging abstinence. The issue of temperance attracted attention for various reasons. Black leaders stressed the dangers of alcohol—from loss of employment to criminal behavior and other social problems—as well as placed temperance within their objective of self-improvement and the elevation of the race. Further, because temperance was a major issue for white reformers, abstinence in the black community was perceived as a way to help make the black race more respectable in the eyes of white society and thus more acceptable.[17]

Buxton's population grew steadily throughout the 1850s. At the Elgin Association's September 3, 1850, annual meeting, the stockholders learned that forty-five families lived in Buxton and that a dozen more were making arrangements to settle there during the upcoming months. In addition, twelve black families had purchased land adjoining the original bloc. By the end of 1852, Buxton's population had increased to roughly four hundred individuals, with about one hundred twenty more arriving during 1853. Subsequent annual reports show continual annual increases in population. From its modest beginnings, the settlement—including both families on the Elgin reserve and those in the surrounding tracts—increased to about eight hundred individuals by 1855 and, according to the Elgin Association reports, reached approximately one thousand before the U.S. Civil War began.[18]

In most respects, Buxton residents typified Canada's black population. The black community that emerged represented a coming together of people from different regions and with diverse experiences. Not all the origins of those who reached Buxton can be traced precisely, but a general composite can be pieced together from various records. As table 5.1 shows, the majority of Buxton's settlers born before 1850 had been born in the United States, whereas the majority of those born after 1850 were native to Canada, suggesting that most of Buxton's residents immigrated to Canada during the 1850s. Additional information can be derived from the birthdates and birthplaces of the children. Definitive conclusions cannot be made for approximately 25 percent of the Buxton population— those adults who had no children—but most were born in the United States, and at least some undoubtedly came to Buxton seeking freedom. Most families with children had at least one child born in Canada, so the ages of those born in the United States and those born in Canada can be used to calculate with considerable accuracy when those families came to Buxton. Of the 687 settlers who resided within the official Buxton tract at the time of the 1861 census, 238 (34 percent), mostly under the age of twenty, listed Canada as their birthplace. Of these, 164, from sixty-five families, were ten years of age or under, which suggests that their families settled in Buxton or somewhere in Canada during the 1850s. Demographic information derived from the Canadian census indicates that at least 50 percent of Buxton's population came directly to Buxton after leaving the United States. The family of Richard and Emily Jones left the United States for Canada between the births of their son, James (age twelve in 1861), and of their daughter, Martha, who was eight in 1861. Cupid and Rebecca Martin's oldest child, Agnes, fourteen years old in 1861, was born in the United States, while her thirteen-year-old brother, James, was born in Canada. Those families who relocated from elsewhere in Canada to Buxton included Isaac and Maria Malone, all of whose children were born in Canada, the eldest in 1847.[19]

A register of marriages performed at St. Andrew's Church in Buxton provides a further glimpse into the origin of some of Buxton's families. Although incomplete and extant only from the late 1850s, these records in many cases indicate place of birth for both the bride and groom in addition to parents' names. This

Table 5.1 Buxton Residents, 1861

U.S.-born before 1850	408	59%
U.S.-born after 1850	41	6%
Canadian-born before 1850	74	11%
Canadian-born after 1850	164	24%
Total	687	100%

Source: Canadian Population Census, 1861

evidence supports the assertion that most of Buxton's families originated in the United States. A significant number of Buxton families apparently came from Pennsylvania (the Freeman, Johnson, Burns, Traves [Travis], Henry, Smith, and Bond families) and Virginia (the Richardson, Clayton, Cooper [Americus], Charity, Dyke, and Boyd families). Franklin Hatter and Rosanna Jones were born in New York (in Niagara and Buffalo, respectively). Isaac Scott and Ellen Bond were born in North Carolina, while Hudosia Dabney was born in St. Louis. Several Buxton families, including those of Mary Ann Poindexter and Eliza Brown, came from Ohio. These records provide no evidence of the circumstances or timing of these families' relocation to Buxton. Few marriage partners during the late 1850s and early 1860s had been born in Canada.[20]

Other characteristics of Buxton settlers, including age, gender, and marital status, can be determined through an analysis of the 1861 census returns. They were, for example, relatively young, with 56 percent twenty years old or under. Twenty-one percent were between twenty-one and forty years old, while only 24 percent were older than forty. Men comprised 53 percent of the population. Of those settlers twenty years old or older in 1861, 71 percent were married, 20 percent were single, and 9 percent were widowed. Buxton was, then, primarily a family community.[21]

It might be assumed that with their previous condition of servitude and a lack of educational opportunities, a majority of Buxton's residents lacked at least a remedial knowledge of reading and writing. According to the 1861 census report, however, 54 percent of Buxtonians over the age of nineteen (and thus most likely to have grown up in slavery or another atmosphere not conducive to literacy) were literate. Buxton's settlers apparently were more privileged than most nineteenth-century blacks, at least in education. These numbers should be taken with some reservations. The census does not define literacy or assess its degree, and it was probably relatively easy to deceive enumerators. Many of those recorded as literate may have been attending Buxton's adult night classes and just learning to read and write. Others may have simply said they were literate to avoid embarrassment. Still others may have been able to read but not write, and some may have been able only to sign their names. Certainly, relatively few would have received a formal education before coming to Buxton.[22]

Several biracial couples lived in Buxton by 1861. During the settlement's establishment, critics of King's plan had stridently argued that Buxton's existence not only would attract blacks to the area but also would encourage amalgamation. If this rejection of amalgamation is taken as the strongest indication of contemporary prejudice, King's racial attitudes and those of the Elgin Association members seem enlightened. King did not use his powers as administrator of the settlement to prohibit interracial marriages or to exclude blacks involved in such relationships from settling in Buxton, and the association's board of directors failed to insist on any such prohibitions. The emphasis on the moral character of Buxton residents suggests that had King or the directors held negative views of interracial relations, such relationships would have been prohibited in Buxton. The apparent lack of protests or violent actions against the partners in these interracial marriages shows white tolerance for what contemporary racists deemed the evilest of all evils.

Although interracial marriages were tolerated in Buxton, such was not the case in some nearby communities. When the Reverend Thomas A. Pinckney, a black man, married Elizabeth King, a white missionary from England, in February 1860, Chatham's whites reacted immediately, distributing handbills urging that special legislation be enacted to prevent further desecration of the white man's "lineage, his breed, his distinctive features and characteristics" in the face of "this violation of the law of God, and our common nature."[23] Though no such legislation was enacted, by the end of the year the whites' hostility had forced Pinckney and his wife to resign their missionary posts in Chatham and leave the area. Since so many Chatham whites vehemently opposed interracial marriages in their township, it is difficult to explain why they voiced little aversion to such marriages in Buxton, at least after the settlement was established. Perhaps they were not concerned about interracial marriages in Buxton as long as the "miscreants" stayed in their own community. Or perhaps the Pinckneys' status as religious leaders caused whites to react differently from how they reacted to lay intermarriage.[24]

Of Buxton's nine interracial couples, one was that of a white male and black female, and seven consisted of black males and white females. The ninth was that of Thomas Scott, a Native American male and Unis, a mulatto female. All but one of these interracial marriages occurred before the couples' arrival in Buxton. Reasons for relocation to the settlement remain unknown, so it is difficult to say whether prejudice against such relationships encountered elsewhere constituted a primary reason for these couples' choosing Buxton. All nine of Isaac (black) and Elizabeth (white) Washington's children were born in Canada, but the oldest was born in 1849, and so the couple must have moved to Buxton from elsewhere in Canada. Charles (black) and Nancy (white) Watts's first child was born in Buxton, and so the couple may have come directly from the United

States to the Buxton area. Adam (black) and Sarah (white) Crosswhite had been married and raised their children in the United States, coming to Buxton in the 1850s and raising their grandchild there. Most of these racially mixed families became long-standing respected Buxton citizens, with eight remaining for at least a decade and five for fifteen years or more. Two couples (Charles and Nancy Watts and Isaac and Elizabeth Washington) were still living in the Buxton area in 1881. Only Henry (white) and Levina (black) Alstead left relatively quickly, for reasons unknown.[25]

The Riley family and King's ex-slaves formed Buxton's nucleus. Four of the freed slaves remained with King as paid servants, while the rest settled on various fifty-acre plots in the settlement. It is surprising that neither King's autobiography nor any of his other writings provide much detail about those men and women whom he once held as slaves. Most of what little is known about their lives in Buxton is pieced together from fragmented records. A close relationship may be presumed to have existed between the former master and his former slaves, who owed their freedom to him. He was now providing them with an opportunity unavailable to millions of other blacks. These fifteen blacks may not have felt truly free but rather beholden to King. It is not known whether King allowed them to decide whether to settle in Buxton, and even if he at least formally offered them the chance to refuse, they may not have felt that they could turn down his offer. And while it can be assumed that they deeply desired their freedom, they may have resented being torn from their East Feliciana Parish community in Louisiana, undoubtedly leaving behind still enslaved family and friends. King's attitude toward his former slaves is also a matter of speculation.

There is conflicting evidence about whether King's ex-slaves were required to adhere to the Elgin Association's financing policy. According to his autobiography, King "placed" the former slaves who did not reside in his household "on farms to support themselves."[26] The precise meaning of his words is unclear, however: Did he provide them the land free of charge, or did he merely help them choose their lots and assist them in the relocation process? King's slaves possessed few resources when they arrived at the settlement. No accounting of the items that they were able to take with them from Louisiana was recorded, but as slaves, they would have possessed little beyond a few personal items. When King sold his property and wrapped up his affairs, he probably sold most of the equipment, and it is not known whether he retained any basic household implements or farming tools and subsequently bestowed them to his slaves. Although the group had spent some time in Ohio on the King family homestead, they probably did not acquire much in the way of tools or save substantial cash reserves. Nevertheless, they would have been in better circumstances than other blacks who came to Buxton. And they certainly had an advantage in that they enjoyed the aid of a white patron.

King's conviction that black settlers were responsible for improving themselves makes it probable that his former slaves generally did not receive special treatment. Edward Coles took a somewhat different approach. He provided his former slaves with one hundred sixty acres of land, but little else. He admitted that the land he was giving them was unimproved land and that they "would not have the means of making the necessary improvements, of stocking their farms, & procuring the materials for at once living on them."[27] Without these provisions, he advised that his slaves "would have to hire themselves out till they could acquire by their labour the necessary means to commence cultivating & residing on their own lands."[28] Coles hired some of these men and women himself but left the rest to seek employment elsewhere. Like King, Coles had a continuing relationship with a number of his former slaves and assisted them when the need arose. On several occasions Coles paid for their medical expenses as well as occasionally purchasing food and other supplies, including clothing. The Randolph and Gist slaves were probably likewise ill-equipped to tackle the frontier. Proceeds from the Randolph and Gist estates were not likely to have been used to acquire much in the way of supplies for the freedpeople. Free black property owners who relocated to Brooklyn or the Beech and Roberts settlements were more likely to possess the necessary farming implements.[29]

A map of the Buxton settlement from some time after 1850 shows fifty-acre lots assigned to Talbot King, Jacob King, Peter King, and Robert (Robin) Phares, all former slaves of William King. None of these lots was marked paid. Rather, each had a dollar amount assigned to it, suggesting that payments were being made. Contradicting this evidence, however, is that only Phares's name appears on the register of land and installments King kept for the Elgin Association. Peter King's name does not appear on the 1861 agricultural census, and so he may not even have been a landowner at that time. Jacob King's and Robert Phares's land was partially cleared and each was worth four hundred dollars in 1861. In addition, the agricultural census records them as possessing between thirty and forty dollars worth of machinery, and so the land was likely in their names and paid for.[30]

Only one of King's former slaves proved either unwilling or unable to live up to King's standard for freedmen. Robert Phares, one of the slaves King inherited from his father-in-law, had initially seemed cooperative. He had stayed and worked on the King family homestead while King was making preparations for the settlement. Phares had then traveled with King's other former slaves to Buxton, presumably inclined to settle there under King's rules. King, whom Phares called his "Moses in the Wilderness," taught his former slave to write a little and to read the Bible. Despite the fifty-acre rule, however, Phares refused to pay for more than twenty-five acres.[31] Single and without a family until 1866, when he married a fifty-year-old widow named Fanny Fraser, also one of King's former slaves, Phares insisted on growing only enough food on his land to feed himself, refusing to raise a cash crop or to find other employment. As a result, he faced the loss of his land through foreclosure. Probably out of a sense of responsibility to his former slave, King loaned Phares money to meet his obligations, and Phares did not work off the debt for almost twenty years. Since King was willing to come to Phares's aid, he may have extended such financial aid to his other former slaves to help with their land payments. Phares may have been assisting King in other ways. Solomon, a young boy whom King had purchased so that he might not be separated from his mother (believed to be either Emeline or Harriet), was listed as part of Robin Phares's household in the 1861 census. Since there is no evidence to suggest that Phares was Solomon's father, it is possible that the boy's mother had died and that Phares had taken the boy in, perhaps at King's request.

Phares's spiritual nature may also have fallen below King's expectations: Phares's name did not appear on the communion roll of St. Andrew's Church, where King was the minister, before 1870. Phares may have been slighting his former master or been reluctant to worship in the same church as King. On the other hand, the 1861 census lists Phares's religion as Episcopal Methodist, so the lateness of his membership in St. Andrew's may have been related to a change in religious practices rather than a lack of them. Widowed shortly after his first marriage, Phares remarried in 1870. His second wife was Barbara Freeman, another widow. Phares's religious affiliation may have reflected his new wife's preference. Despite Phares's rebelliousness, King did not abandon his former slave. Phares was the only one of King's former slaves still alive and in the area when King died in 1895. King's will stated his desire that "'old Robin' should not suffer through the need of any of the necessities of this life."[32] King provided financially for Phares and arranged that he would not be turned off his land for any reason.[33]

It is more difficult to recover the lives of most of King's other former slaves. Benjamin Phares was a minister in one of the settlement's Baptist churches for a short time but completely disappears from the community records by 1857. Stephen Phares, who was in his seventies when he came to Buxton, married Maria, a woman two years his junior. While it seems that the couple settled on a fifty-acre plot on the Elgin tract, tax assessment records show that by 1859 Stephen had become a householder rather than a freeholder and resided on only five acres of land. Stephen Phares disappears from the land records of Buxton after 1861, and by 1873 his land had reverted to William King, which may signify that King had financed the purchase.[34]

Talbot and Jacob, the first two slaves King owned, took King's surname and settled next to each other on the tenth concession. Jacob married a woman named Ellen who had been born in the United States. Together they had a son, James. Jacob and his family were last recorded on their land in 1863. Jacob enlisted in the Union Army during the Civil War, and so he and his family may have returned to the South after the war. Talbot also served in the Union Army; because his name disappears from the Buxton records, it is possible that he too remained in the United States rather than returning to Canada after the war, or he may not have survived the conflict, although no explicit evidence points to his death.[35]

The 1861 census lists Mary King, age fifty, as the only nonfamily resident of William King's household. During the mid-nineteenth century, the names Mary, Mollie (Molly), and Amelia were used interchangeably, and this woman is probably Amelia, the nanny of King's first wife. Although King also owned a slave named Mollie, she appears to have been much younger than Mary/Amelia: when King purchased Mollie in 1843, she had an eight-year-old child. What became of that child remains a mystery.[36]

Fanny, one of the blacks originally from King's Louisiana farm, was one of the four women who initially remained with King as servants. She was single, with at least one child, until she married Luke Fraser and presumably left the King household. Sometime between 1861 and 1866 her husband died, and Fanny married Robert Phares. She died a few years after her remarriage. A simple stone with a willow-and-rose motif marks her final resting place in the South Buxton Cemetery. The 1861 census lists Cornelius King, then seventeen, as living with Fanny and Luke Fraser. Fanny's son, Cornelius, although nowhere listed as one of King's slaves, was born in 1844, a year after King's purchase of Fanny. Cornelius served in the Union Army and returned to Louisiana after the war.[37]

Peter and Sarah King, the two children whom King acquired with the purchase of his Louisiana farm, remained in Buxton in 1861. Both were in their early twenties and single. What is known and not known about Peter and Sarah provides evidence of one of the cruel characteristics of slavery that would have extensive repercussions for generations—the fragmentation of family unity. The maternity of Peter and Sarah is shrouded in uncertainty, and it is not even clear whether they were brother and sister. Mollie and Fanny were also slaves obtained by King as a by-product of his 1843 plantation purchase. Thus, either of these women may well have been the mother of one or both children. Yet neither child is listed with either Fanny or Mollie in any of the records, and no other evidence ties any of them together. So it is also possible that the children were born to another, unknown woman or women and that the children had been separated from their mother or mothers before their purchase by King. In any event, the 1861 census shows Peter and Sarah to have been nonfamily residents of the Mary Brown family. Mary, not believed to have been one of King's slaves, was a fifty-three-year-old widow with three children, two of whom were close in age to Peter and Sarah. Existing marriage or cemetery records provide no information on Peter's or Sarah's later life.[38]

Little else is known about the rest of the settlers who had once been King's slaves. No specific mention can be found of Isaiah, Harriet, Emeline, Eliza, Mollie, or Amelia. According to the *New York Tribune,* three of the fifteen had died by 1857. Another, presumably a woman, was married and living in Chatham, and three others were living in Detroit. Since Talbot is known to have been alive at that time, he was likely one of the three in Detroit. Benjamin had disappeared from the records by 1857, so he was probably one of the deceased, as was Stephen. Eliza had been the childhood companion of King's first wife and was probably born about the same time as Mary Phares, which means that Eliza would have been close to or in her forties in 1857. She might have married and moved to Chatham, moved to Detroit, or died. The ages of Emeline and Isaiah are unknown, which makes it impossible to hazard any sort of accurate guess about their whereabouts in 1857, if they indeed remained alive.[39]

Black individuals and families came from diverse backgrounds and chose to settle in Buxton for a variety of reasons. Freeborn and fugitive blacks who had been living in either the United States or Canada moved with their families to Buxton because of their need for a haven, their sympathy with the purpose of the Elgin Association, or their desire to secure for their children the advantages afforded by the schools being built there. Others came to Buxton to join family and friends already settled in the community. Many were fugitive slaves fleeing from their masters and sought the security that Buxton offered. Motivations for resettlement ranged from increasing racial tensions and decreasing rights and privileges to declining economic opportunities. The theme of migrating to improve economic standing and escape increasing racial tensions was common. Settlers were driven by impulses to improve their families' economic fortunes and to preserve and maintain ways of life that were, for whatever reason, threatened in their former locations. Decisions to migrate were never easy. Deteriorating circumstances and disillusionment with future prospects had to be countered with trepidation of venturing to a new place—in Buxton's case, a new country—leaving behind family, friends, and community.

Such fugitive slaves who had lived in the free northern states as Henry K. Thomas, Joseph Liason, Tom Gordon, and Daniel Ducket sought protection from the 1850 Fugitive Slave Law. Other fugitives, Eliza Brown and Dick Sims among them, came to Buxton directly from the clutches of slavery, often assisted by American abolitionists and others sympathetic to their plight. Buxton was, above all else, a place of refuge. Families such as the Rileys and Rapiers desired quality education for their children. So did Wilson Ruffin Abbott, a wealthy black

Toronto real-estate investor who moved with his family to the settlement so that his children could attend the Buxton school. Robert VanRankin, who established Buxton's first store, saw Buxton as a business opportunity. Buxton's land policy offered blacks a chance at independent living. The availability of cheap land also attracted settlers such as the Washington family. Some viewed the available land as an investment opportunity. John Rapier Sr. purchased a fifty-acre lot and kept up the property as it appreciated in value but—although he visited on several occasions—he himself never moved to Buxton. Freeborn blacks Elijah Doo and Ezekiel Cooper settled in Buxton with the hope of escaping the prejudicial attitudes and discrimination that hindered their efforts to live a truly free life in the United States. Ezekiel Cooper had come from Northampton, Massachusetts, with his wife, Louisa, and their three children. They settled on fifty acres of land in the eighth concession. The exact circumstances surrounding the Coopers' move are unknown, but he hinted at his motivations in a letter written to the *Liberator*: "I consider that Canada is the place where we have our rights. We might stay in the United States and preach for rights and liberty . . . and the result will be that our children will still be under the yoke."[40]

The Liberty Bell hanging from St. Andrew's Church, a gift from the black residents of Pittsburgh, symbolized the freedom blacks found in Buxton. William King recorded that the bell was rung for each fugitive to reach Buxton, proclaiming "Liberty to the captive."[41] More than other black communities, Buxton provided a place of refuge for runaways. Unfortunately, it is impossible to determine exactly how many of Buxton's residents were runaway slaves and how many were free blacks, and it seems unlikely that the Liberty Bell was literally rung for every fugitive, as King claimed. Rather naturally, fugitive slaves may have been reluctant to broadcast themselves as runaways.

Buxton's population does not match the typical composite for fugitive slaves in that the majority of runaway slaves were single adult males, whereas the settlement's population was split almost evenly between men and women and mostly included family units. There is no doubt, however, that many Buxton residents were fugitive slaves who arrived as intact families. As mentioned earlier, Buxton's first residents, Isaac Riley and his family, were fugitive slaves. Another example was the family of William Isaac and his wife, Jane Serena Lewis. William had been a slave on a Maryland plantation when Harriet Tubman assisted him on the path to freedom. Living as a fugitive in Marshall, Michigan, he met his future wife. Like many others, they decided they were no longer safe in the North after passage of the 1850 Fugitive Slave Law and consequently decided to go to Canada. Sometime during their travels, William and Serena shed the name of his former master and chose a new surname, Rhue. They settled in Buxton and raised their family, which eventually grew to include sixteen children. Likewise, Thomas W. Stringer brought his family to Buxton when he moved there and took up residence on the twelfth concession. Stringer had escaped slavery in Mississippi as a boy, living in Ohio until adulthood. Exactly why he left Ohio is not known, but it might have had something to do with the Fugitive Slave Law, since he and his family arrived at Buxton in the early 1850s. Statistics and family stories such as these and others show that a significant number—perhaps even a majority—of Buxtonians were runaways or were closely connected to fugitive slaves. Part of Buxton's success can thus be attributed to population growth caused by increased emigration from the United States in the wake of the Fugitive Slave Law, providing a stable source of new residents that Wilberforce and Dawn had lacked and whose absence caused those earlier settlements to falter for a want of settlers.[42]

Direct information can be found for many of Buxton's residents. For example, Joseph Liason, one of Buxton's earliest settlers, was born a slave in Kentucky, where he married and had a daughter before the family escaped to Indiana. There they lived for many years and accumulated some property. When the Fugitive Slave Law was passed, he "saw there was no safety in a free state" and sold his property and took his family to Buxton, where the Liasons purchased a fifty-acre farm.[43] Tom Gordon, also a slave from Kentucky, escaped from bondage before passage of the Fugitive Slave Law and lived as a free, albeit fugitive, man in Ripley, Ohio. Gordon's master discovered his former slave's location and hired some men to bring him back under the provisions of the new law. Luckily for Gordon, one of the agent's horses needed attention, and the blacksmith to whom the agent brought the animal was none other than the object of his search. Gordon recognized the man as a neighbor of his former master, and, under the pretense of retrieving a tool, escaped, ultimately settling in Buxton.[44]

Some residents came to Canada and subsequently the Buxton settlement directly fleeing the Fugitive Slave Law—that is, without first living in a free state or living in the northern United States even briefly. Shadrach Burgee (Burger), Eliza Brown, and Dick Sims are cases in point. Abolitionists purportedly rescued Burgee from a Boston courthouse in February 1851. According to contemporary accounts, a fugitive slave from Norfolk, Virginia, named Shadrach was captured by John Capehart, an agent of Shadrach's master who attempted to enforce the Fugitive Slave Law and return him to slavery. According to Buxton lore, Shadrach's rescuers spirited him off to Canada, where he settled in Buxton, taking up land on lot six of the eleventh concession. Approximately a year after his arrival in Buxton, Burgee, with the help of friends, returned south to free his wife, Rebecca, and child. Shadrach Burgee lived with his family in Buxton until his death in 1858. Rebecca Burgee appears on the land records until 1861, when she wed her neighbor, Milton Ragland.[45]

Eliza Brown and her young daughter escaped from a Kentucky plantation in 1852 when she learned that her master, Edward Thompson, was planning to sell her. The pair reached Ohio, where sympathetic abolitionists helped the fugitives hide from slave hunters hired by Thompson. William King happened to be in the vicinity and offered to take Brown and her daughter to Canada because he knew that U.S. soil would offer no protection if their master discovered their whereabouts. Before they could depart, Thompson and his agents became suspicious of King. He therefore returned to Buxton without the fugitives, hoping that local abolitionists could arrange another escape plan. Eliza Brown reached Buxton three weeks later, "with her girl dressed in boys clothes and herself well dressed and concealed with a thick veil so that she could not be distinguished from a white woman."[46]

King personally assisted several fugitives in their quest for freedom. In 1853 Dick Sims, a mill hand at a Savannah, Georgia, sawmill, offered a crew member on a Boston-bound vessel his entire savings (sixty dollars) to stow him away. The mate took the money and hid Sims in the ship's hold. When the vessel reached its destination, however, the crewman surrendered Sims to authorities. Ironically, the Fugitive Slave Law at first worked in Sims's favor. In the absence of an affidavit or anyone who could testify that he was a slave, Sims was set free, at least temporarily. By chance, King was in Boston at the time, having come to the area as a guest of Harriet Beecher Stowe. Approached by abolitionist Wendell Phillips, King agreed to help Sims and subsequently departed for Canada accompanied by a "servant." As the story goes, the two men narrowly escaped capture at the border. An order had been sent out to inspect all trains bound from Boston to Canada, but fortunately for King and Sims, their train stopped for repairs just east of the suspension bridge where the inspections were taking place. For some unknown reason, King changed his plans and boarded a train destined for Buffalo. After spending a few hours there, the two men boarded yet another train bound for Niagara Falls, New York, and late that evening King and Sims walked across the bridge to Canada. King described Sims's walk to freedom: "When half way across I showed Dick the line that divided the United States from Canada and when we crossed that line[,] . . . I told him he was now free and all the power in the United States could not take him back. . . . The poor fellow was frantic with joy to think that he was now free from his master."[47] The two men then continued their journey to Buxton, where Sims settled, married, and had four children.[48]

King also aided a young girl, Anna Marie Weems, in the final stage of her journey to freedom. Weems was only twelve years old in 1853 when she ran away from her master in northeastern Virginia shortly after both her mother and father had been sold to the Deep South. Dressed as a boy, the young girl eluded slave catchers hired by her master and eventually the Underground Railroad assisted her flight to the free states. Her journey took her through Wilmington, Delaware, Philadelphia, and finally Buffalo, New York. King arranged to travel to Buffalo to meet the runaway and bring her to Canada. Successfully evading detection and capture, the two walked across the border. King brought Weems to Buxton, where she was adopted by Joseph and Julia Liason, fugitives themselves.[49]

Many fugitives, such as Henry K. Thomas, gave up businesses to start afresh in Buxton. The son of a slave woman named Sally and her master, John Thomas, Henry escaped in 1834, when he was seventeen, at his mother's urging. Thomas was captured in Louisville, Kentucky, and confined to a guardhouse. He managed to work off his leg chains one night and steal down to the Ohio River, where he untied a boat and drifted over to the northern bank and free soil. Residing for short periods in various northern states, he finally settled in Buffalo by 1842, where he married a free black woman named Maria and started a barbershop in the basement of the Hotel Niagara. Thomas's earnings were enough to allow him to purchase real estate, including a lot in Buffalo and a small tract of land along Lake Erie that had been part of the Seneca Indian Reservation. In 1852, fearing the Fugitive Slave Law, Thomas gave up his business and left Buffalo with his family. With the express desire to educate their children, who would eventually number seven, Henry and Maria traveled to Buxton. Henry purchased one hundred acres on the tenth concession of the Elgin tract. In time he became a prominent citizen of Buxton, joining St. Andrew's Church and serving on the board of directors of the first black-owned and -operated corporate venture in Canada, the Canada Mill and Mercantile Company. Although at times impoverished and barely able to hold onto his land, Henry stayed in Buxton until after the U.S. Civil War. Part of his family remained in Buxton, while others lived out their lives in the United States.[50]

Daniel Ducket (Ducat) fled his master's Kentucky plantation years before the passage of the 1850 Fugitive Slave Law. After his escape, he settled on a farm in Michigan, where it was well known locally that he was a runaway slave. His master did not attempt to retrieve his property, in view of the difficulty of recovering a slave under the 1793 law. Upon passage of the new law, however, Ducket's owner decided to claim his slave. Ducket was warned of his former master's impending arrival and fled to Canada, taking with him only two horses and two hundred dollars in cash. Accepting the almost complete loss of his savings and land, Ducket started life anew in Buxton but never achieved the relative prosperity that he had experienced in Michigan. By 1861 Ducket had cleared only three of his fifty acres, planting one and using two for pasture. One possible explanation for Ducket's having improved so little land is that he was unmarried and had no children. Therefore, he had access only to his own labor, and his subsistence and material needs were also low. Although no marriage record exists, the 1873 assessment rolls list two persons in the family, and his cleared acreage had increased to twenty acres. His farm was then worth three hundred sixty dollars, compared to two hundred fifty in 1859.[51]

Perhaps the most famous of Buxton's fugitives was William Parker, a former slave who had escaped from Anne Arundel County, Maryland, in 1848 and fled to Pennsylvania. Parker won international acclaim for his actions in Christiana, Pennsylvania, on September 11, 1851, when Edward Gorsuch, a Maryland planter and slave owner, was killed and his son, Dickinson, seriously wounded during an all-night siege at Parker's home. The siege was the result of a manhunt for four escaped slaves who had taken refuge with Parker. Parker's role in the Christiana Riot, as it quickly became known, forced him, along with several other resistance leaders, including his neighbor Abraham Johnson, to flee, eventually arriving in Toronto.[52]

In Parker's haste to escape, he left his wife and children in Pennsylvania. Eliza Parker did not join her husband in Canada until November 1851, and their children remained in the United States in the care of friends until the Parkers became settled. By March 1852, Parker and Abraham Johnson decided, largely as a result of difficulties in finding and sustaining employment, to settle in Buxton. Assisted by funds provided by sympathizers from the Canadian Anti-Slavery Society, Parker and Johnson traveled to Buxton in early June. The two men had originally planned to take one lot between them, but "when we saw the land," stated Parker, "we thought we could pay for two lots. I got the money in a little time. . . . I built a house, and we moved into it that same fall."[53] According to a land register for the Elgin Association, Johnson signed for a section of lot ten in concession thirteen, and Parker registered for part of lot twelve of concession twelve. Johnson later married Clarissa Bristow, a runaway slave who had escaped from her Louisiana owners at the age of twelve. The couple had eleven children, nine of whom died before reaching adulthood.[54]

Parker became a prominent member of the community. Illiterate when he first settled in Buxton, Parker attended night classes for adults, eventually learning both to read and to write. He later represented Buxton on the Raleigh Township Council. At least three of Parker's children, William, Charleat, and Alfred, were born in Buxton. Parker later published in *Atlantic Monthly* an account of the Christiana Rebellion, his escape, and his arrival in Buxton. Eliza Parker died in May 1899, at the age of eighty-two, and her grave marker still stands in the Methodist Church Cemetery in North Buxton. Her husband lies beside her, having died sometime before 1881. At her death, Eliza resided on a part of the land on which she and her husband had taken up residence when they arrived in Buxton—the original fifty acres had betweentimes been divided among members of the Parker family. Eliza's will stipulated that her section of the land be divided between her son, Francis, and her daughter, Cassanda Goodall. Her will also shows that, although not wealthy, the family had accumulated possessions. Eliza left household furniture to Francis and left two horses and a wagon to her son, Samuel. Another son, Alfred, received all the farming implements as well as the bulk of her estate. She also bequeathed one dollar to each of her two children, William and Mary.[55]

Buxton's residents did not actively participate in the abolition movement. The various societies established within the community did not include an abolition society. Nor is there any indication that any Buxton residents were members of any of Canada's antislavery organizations. Blacks were generally preoccupied by their daily struggles and had little time or energy to devote to the antislavery cause, which was, realistically speaking, out of their control. Survival came before community and political activity.

Transience was a facet of life in frontier areas. The decennial persistence rates of communities in the American West were 30 percent or less—approximately two-thirds of the heads of household moved elsewhere during the course of each decade. And other families came and departed between decennial censuses. A certain level of transient residents is to be expected in any new area of settlement. Migration patterns typically include squatters staking out a claim, growing crops for a season or two while judging farming prospects and assessing the nature of the community, and then deciding for whatever reason not to stay permanently. Buxton had its share of transients among its more permanent settlers.[56]

In contrast, a majority of those who took up land on the Elgin tract stayed and worked the land, built houses, and raised children. Landownership was a key to this success. King's conviction that landownership would enhance stability was confirmed. Of the 126 families traceable with a reasonable degree of accuracy, 29 (23 percent) remained in Buxton less than five years. Eleven families (9 percent) settled in Buxton for five to nine years. The rest of the families lived in the settlement more or less permanently—ten years or more—with 36 families (28 percent) remaining for ten to nineteen years and 50 families (40 percent) staying for more than twenty years. In short, despite periodic influxes and exoduses, the community retained a core group of families. As with other black settlements of at least moderate success and longevity, Buxton's core set of landowners provided the settlement with a sense of identity and cohesion as it developed into a community. Names such as Riley, Hatter, Doo, Cooper, Thompson, Johnson, Shadd, Chase, Prince, Toyer, Steele, Scipio, Geals, and many others became so much a part of the community that no study of Buxton and its history can be made without them. This core family group built the social institutions and created the community consciousness so vital to Buxton's survival—they were the Buxton settlement.[57]

Map of Buxton and the surrounding environs. (Prepared by Jay Flynn, Radford University.)

Reverend William King, founder of Buxton. (Courtesy of the Buxton National Historic Site and Museum.)

This Indenture

made the first day of January in the year of our Lord One
Thousand Eight Hundred and sixty six in pursuance of the
Act passed in the Thirteenth and Fourteenth years of the
Reign of Her Majesty Queen Victoria Chapter one hundred and
fortyfour entitled "An Act to incorporate the Elgin Association
for the settlement and moral improvement of the coloured
Population of Canada" Between The Elgin Association
of the first part and Levi Anderson of the Township of
Raleigh in the County of Kent yeoman of the second part
Witnesseth that the said Elgin Association for and in consideration of the sum of Three Hundred Dollars
of lawful money of Canada now paid by the said party of the
second part the receipt whereof is hereby acknowledged the
said Elgin Association doth grant unto the said Levi Anderson his heirs and assigns forever All and Singular
that certain parcel or tract of land and premises situate
lying and being in the Township of Raleigh in the County of
Kent being Composed of the northwest half of lot number six
in the thirteenth concession containing one hundred acres
more or less To have and to hold unto the said Levi
Anderson his heirs and assigns to and for his and their
sole and only use forever Subject Nevertheless to the reservations limitations provisoes and conditions expressed in
the original grant thereof from the Crown The said Elgin
Association covenant with the said Levi Anderson that

Elgin Association Contract. (Courtesy of the Buxton National Historic Site and Museum.)

Isaac Riley, first settler at Buxton. (Courtesy of the Buxton National Historic Site and Museum.)

Reverend John R. Riley, son of Isaac Riley. (Courtesy of the Buxton National Historic Site and Museum.)

The Liberty Bell, hung in St. Andrews Church. (Courtesy of the Buxton National Historic Site and Museum.)

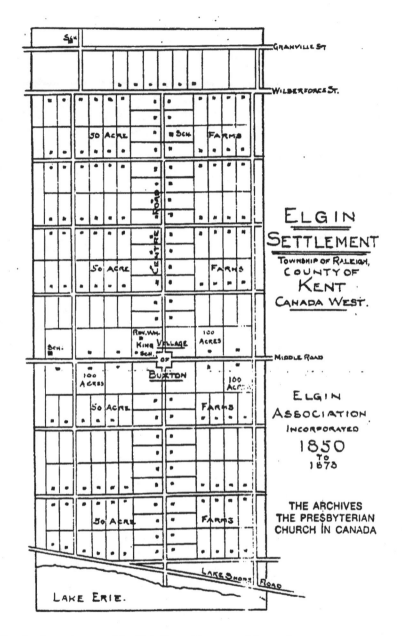

Plan for the settlement of the Elgin Tract. (Courtesy of the Presbyterian Church of Canada Archives, Toronto.)

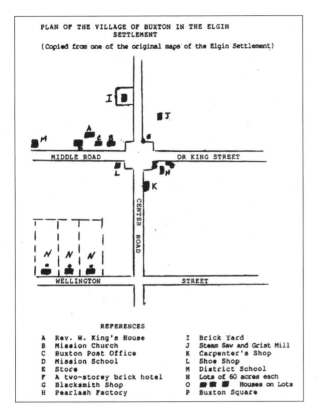

PLAN OF THE VILLAGE OF BUXTON IN THE ELGIN
SETTLEMENT

(Copied from one of the original maps of the Elgin Settlement)

MIDDLE ROAD   OR KING STREET

CENTER ROAD

WELLINGTON   STREET

REFERENCES

A Rev. W. King's House
B Mission Church
C Buxton Post Office
D Mission School
E Store
F A two-storey brick hotel
G Blacksmith Shop
H Pearlash Factory

I Brick Yard
J Steam Saw and Grist Mill
K Carpenter's Shop
L Shoe Shop
M District School
N Lots of 60 acres each
O ▪▪▪ Houses on Lots
P Buxton Square

Buxton Square. (Courtesy of the D. B. Weldon Library, University of Western Ontario.)

St. Andrew's Church. (Courtesy of the Buxton National Historic Site and Museum.)

The British Methodist Church in Buxton. (Courtesy of the Buxton National Historic Site and Museum.)

Buxton Schoolhouse. (Courtesy of the Buxton National Historic Site and Museum.)

6

Family and Community Structure

Nineteenth-century African Americans placed great value on family ties and community cohesion. Both in slavery and in freedom, they depended on the affection and support they received from family ties in their continuing struggle to survive the dangers and humiliations to which they were subjected. Family, household, and community structure provided African Americans with defenses. The family and the household were the building blocks of society at Buxton as elsewhere. An important principle of social life, kinship provided an organizing force that brought settlers together. In some ways, family and kinship cohesion were even more important in freedom than in slavery because free blacks' basic needs were not supplied by owners, increasing the dependence of blacks on each other. The virulent race prejudice that free blacks encountered encouraged them to bind together in supportive units. Individuals, family, and kin became welded into a cohesive unit—community. The most important and enduring institution in the free black community, family and kinship ties provided blacks with vital support, security, and a sense of belonging. Ann Patton Malone's contention that the strength of the slave community "was its multiplicity of forms, . . . its adaptability, and its acceptance of all types of families and households as functional and contributing" can be applied to the success of an all-black free community.[1]

Family fulfilled far more than basic functions. The family constituted society's basic economic unit, cared for the elderly, and reared and socialized children, instilling in them appropriate and necessary behaviors for survival in a hostile society. Marriage further played a social function in that weddings were often highlights of the rural social season, celebrating both the joining together of a new couple and their entrance into the community. Weddings brought together the community for celebration and fellowship. In Buxton, no less than elsewhere, life and culture revolved around family relationships. The institution of family did much to ensure the settlement's stability during its critical first decade.[2]

Data from the 1861 census allows an examination of Buxton's family structure and domestic organization. Fairly complete profiles of household composition are available from these records, albeit only as a snapshot in time. A typology accepted by many historians defines a simple family as the elementary or biological family in which a conjugal link (husband-wife or parent-child) must be present. The simple family includes married couples without resident children, married couples living with children, and single-parent families. This classification of family structure is employed in the following analysis. The simple family, encompassing all classifications of that type, was the dominant household type among both slave and free black populations of the nineteenth century, as in Buxton. Eighty-one Buxton households were two-parent families with children. Of these, fifty-seven were considered standard nuclear families, consisting of parents and children only. Eighteen were augmented nuclear households consisting of parents, children, and nonfamily residents. The remaining six families were extended household units with parents, children, and other family members in residence. Of these, three households included both kin and nonkin residents in addition to the parents and children. The Henry Thomas household, for example, included Henry, his wife and their children, one of his nephews, and two nonrelatives.[3]

Buxton had thirteen single-parent households (seven male and six female) in 1861. This nearly equal gender division is not a characteristic common to black communities; especially urban communities typically contained larger percentages of female-headed households. These truncated families, although often termed single-parent households, are nonetheless nuclear family units. Numerous circumstances may explain single-parent households, most frequently death of or separation from a spouse. Nine (69 percent) of Buxton's single-parent households were headed by widows (four) or widowers (five). Census returns show both Louis Carter and Ann Jones as married, but there is no indication of the locations of their spouses. Harriet Roth's marital status is unknown, but since her two children were fifteen and eighteen years old, it is likely that she was a widow or otherwise separated from her spouse. One male head of household, Robert Phares, was listed as single with a minor, Solomon, age seventeen, who was not Robert's child although both men had the same surname. As previously mentioned, both Robert and Solomon were former slaves of William King, and Robert had apparently taken Solomon in at King's behest, presumably after the death of his mother. Mahala Hampton, a widow only twenty years old, also cared for two minors who were not her children, Berriman and Abraham Mathews, ages eighteen and five, respectively.[4]

Single parenting should not be construed as a reflection of immorality or the breakdown of the institution of family. Despite their single-parent status, several of these households give testimony to the strength of marital relations. Single father William Burger's five children ranged in age from two to seventeen, showing a marital commitment of at least seventeen years to his recently deceased wife. Sometime in the twelve months before the 1861 census, William Garle's wife had passed away after an obviously long-lived marriage, leaving him to raise four of their seven children, who were under the age of eighteen at the time of her death. Widows Nancy Geals and Julian Henry also had children as young as age two and as old as seventeen and eleven, respectively, illustrating their long-standing marriages ending only with the death of their partners. (Julian's forty-one-year-old husband had died from consumption in 1860.)[5]

A number of Buxton's single-parent households provide evidence of the economic needs of black families. Of the thirteen single-parent residencies, four (31 percent) had children over the age of eighteen residing with them, an arrangement not uncommon throughout the community. Two of Mary Brown's resident children were twenty-five and twenty years of age. She had recently lost her husband, and at the age of fifty-three, was unlikely to have been capable of supporting herself alone. Of William Garle's seven children, two were over the age of eighteen, and Amariah Scipio's thirty-one- and twenty-nine-year-old sons still lived with him. This was not an uncommon situation in the nineteenth century, when children generally did not maintain independent living arrangements until they married. Unmarried children often lacked the financial resources to set up independent households and could not muster the labor necessary to begin farms of their own. Older children remained in the parental family to help support their parents and siblings.[6]

Free blacks, like slaves, had a high incidence of intergenerational and multisurnamed members in their households. These phenomena were important survival mechanisms. Extended kin networks were vital to free blacks because they provided supplemental financial and emotional support. Beset by economic difficulties, blacks often augmented the nuclear family unit to create expanded household structures. Extended nuclear families often remained together for years as a result of both economic expediency and deep emotional ties. Such relationships provided not only material support but the sharing of child-rearing duties and an emotionally rich family environment.[7]

Several domestic organizations can be classified as extended family units. Extended family households consist of a conjugal family unit with the addition of one or more relatives other than offspring. Households exhibiting upward extensions include a relative from an older generation residing in a household headed by a younger-generation relative—a husband and wife absorbing one of their parents into their household, for example. A couple with a grandchild whose parents were absent would be considered a downward-extended household, and a laterally extended household would have a same-generation relative living with a simple nuclear family—for example, a couple living with one spouse's sibling. Other domestic organizations included multiple-family households—two or more conjugal units connected by kinship or marriage. Once again, the secondary unit, or second family, could be extended upward, downward, or laterally. The most frequent type of multiple family was a nuclear family incorporating a daughter with children of her own, the later forming the second family. Examples of all these family structures existed in Buxton.[8]

Multigenerational households were fairly common in Buxton. At least five Buxton households included three generations. London Harris's household featured himself; his second wife, Elisa; two adult children from his first marriage; and his younger son's wife and their four children. Henry Herrington likewise presided over an extended family. Living with him in 1861 were seven individuals, all with the surname Freeman. Despite the two surnames, evidence suggests that Henry and Amanda were married. Both were listed as married and residing in a one-story log cabin, and only Herrington appears on the agricultural census where heads of households are listed. Regardless of whether Herrington and Freeman were married to each other or to other, nonresident spouses, three generations of the Freeman family lived with Henry Herrington: Amanda; her children, Julian and Elizabeth, both single; Jeremiah Freeman and his wife, Maria, and their two young children. Other extended families whose lineages are discussed elsewhere include the Watts, Henrys, Crosswhites, and Liasons.[9]

Both financial needs and cultural patterns encouraged blacks to maintain extended family households and take in boarders. Poverty prevented many blacks from establishing households and encouraged householders to take in boarders. Black households in New York and Philadelphia, for example, often included dwellers who were not family members. Besides the obvious economic advantage, there is another reason for boarding, especially in cases involving children. Boarding became an aspect of the socialization and education process for some blacks, as in white society. Although this was more common among the black elite than the black masses, children were sometimes sent to the homes of friends or relatives.[10]

At Buxton as elsewhere, distinctions also existed between households and housefuls. Persons who were not part of the same family household or even kin group sometimes occupied the same dwelling, making up a houseful but not constituting a household. Economic considerations were implicit in such arrangements, but friendship and family relationships also played a part. It was common for individuals who had lost their spouses to reside with relatives and particularly with their adult children. Sixty-year-old Buxton widower Stephen Ambleton, for example, lived with his son, Jasper, and Jasper's wife, Charlotte.

Patty Chatham likewise resided with her adult son, Prince. Widow Cathrine Johnson sought financial and emotional stability in the home of her son, Samuel, and his wife, Maria. Of the twenty-five widowed individuals in Buxton at the time of the 1861 census, twelve were heads of household—although not necessarily living alone—while thirteen lived in other households, five of them with family. Martha Elsey, age thirty-one, and Hardenia Fields were the only two who appear to have been living alone. It is difficult to determine whether any of the remaining eight resided in households of family members because of different surnames, but it is probable that some did. A case in point is the household of Joseph Liason. Residing with Joseph and his wife, Julia, was a widow, Julia Munroe, and her daughter, Lucinda. Several things point to the strong possibility that Julia Munroe was Joseph and Julia's Liason's daughter. Joseph and his wife were seventy and sixty-nine, respectively, while Julia Munroe was twenty-seven, a reasonable age difference between parents and child. Furthermore, the similarity of the first names suggest that Joseph and Julia followed African and African American custom by naming their daughter after her mother. A daughter might well return to her parents' home if the death of her husband resulted in dire financial straits.[11]

Buxton circumstances reveal that multifamily households did not always result from children taking in widowed parents. Rather, the widowed adult often remained the head of household. Such was the situation with widower Amariah Scipio, age fifty-eight, who had two of his single adult sons, twenty-nine-year-old James and thirty-one-year-old Dalmanintha, residing with him. Benjamin Crosswhite, widowed at the young age of twenty-five, apparently moved back in with his parents, Adam and Sarah, and sister, Frances, after the death of his wife. It is unclear whether six-year-old John Crosswhite, another resident in the household, was Benjamin's son or his younger brother, but since Sarah Crosswhite was then sixty years old and since Benjamin and John were listed together on the census, they were probably father and son.[12]

Skilled craftsmen sometimes resided with one another, as was the case in shoemaker Thomas Scott's household, which included himself, his wife and two children, one of them a twenty-one-year-old shoemaker; and William Hookman, a single thirty-five-year-old whose trade was also shoemaking. Richard Jacobs and George Radclif, both of whom were recorded as married, boarded with Thomas Stringer. Jacobs and Radclif were in their late forties and were skilled carpenters. The location of their wives is unknown. Blacksmith Francis Lasse also had two laborers residing with him, presumably working in his blacksmith shop. These households may reflect apprenticeship arrangements, with room and board as part of the agreement, or simply employer-employee relationships in which laborers resided with their bosses, a not uncommon situation in the early nineteenth century.[13]

Buxton and other black communities in slavery and freedom adapted a fictive kinship system from their West African heritage to ensure that those without relatives had a family with which to live and from which to draw emotional and financial support. Inadequate family resources or family separation (whether through sale, death, or other circumstances) often necessitated informal adoption and placing of kin in households of other community members. This extensive support network became central to fulfilling societal obligations, the primary means for caring for those in need, especially children.

A number of Buxton families opened their households to children in need, family and nonfamily alike. One visitor to Buxton commented on the home of an unnamed fugitive settler who had married after coming to Buxton. Living with this man was his wife, "with a couple of small children, her relations, to whom the couple afforded a home."[14] The 1861 census records show thirty children living in households with which they did not share the family name. The twenty-two families who provided a home for these thirty children included twelve couples who had no children of their own currently living with them. They had numerous reasons for augmenting their households in this way. Prince Chatham, for instance, may have been seeking assistance for his elderly mother when he offered shelter to young Elisa Brown, an eight-year-old girl with no apparent family in Buxton. Elisa may have been the daughter of the Eliza Brown whom King had tried to assist to freedom. The names *Eliza* and *Elisa* were interchangeable, and one or the other may have been misspelled or changed in the transcriptions of the records over the years. There are no Eliza Browns on the 1861 census, and so, unless she married after settling in Buxton, she had probably died by that time, offering a possible explanation for how young Elisa had come to live with Prince Chatham and his mother. Robert Van-Rankin and his wife had five unrelated children, ranging in age from eight to seventeen, living in their two-story brick house. The children likely helped out in VanRankin's fields and store. The arrangement gave the VanRankins, who had no children of their own, much-needed labor and provided the children both their material and their emotional needs. Elderly couples such as William and Sarah Wright, Peter and Sally Grey, and Luke and Fanny Fraser likewise needed extra hands in the fields and house. All three of these couples had no resident children of their own and took in children for both labor and companionship. Those Buxtonians with children of their own, such as Norris Burford, whose expanded household included his wife and their four children in addition to two unrelated residents, may have welcomed nonrelatives for financial and other motives. Henry Thomas's income was supplemented by funds sent to him by his brother John Rapier to defray the living costs of Rapier's two sons who, at different times, lived with Thomas. Buxton residents even took in adult siblings. Uriah Wilson and his sister, Deborah, twenty and eighteen years of age, respectively, resided with Absalom and Cintha Johnson.[15]

One especially interesting case is that of three children—Cathrine (fifteen), Ann (fourteen), and Joseph (thirteen), whom the 1861 census recorded as residing in three separate households. The children's surnames were listed as Micham, Milcham, and Mitcham, respectively. Because of the imprecision of census enumerators, the nature of nineteenth-century handwriting, and the poor quality of the medium, it is plausible that these three children were siblings and that their slightly different surnames were actually the same. Cathrine resided with Thomas Stringer's family, Ann lived with Charles Watts and his family, and Joseph resided with Peter and Sally Grey. It is unclear whether these children's parents had ever lived in Buxton or what happened to them, but although unable to remain together, the three children apparently were fortunate enough to remain within the same nurturing community. Peter and Sally Grey were an elderly couple with no children of their own then in residence. Thomas and Mamie Stringer likewise had no children of their own living with them, but they did open their home to numerous nonkin. In addition to Cathrine, the Stringers' augmented household included an elderly widow and her three teenage children, a single man in his early twenties, and two married men in their mid- to late forties (with no indication of their wives' whereabouts). The demographics of this household suggest a boarding arrangement that supplemented the Stringers' income. The Watts residency was likewise an augmented family household. Residing with Charles and Nancy Watts were their four children, a related married couple, Benjamin (probably their son) and Maria Watts, and Ann Milcham. No further record of these three children has been uncovered.[16]

Another type of domestic organization in the community was children of Buxton families residing in households other than those of their parents. For example, census enumerators twice recorded thirteen-year-old Sarah Enos—once with her family and again in the household of Peter and Catherine Simmons. A reasonable explanation for this dual entry is that Sarah was temporarily residing with the Simmonses to help them care for their infant son, Levi. The Enoses had nine other children residing with them, so economic need may have required them to hire out their daughter as a nanny. Of course, financial matters may not have played a role: Sarah may have gone to assist the Enos family purely as a neighborly gesture. Robert Garle, a young teenager, was also listed in two households, that of his father, William, and that of John Glen.[17] John and his wife, Sarah, had no resident children, and though they were only in their early forties and presumably capable of providing for themselves, they may have hired Robert as a laborer in their fields and provided him with a place to stay.[18]

Residency arrangements were often determined by several variables: the special needs of some community members; the sharing of domestic duties; for security; or, in the case of the sick, old, young, or pregnant, for care and nurturing. Profiles of household composition reveal that blacks often ministered to the needs of family members, orphaned kin, and unrelated dependents. In Buxton as in other black communities, kinship helped support households and nuclear and augmented families, providing blacks with continuity, stability, and economic assistance. During the early years at the Beech and Roberts settlements, residents relied heavily on kin and friends already in the area, naturally seeking out help from those with whom the new arrivals were already acquainted. Whereas such assistance for most new arrivals at the Beech and Roberts areas came from past relationships, it came to a lesser extent from families and kin at Buxton simply because of the lack of preexisting connections among the settlers, at least early on. As the settlement built momentum during the 1850s, newcomers began to arrive at Buxton who had relationships with settlers already there. George Hatter and his first wife, Mary, had been living in Buxton for several years before the arrival of George's brother, Franklin, and his family. Abraham Johnson and William Parker had been neighbors in Pennsylvania before relocating to Buxton. When James Rapier's father sent James to Buxton, he lived with his uncle, Henry Thomas, even while purchasing a plot of land and making arrangements to build the required homestead on it. Other, similar relationships certainly existed, but not to the same extent as in some other black communities.

As alluded to earlier, further evidence of economic pressure on black families is seen in the considerable number of adult children remaining in their parents' homes or other households instead of establishing separate households. Only six single persons lived alone in Buxton in 1861. Two, Hardenia Fields and Martha Elsey, were widows. Both these women were thirty-one years old and apparently had no children. It is unknown when they lost their husbands. The other four settlers who lived alone were single adult men. Daniel Ducat and Fredrick Davies were in their forties, William Taylor was a fifty-eight-year-old bachelor, and Henry Colbert was a thirty-five-year-old whose occupation was listed as sailor. Forty-three single individuals twenty years old and older lived with family, most often but not always their parents. Fifteen single adults resided in other households, perhaps as boarders.[19]

Indicative of the high mortality rates among blacks during the mid-nineteenth century is the number of marriages with a significant age difference between spouses. The pattern generally found in free society of the period was husbands and wives differing in age by six to eight years or less. Where a notable age discrepancy existed, husbands tended to be older than their wives. The Buxton community experience was somewhat outside the norm. In 1861 thirty-six married couples in Buxton showed a difference of more than ten years. In a large majority (88.8 percent) of these marriages, the husband was the older spouse. Twelve (34.3 percent) of those couples differed in age by eleven to fifteen years, another twelve had sixteen to twenty years separating them, nine (25 percent) had age differences ranging from twenty-one to thirty years, and three couples (8.3 percent) were separated by more than thirty years. Eighty-one-year-old London Harris and his thirty-eight-year-old wife, Elisa, had a forty-three-year age difference. Rosana Lewis, age one hundred four, was forty-one years older than her husband, Isaac. William Winfria's second wife, Mary, was forty years his junior. Buxton thus exhibited a pattern of large age differences in marital relations. Beyond mortality, a limited choice of marriage partners resulting from age or gender imbalances also helps to explain these significant age differences. Table 6.1 shows the breakdown of marriages in Buxton according to the 1861 census.[20]

An analysis of Buxton's adult population (seventeen years of age and older) provides insight into the pattern of age differences in marital relations and illumi-

Table 6.1 Marital Status of Buxton Residents, 1861

Age	Marital Status	Number	Percentage	Marital Status	Number	Percentage
17–25	Male				Female	
	Single	46	96%	Single	38	78%
	Married*	1	2%	Married	9	18%
	Widowed	1	2%	Widowed	2	4%
	Total	48			49	
26–34	Male				Female	
	Single	9	43%	Single	0	0%
	Married	11	52%	Married	25	89%
	Widowed	1	5%	Widowed	3	11%
	Total	21			28	
35–45	Male				Female	
	Single	5	12%	Single	1	3%
	Married	34	83%	Married	35	87%
	Widowed	2	5%	Widowed	4	10%
	Total	41			40	
46 & Older	Male				Female	
	Single	2	2%	Single	0	0%
	Married	71	90%	Married	46	87%
	Widowed	6	8%	Widowed	6	11%
				Unknown	1	2%
	Total	9			53	

*The census records John Riley, age nineteen, as married, but other evidence suggests that this is inaccurate, perhaps a mistake by the census enumerator. No wife was recorded with him, and family records show that he was single in 1861.

Source: Canadian Population Census, 1861

nates further characteristics of the community. In this analysis, the adult population was broken down by gender and age (seventeen- to twenty-five-year-olds, twenty-six- to thirty-four-year-olds, thirty-five- to forty-five-year-olds, and those over forty-five) to reflect primary reproductive groups. No significant gender imbalance exists in the first three age groups. The group of adults forty-six years old or older contained twenty-seven more males than females, a considerable discrepancy. This gender imbalance suggests a greater life expectancy for men, likely as a result of the dangers of childbirth, which gave women of childbearing years a higher mortality rate than men of comparable age. Childbirth was frightening and dangerous for mothers of any race or class in the mid-nineteenth century. The health risks for women made pregnancy and childbirth a time of anxiety and ill health. Widower William Burger's youngest child, Elizabeth, was two years old at the time of the census, which does not record his wife as having died during the preceding twelve months. These facts make it reasonable to assume that his wife died from complications related to the girl's birth. Likewise, Benjamin Crosswhite's wife may well have died giving birth to their only child, John, since Benjamin was widowed before he reached the age of twenty-five and John was only six in 1861, which probably indicates that his wife died in her late teens or early twenties.[21]

Other explanations for the gender imbalance in the Buxton community among certain age groups are also possible. The numbers may in part reflect a greater propensity of men—generally young men—to migrate to new areas. Men tended to outnumber women on western frontiers. The imbalance may also partly reflect the general profile of fugitive slaves. The typical runaway was a young male, in his late teens or early twenties. Young men ran away in greater numbers because often they had not yet married or begun a family, because young men were more willing to defy their masters, and because they could better defend themselves. Arguing for a different explanation is the fact that the U.S. free black population was predominantly female, whereas both the white and slave national population was predominantly male. The preponderance of females in the national free black population resulted largely from high black male mortality rates. Since the 1861 census shows that Buxton's overall population was nearly evenly divided between men and women, the male dominance in the oldest category may reflect fugitive slaves who escaped as young men.[22]

Regardless of its causes, the gender imbalance among Buxton's older residents may explain the most noticeable characteristic in this analysis—that is, the near absence of single women over the age of twenty-five. Of the forty-nine women between the ages of seventeen and twenty-five, nine were married and two were widows; in the same age group, only one male was recorded in the 1861 census as married, and his marital status is questionable (see table 6.1). Benjamin Crosswhite was the lone widower in this age group. It seems then that Buxton women tended to marry at a younger age than did men. Since only two men over the age of forty-five were single, they were clearly seeking and finding marriage partners from outside their age group. The age difference between the spouses of the married women in the seventeen-to-twenty-five group bear out the conclusion that older men attracted marriage partners despite the limited number of perspective partners of their own age. Older, propertied men were thus able to marry younger women. Of those nine married women, only two were married to husbands who were within ten years of their age. Five had husbands more than ten years older than themselves, and two were married to men who were ten years older. The largest age discrepancies involved the marriages of William (sixty-five) and Mary (twenty-five) Winfria; Henry (forty) and Mary (nineteen) Moore; and Thomas (forty-five) and Unis (twenty-four) Scott.[23]

Although census records do not recognize second marriages, it seems likely that a number of the older men, particularly those married to much younger women, had been previously married. The 1861 census records Thomas and Unis Scott as having two children living in their household: William, age twenty-one, and Robert, age four. Since Unis was twenty-four years old at the time, William could not have been her son, and it is consequently reasonable to conclude that Thomas had been previously married and had lost his wife, possibly in childbirth, from Thomas's age (forty-five, which would have made him twenty-four or so at the time of William's birth) and the fact that there seem to have been no other children born of that marriage (young Robert presumably was Unis's son). Likewise, William Winfria had been married before his union with Mary, whom the census listed as twenty-five years old, since their household included three children fourteen, seven, and six years old. While the two younger children may have been Mary's, the oldest one was not. These two family scenarios further provide evidence of the young age at which women married—Unis and Mary would have married sometime between the ages of seventeen and nineteen. Buxton women commonly bore their first children during that age span. According to census data, Ann Simms, Sarah Crabtree, America Gross, Abigail Due, Martha Robinson, Susan Smith, Jane Taylor, and Cintha Johnson, among others, were approximately nineteen when their first children were born. Mary Moore, Nancy Wickham, Eliza Parker, and Lucy Brooks were eighteen when they had their first children. Rebecca Martin was seventeen when she first gave birth and had had six children by the time she was thirty-one. Hampton Bailey had six children alive in 1861, when she was only twenty-eight years old; she had first become a mother at age sixteen. The census does not allow a determination of whether Buxton women followed a not uncommon slave practice of bearing a child before marriage; that circumstance seems unlikely, however, because of King's and the community's stance on morality.[24]

Rebecca Martin and Hampton Bailey bring to the fore the issue of family size.

As was the case elsewhere during the nineteenth century, Buxtonians had large families. Because nearly all farm labor came from family members, having a large number of children represented a substantial asset, merging reproduction with economic production. Numerous variables—from large families whose oldest children no longer lived with their parents to families who were separated while enslaved or during the process of acquiring freedom—make it difficult to accurately re-create each and every family. Nevertheless, it is possible to make generalizations about family composition among Buxton residents. Taking into consideration only those families for whom adequate data is available from the 1861 census, Buxton seems to have had fairly typical family characteristics for the mid-nineteenth century. Women commonly bore their first child within a year of marriage and their last in their early forties. During those twenty or so years, women gave birth at fairly consistent intervals of two to three years. Buxton families with resident children ranged in size from one to fifteen children, while most had between one and seven children. These findings do not take into account children who no longer lived with their parents in 1861 or infant/child mortality.[25]

Typical of Buxton families were Richard and Emily Jones, who had six children, ages two to nineteen; George and Nancy Hatter, with their five children, ages sixteen and under; and George and Jane Taylor, who had four children, all of them under fifteen. Mothers twenty-five years of age or under and those older than forty-five had the fewest resident children: Those in the younger range were still in their prime reproductive years and might subsequently have more children, while those in the older cohort had probably ended their childbearing and had had children who had left the household. In the 1861 census, the ages of mothers range from nineteen-year-old Mary Moore, whose son, Josiah, was one, to sixty-five-year-old Ellen Overton, whose youngest two children, thirteen and fifteen, lived at home but who undoubtedly had older children who had left the nest. Forty-six-year-old Rebecca Carter and her husband, John, had fifteen children, ranging in age from two to twenty-four, living in their one-story log home. Table 6.2 shows the ages of Buxton's mothers and the average numbers of children in their households according to the 1861 census.[26]

The family of Isaac and Marie Malone demonstrates the typical pattern of childbirth every two to three years. The Malones' nuclear household included Isaac (two), Malseny (four), Susan (seven), Mahala (nine), Elmira (twelve), and Robert (fourteen). Robert and Mary Harris and their four children (ages two, five, eight, and eleven) are also representative of Buxton families. Less common were David and Maria Stuart and their closely spaced children—ages one, three, five, six, eight, and nine years of age in 1861. A basis for further analysis is provided by using families with four or more children, of which the Buxton sample contains forty-four. More than half (23) of the families analyzed here had at

Table 6.2 Motherhood and Children in Buxton

Age of Mother	Average Number of Children in Household
19–25	2.1
26–30	5.6*
31–35	4.4
36–40	6.6 (5.8)**
41–45	4.1
46 & older	3.0

*There were three women in this age group whose household included one child who might not have been theirs but rather the product of their husbands' first marriages. If those children are removed from the equation, the average number of children in the household would be 5.3.

**In this age group, one mother, Rebecca Carter, had fifteen children. The first number represents the average with her included; the number in parentheses is the average if she is removed from the calculation.

Source: Canadian Population Census, 1861

least one gap of four or more years in the ages of their children. Several factors can account for such interval patterns. Richard and Emily Jones's youngest four children were spaced every two years (ages two, four, six, and eight) but their oldest two children were twelve and nineteen. Emily may have suffered one or more miscarriages that explain the gap, or the couple may have experienced the not uncommon pain of losing a child. The mid-nineteenth century saw high infant-mortality rates, and parents black and white lived with the reality that some of their children would likely not live to adulthood.[27] When the census enumerator visited them in 1861, Edward Calahan and his wife were still grieving the recent loss of their two-year-old from a lingering illness. Thomas and Unis Scott were recovering from the death of their eighteen-month-old daughter as a result of scarlet fever.[28]

At first glance, it might seem that Henry and Matilda Dabney had more than their fair share of heartache. The 1861 census shows several large gaps in the ages of their children, Ida (eleven), Henry (fourteen), Theodocia (twenty-one), and Josephine (twenty-seven). The significant age differences between Henry, Theodocia, and Josephine do not necessarily signal miscarriage or death, however, but may merely indicate that the children born between those remaining at home had married and left the household. Or the marriage may have been the second marriage for one of the partners, and the older children were the product of an earlier marriage. Alfred and Juliet Hooper had buried at least one and perhaps more of their children. Living in their household in 1861 were five children, ages twenty-three, twenty-two, nineteen, seven, and six. Recorded as having died during the previous twelve months was an eighteen-year-old son who had succumbed to scarlet fever. Gaps between the ages of younger children, though, are likely the result of mortality. Nancy Geals, a widow, had four children between the ages of two and seventeen, but a ten-year gap existed between her youngest child, Leroy, and the next oldest child, twelve-year-old Matilda. Likewise, the Lightfoot, Hatter, Henry, Parker, Goodson, and Brooks families all had age gaps of four or more years, indicating probable miscarriages or infant death. Fifteen-year-old Martha Lightfoot was eight years older than William, her younger sibling. Four years separated Pricilla and Barbara Hatter and Alfred and Charleat Parker. Evilda and Avon Henry were five years apart, as were Amanda and Dinah Goodson, while Ester Brooks was seven years older than her brother, John. In some cases it is possible to determine that the death of a child was the cause of such age gaps. This is the case with Levi and Mary Jackson's family. The 1861 census shows the couple with five children, ages fifteen, twelve, ten, nine, and one. The large gap between the two youngest children suggests misfortune, which is verified in the marginal comments to the census, which note the recent death of their three-year-old son as a result of "cold." Other possible explanations for such gaps in childbearing include temporary separation of spouses or death and subsequent remarriage.[29]

As Buxton's primary social institution, the family served as the repository for African cultural traditions. Naming was of great significance in African societies, and African Americans actively sought to preserve that aspect of their cultural heritage. Naming practices enabled blacks to express their respect for kinship ties and cultural continuity and to preserve their African linguistic heritage. Sharing a kin name was a useful device for fortifying generational ties, for connecting children with their past and placing them in the history of their families. First names in particular served as important connectors between fathers and sons, mothers and daughters, grandparents and grandchildren. More than anything else, names linked one generation to another, helping to define an African American identity based on a common heritage and experience.[30]

As would be expected by the mid-nineteenth century, the Buxton census records reveal little perpetuation of names of unmistakably African origin, but several probable anglicized versions of African names are present. Born in the United States in 1819, Abigail Doo may have been given the Americanized version of Abba, a traditional day name for female children born on Thursday. Born in 1838, Cintha Johnson's name is likely derivative of the African name Cinda. Likewise, Jemina Lewis's parents could have been trying to perpetuate an African namesake, Jeminah. Kiniah Enos's name may have been of African origin, as may also have been the case of Kincheon Brooks's name.[31]

By the nineteenth century, most blacks had rejected the place-names and classical names common in seventeenth- and eighteenth-century slave societies. Place-names were almost nonexistent at Buxton: The 1861 census lists only three, America Gross, Manchester Roper, and London Harris. Classical names were somewhat more common. Buxton's 1861 residents included Cupid Martin, Jasper Jackson, Clementine Calahan, Augustus Brooks, and Prince Chatham.

Among women, the names Flora, Delia, Juliet, and Dinah—all common names throughout the slave era—appear numerous times in the Buxton records. Also by the mid-nineteenth century, Anglo-American and biblical names had largely replaced classical, place-, and day names among blacks. Names of biblical origins are prominent among Buxtonians. Old Testament names such as Solomon, Isaiah, Isaac, Immanuel, Elijah, Hezekiah, Ezekiel, Hannah, Ester, Rebecca, and even Shadrach, Zachariah, and Tamar appear in the Buxton records. Other biblical names such as John, Abraham, Peter, David, Rachel, Sarah, Martha, and Mary were so commonly used that they lost much of their biblical connotation.[32]

Reflecting their status as freedpeople and to emphasize the self-esteem that accompanied freedom, blacks often elevated their names from the informal to the full form. This characterization can be seen in Buxton, where Samuel, Richard, William, Joseph, James, Robert, Edward, Charles, Franklin, Benjamin, Victoria, Rebecca, Elizabeth, Catherine, Martha, Josephine, and Margaret appear rather than their diminutive counterparts often seen in slave record books. Some distinctive names in Buxton included Wellington Stone, Evilda Henry, Morlene Smith, Dalmanintha Scipio, and Green Due. Henry and Elizabeth Johnson whimsically named their children Elsina, Thosdosia, Mahala, Adelia, Chelia, and Flora.[33]

Of the ninety-one Buxton families with children in residence in 1861, thirty-four (37 percent) named one or more of their children after a parent. Among these, several families passed their names on to both their sons and daughters. Charles and Nancy Watts, for example, named their second son Charles and their third daughter Nancy. Likewise, two of Joseph and Senneth Elliss's children bore the names of their parents, as did two of Henry and Maria Thomas's children. John and Catherine Morris similarly named a son and a daughter John and Catherine. A preference for paternal kin names is indicated in the frequency with which sons received the names of their fathers. Kin naming was not practiced as intensely for daughters. Only twelve (15 percent) of the seventy-nine families with one or more daughters named a child for her mother, while twenty-four (26 percent) of the seventy-nine Buxton families with sons passed on the father's name to the next generation. The more frequent naming of sons after fathers reflects the patriarchal structure of families. Naming practices were a way to solidify family ties—a carryover from enslavement, where fathers were more likely than mothers to be separated from their children. In Buxton as elsewhere, the larger the family, the greater the likelihood of more familial connections. Second-born sons or daughters were most likely to be named for their parents: Eleven of the twenty-four sons who bore their fathers' names were the family's second male child, while five of the twelve daughters who received their mothers' names were the second female children.[34]

In most cases, not enough is known about the extended family of Buxtonians to determine whether children were named for kinfolk other than their parents. In some instances, however, extended kin relations of early Buxton residents can be re-created, and connections can be seen between grandparents and grandchildren and aunts and uncles and nieces and nephews. At least two firstborn female children were named after their grandmothers: Both Sarah Freeman and Julia Hooper received their paternal grandmothers' names. Benjamin Crosswhite passed on the name of his mother when he named one of his daughters Sarah. Richard Thomas, the third son of Henry and Maria Thomas, was named after a cousin who was twenty years his senior. Henry and Maria named another of their sons John after Henry's brother and nephew. The firstborn son of George Hatter and his first wife, Mary, bore the name of George's brother, Franklin, which may have been a family name, perhaps that of a grandfather. Buxton families would continue the practice of passing family names on to new generations. For example, William Goodhall was named after his grandfather, William Parker. He was the family's third generation to bear the name *William*.[35]

Personal relationships, the bonds woven among its members, were the building blocks of community at Buxton. Community identity at Buxton, as elsewhere, was rooted in mutual experiences of racial oppression and common culture based on nationality. Numerous facets of interlocking relationships developed as Buxtonians were involved in kinship, occupational, and organizational matrixes. These reinforcing relationships augmented the development of the close bonds necessary for a cohesive, well-organized, and stable community. United by shared circumstances and living conditions and a common set of cultural values, the residents in Buxton developed relatively quickly into a supportive community.

Marriage assisted in the formation of a cohesive community at Buxton. Kin relations bound Buxton households into kinship communities. Marriages united two sets of kin, creating larger extended family networks and increasing the number of interfamily relations from which community interconnectedness grew. In time, many of Buxton's families became related to one another through blood ties. Two of Buxton's founding families were united when Ann Watts, the eldest daughter of Charles and Nancy Watts, married George Hatter, son of Franklin and Rebecca Hatter. Members of the Hatter family first came to Buxton in 1850, when Franklin's brother, George, relocated from the Niagara area, where he had settled after escaping from his master in what is now West Virginia in 1837 at the age of nineteen. As has been previously mentioned, the Wattses were one of nine interracial families living in Buxton during the 1850s. Charles, born a slave, had been manumitted for saving his master's son's life during the Mexican War. The Wattses merged with another Buxton family with the marriage of son David to Hanna Kersey, the daughter of John and Martha Kersey, who came to Buxton in the mid-1850s. The Hatter family united with yet another founding Buxton family when their daughter, Pricilla, wed William Carter. Likewise, the Carters combined with the Morris family when Catherine, the daughter of John and Catherine Morris, married James Carter. Ezekiel and Louisa Cooper, a black family that migrated from Maryland, linked with the family of James and Matilda Dabney, who came to Buxton in 1851, when Elizabeth Cooper married Henry Johnson Dabney. William and Eliza Parker's daughter, Cassanda, married Squire Goodall, son of James and Mary Goodall, who numbered among Buxton's founding settlers and who owned two hundred acres of land by the mid-1850s. Numerous other marriages served to create and strengthen kinship ties in the Buxton community.[36] If "the degree to which a society's inhabitants enter into marriages, maintain lasting relationships, promulgate families and develop extensive kinship systems" reveals much about a community's cohesion, then Buxton had become a cohesive, stable community within the first decade of its existence.[37]

Despite being an all-black community and segregated in its residential patterns, Buxton did not exist in a void, cut off from its surroundings. Buxton residents had considerable connections with blacks (and whites) throughout Upper Canada. Buxton's experience was, to a certain extent, intertwined with those of nearby communities. Marriage records kept by the congregation of St. Andrew's provide evidence of such interaction. Buxtonians apparently did not find marriage partners only within their immediate community. Most of the unions between a member of the Buxton community and an outsider tended to involve someone from a neighboring community in Raleigh Township. Jeremiah Freeman, then living in Raleigh, married Maria Carter of Buxton in December 1857. In December 1861 George Charleston of Raleigh married Buxton's Hudosia Dabney, and the couple took up residence in Raleigh. Raleigh's Americus Cooper married Buxton's Mary Ann Poindexter a year later. John Carter of Buxton and Raleigh Township's Hariet Dyke married in 1863. Most such unions in Buxton's records involved women from Buxton and males from elsewhere, which may reflect a lack of potential male spouses in Buxton or simply the tradition of a bride holding the marriage ceremony in her home location. (That is, the marriages of Buxton men and women from other communities would have taken place in those other communities and thus would not have been recorded in Buxton.)[38]

Some relationships developed over a greater distance. In November 1862, Rosanna Jones, a Buxton resident, married William Clayton, who was living in Ingersoll, approximately one hundred miles northeast of Buxton, between London and Hamilton. Evidence suggests that William had a previous connection to Buxton. According to the 1861 census, Nancy Clayton, age fifty-six, and Charles Clayton, seventeen and presumably her son, lived in the household of Henry K. Thomas. The exact relationship between the Clayton family and the

Thomas family is unknown. It is not even clear whether William Clayton was related to Nancy and Charles, although it seems likely that he was. If Nancy and Charles had moved from Ingersoll to Buxton, William may have visited them and thus met and courted Rosanna. About a year after William and Rosanna married, Thomas Wilson and Mary Ann Charity exchanged vows at St. Andrew's. The Virginia-born Mary Ann was a resident of Buxton, while the groom listed Detroit as his place of residence and Ohio as his place of birth. Again, census records show a possible connection between Thomas Wilson and Buxton. The 1861 census shows Uriah and Deborah Wilson, ages twenty and eighteen, respectively, living in the household of Absalom Johnson's family. There was also a widower, Hugh Wilson, who lived with his two sons, Jesse, fourteen, and Robert, twelve. It is unclear whether Uriah and Deborah were also Hugh's children, just living in another household. Perhaps Thomas was Hugh's son and had gone to Detroit looking for employment, in which case Thomas and Mary Ann may have carried on a long-distance relationship for a couple of years before deciding to marry.[39]

The process of building new communities involved the coming together of people from a variety of locations and cultural backgrounds. Differences of both experience and heritage undoubtedly separated people. A fugitive slave, to cite an example, had grown up in a world quite removed from that known by a freeborn black. Although such distinctions existed among Buxton settlers, it does not appear that they caused debilitating divisions, probably because such differences were offset by factors that tended to encourage the development of a new, shared sense of community. Buxton settlers knew that getting ahead would require them to depend on one another and keep personal disputes to a minimum. Their sense of community would help sustain them in trying economic times. Despite their different experiences, the diverse community at Buxton, as in black communities elsewhere, was less divided internally than white society. Fewer economic, religious, and social distinctions separated the residents of Buxton, largely because, regardless of their differences, they were bound together as an oppressed people in a white-dominated society.

Most of Buxton's peer communities benefited from the identity and stability of preexisting connections. One of the strengths of the Gist settlements was that their social organization was based on preexisting families and communities. They did not have to create a new kin structure. The Randolph slaves, too, had been a community for more than half a century, and even after their dispersal in 1846 they retained a sense of group identity. Their survival as a single physically united autonomous community had been prevented, but the sense of a unique communal identity had not been lost. Ties of kinship and community already existed among many of the Beech and Roberts families and were strengthened on the frontier. In these and other locations, many of those who became core families came with their relations and established family and kin connections. Communities were, in other words, built by families in association. One area in which such preexisting community ties greatly aided new arrivals was in financial matters. Familial connections played an important part in providing new arrivals with the wherewithal to remain.[40]

Unlike some of these other antebellum black communities, Buxton was not established by a group of interrelated families. Granted, King's fifteen slaves, the core founders of Buxton, were part of a community prior to their relocation, but in the larger context of the settlement, those fifteen individuals did not represent a community foundation on which the settlement could build. Buxton residents therefore lacked a preexisting sense of community. It had to be developed, and to their credit, Buxton residents did so within a decade.

7

Making a Living

Buxton's land was heavily timbered, with elm, hickory, oak, maple, and ash, all of which had to be hewn and cleared before an ear of corn or a blade of wheat could be raised. An abundance of animal life—fox, wolves, bear, deer, raccoon, and turkey—shared the Elgin tract with the human settlers. Looking at the primitive nature of their land and homestead sites must have discouraged many, particularly those settlers who grew up in long-settled regions of the United States. They would soon be engaged in a constant struggle to gain the upper hand against nature and tame their land. The task confronting settlers on virgin land was formidable. Moreover, Buxtonians encountered obstacles that white pioneers did not face.

Regardless of their backgrounds, all blacks coming to Buxton faced similar circumstances after arriving. Fugitives, often equipped with only the clothes they wore at the time of their flight and whatever supplies or funds friends and sympathetic strangers along the way might have provided, were ill prepared to sustain themselves, pay their first installments on parcels of land, begin clearing the land, and build houses, all before the first crops were harvested. The circumstances of those blacks who came to Buxton from other parts of Canada or from the northern United States were usually somewhat less urgent than those of fugitive slaves coming directly from the shackles of slavery. Yet even these people were sometimes little better prepared for the task before them than were recent runaways. Only a handful of the arrivals held property before reaching Buxton.

William King and the Elgin Association envisioned Buxton as an interactive community based on self-reliance and independence, a model for blacks throughout North America. Economic stability was central to King's aspiration of improving "the social and moral condition of the coloured population of Canada."[1] Land in and of itself was not adequate to accomplish the lofty goal of an independent, financially secure existence. Throughout its existence, the Buxton community fluctuated between periods of hardship and relative ease, with the former more prevalent. The zeal with which many new arrivals entered the settlement often diminished, at least temporarily, when they confronted the immediate need for food, money, and supplies. Faced with such basic necessities, new settlers often left their land temporarily and sought work as day laborers. Many found employment with the growing Canadian railway system. Not finding that work to their liking or meeting their needs, however, most of these people returned to Buxton with renewed determination to farm their land. Even so, they, as well as other Buxton settlers, found it necessary to supplement family incomes with part-time employment outside the settlement. In Buxton as elsewhere, the general poverty of the free black community often meant that all family members worked, sometimes outside the household. In the early years men commonly obtained work as laborers, while women worked as house servants for local white farmers: Wages thus earned "were carefully husbanded to maintain the family while chopping down the bush and clearing the land during the winter."[2]

This pattern undermined a primary function of Buxton as a viable community and concerned all those involved in the settlement. King believed that to progress, black people required family to provide social unity and a consciousness of civic responsibility to provide political cohesion. A stable community could provide both ingredients. Buxton could offer blacks the opportunity to establish that stable community only if its natural resources were exploited in a way that would enable settlers to stay on their farms to enjoy that family unity and exercise that civic responsibility. The solution was to create local industries based on those resources. By providing part-time employment, such industry would make it unnecessary for settlers to go outside their community to find work. Buxton would not be the only all-black settlement in Canada to try its hand at industry. In 1847 Josiah Henson established a steam sawmill at Dawn with the financial support of Boston merchants Ephraim Peabody, Samuel Elliot, Amos Lawrence, and H. Ingersoll Bowditch. The land on which the British-American Institute was situated contained extensive stands of black walnut timber that Henson wanted to market rather than burn in land clearing. King may have gotten the idea for a sawmill in Buxton from Dawn's example. Other industries followed in Dawn. Two fugitives from Virginia and North Carolina erected a ropewalk at which they manufactured cordage with hemp they cultivated. At least two blacksmiths and a millwright also settled in Dawn and engaged in their crafts. To be truly successful, however, Buxton's industrialization needed to be more extensive and productive than that in Dawn or for that matter in any other black community in North America.[3]

As was customary in Buxton, a public meeting was called to discuss possible approaches to establishing an industrial base. Among those in attendance were two men who had formerly made bricks in the United States. They pointed out that clay, wood, and labor, all of which were in abundance at the settlement, were all that was needed to begin the production of brick. These two men subsequently opened a brickyard just outside Buxton's center square. During the first year of operation, the Buxton kilns reportedly fired three hundred thousand bricks, which they sold both to residents of the settlement and to blacks and whites as far away as Chatham. The first brick building in Buxton was a two-story hotel run by Alfred West. In 1854, during the brickyard's second year of operation, Robert VanRankin built the first brick home, and by 1866 others had been erected. At least one of the community's schoolhouses was built from brick made by the settlers. Sufficient quantities of brick were sold to keep the brickyard in business throughout the 1850s, bolstering Buxton's economy and contributing to its stability.[4]

Because timber and especially elm and oak abounded throughout the Elgin tract, a lumber mill was a logical business venture. The nearest such facility was in Chatham, too far for Buxton's inadequate transportation facilities to conveniently and economically carry timber for milling. In 1849 only one road cut through the Elgin tract, and it was of poor quality. Additional roads had been mapped out, but they would not be completed for years, and even then they were to be hardly more than wide lanes. As a result, Buxtonians at first cleared land and then watched as most of the valuable trees were burned rather than converted to cash, although some of the wood was used for buildings and fences. The lack of a potash or pearl ash factory to utilize the by-products of the burning meant that the ashes were simply left to disintegrate. As a result, the possibility of establishing a sawmill consumed a major part of the discussion at the initial community meeting on industrial pursuits. Lacking the necessary financial resources to launch such an enterprise on their own, Buxtonians sought outside assistance. Henry Thomas and Wilson Abbott, who had engaged in various business activities before relocating to Buxton, agreed to aid in the promotion of new industries in Buxton.

Traveling to Buffalo and Toronto, Thomas and Abbott raised more than three thousand dollars, mostly from black businessmen who purchased stock for one hundred twenty-five dollars. By September 1852, thirty shares had been sold. With this investment, the entrepreneurs formed the Canada Mill and Mercantile Company (more commonly referred to as the Buxton Company) in March 1852, with the purpose of establishing a "Saw Mill, a Grist Mill, and a good Country Store" so that Buxton might become "independent and respectable in business transactions."[5] Unlike the Elgin Association, the majority of the Buxton Company stockholders and its board of directors were black men. Only two white men, William King and George Brown, served on the company's board of directors. Brown, the publisher of the *Toronto Globe*, the largest and most influential Canadian newspaper of the time, ardently supported Buxton and contributed substantially to this venture.[6]

The Canada Mill and Mercantile Company was well received by the general public. The editors of the *Voice of the Fugitive*, a black newspaper published in Windsor, approved of the company's management and objectives, writing that the objectives seemed "to have been well digested and taken hold of in a business like manner, by men who have not only the brain[s] but the means also to carry it forward."[7] The editors further heralded the formation of the Buxton Company as a sign that "our people are getting their eyes open, and are now beginning to strive for something higher than perpetual begging."[8]

The new company's board of directors appointed a three-man committee consisting of King, Abbott, and another local black man, John M. Tensley, to oversee the construction of a sawmill. King was delegated to travel to Detroit to purchase the necessary machinery. Demonstrating the community effort that went into most Buxton projects, Abbott granted the company land on which to establish the mill; settlers built the frame from trees cut from nearby acreage; and the Buxton's brick factory produced the bricks for building. Only the mill machinery, which King donated as his investment in the company, came from outside the settlement. By 1853 the sawmill was in full operation. Later, a corn mill was obtained from Cincinnati and attached to the sawmill engine by a belt so that the two mills could run simultaneously. By 1858 the operation included a siding machine and a shingle factory, all of which joined the existing wagon, carpentry, and blacksmith shops of Buxton's village square.[9]

By the mid-1850s, then, Buxton had readily available lumber and brick for building purposes. Soon marked improvements appeared, helping to give the community a more permanent character. The dirt floors of early settlers' homes gave way to oak flooring, brick chimneys replaced primitive ones made of mud, and frame and brick buildings grew alongside log cabins. The sawmill and brickyard improved Buxton in other, perhaps more vital, ways. Income from these business ventures made it less necessary for Buxton residents to seek employment outside their community. By 1855 the settlers "manifested a more fixed determination to support themselves without going abroad for work."[10] Settlers converted their cleared timber into cash or useful building materials, resulting in a substantial increase in the amount of land cleared for agricultural purposes.

The sawmill performed fairly well, at least for a time. The Canada Southern Railroad, paying seven cents each for ties, initially provided a good deal of business as the rail line through the area was constructed. The mill's oak staves also found a market as far away as England. In 1866 Anderson Ruffin Abbott, a prominent black man from Toronto, visited Buxton and reported that the mill had turned out eight hundred thousand feet of lumber during the previous year. By then, it was also cutting sycamore lumber for the manufacture of cigar boxes, with the tramway carrying the timber to Lake Erie for shipment. Little is known about the profitability of the gristmill venture; but the ability to convert wheat and corn into flour and meal for home consumption aided the settlers because they no longer had to transport their grain to Chatham for grinding.[11]

Drawing once more on the skill of one of its members, the community at Buxton explored another moneymaking venture based on lumber, their most valuable and abundant natural resource. One Buxton resident, a fugitive from Georgia, had made pitch-pine barrels as a slave. He now utilized that skill to provide income for himself and his family. Several men learned the skill from him and helped support their families in this manner. By the mid-1850s, barrel staves produced in Buxton were sold as far away as Cincinnati and Buffalo.[12]

Other industrial activities arose in Buxton, some of them taking advantage of the salable commodities produced from their timber resources. While in the United States to procure machinery for the sawmill, King had journeyed to Delta, Ohio, to consult with F. Gates, a white man experienced in making pearl ash, which was used as fertilizer. King persuaded Gates that Buxton held financial promise, and he and his family moved to the area and settled just outside the Elgin tract. There he began teaching his craft to interested Buxtonians. A pearl ash factory was up and running in Buxton even before the completion of the sawmill, providing yet another source of income for the settlement's residents. King undoubtedly exaggerated when he claimed that "the salts made from the ashes [were] found sufficient to pay for the clearing of the land."[13] The selling of pearl ash alone would not have supplied the settlers with enough income to support themselves. Nevertheless, pearl ash sales may temporarily have been the settlers' principal source of cash, at least until the sawmill began operating and the brickyard became better established. The pearl ash facility also benefited the settlement for a time by using an otherwise worthless by-product. Ironically, however, the pearl ash factory was eventually abandoned because it necessitated the destruction of too much timber, thus taking away necessary supplies from the sawmill.[14]

Potash, a silvery-white substance, was used for glassmaking and as fertilizer. James Rapier, an enterprising young Buxtonian, opened a potash factory in late March 1857. Rapier chose to start such a business because potash had "arisen to enormous Prices—from $25 to $50 per Barrell."[15] With one kettle and two assistants, he could manufacture three barrels of potash a week, which, he believed, could be sold for an attractive profit. Little more is known about his business, but Rapier left Buxton during the early 1860s, and so the business venture apparently did not live up to his expectations. Perhaps a shortage of readily available timber hampered his efforts, just as it had the pearl ash factory.[16]

Buxton's industrial pursuits created a need for improvements in the transportation system. Lumber, barrel staves, and other products sold to outside markets had to be transported to the lakefront, which bordered the Elgin tract on the south. Buxtonians first worked as a community to complete Center Road, thus opening a path straight to Lake Erie. Center Road, however, was besieged with water problems. In an 1848 survey of the land, Richard Parr noted that the "present value [of the land] is much depreciated for want of roads and a thorough drainage." Parr further noted that the lack of "a proper channel to carry [the water] off" creates "an obstacle to the construction of roads" and "renders it impossible to reach a market . . . without following a circuitous route of several miles."[17] With every rain, the road became a morass of mud, difficult to traverse with heavy wagon loads for much of the year. The Buxton community collaborated on the construction of a wooden tramway from Buxton Square to the edge of Lake Erie on the tract's southern border. When the route was completed, Buxton goods could easily reach a water outlet, traveling atop wagon beds rolled along the wooden rails.

Other efforts were made to bring the benefits of economic diversification to Buxton. As it celebrated its tenth anniversary, Buxton boasted three shoemakers, two carpenters, a printer, a blacksmith, and at least one shopkeeper. In addition, the 1861 census recorded several young Buxton men as laborers who resided in the households of artisans. Francis Lasse, a blacksmith, had three single men in their mid-twenties listed in his household, presumably working for him and learning the blacksmith trade. One of those apprentices was Peter Daly, a (white) Irish laborer. By 1860, the community also included Alfred West's brick hotel and a grocer's store. The store apparently encountered trouble from the start. Probably because of transportation and other expenses, the owner, Robert VanRankin, charged prices that were as much as 25 percent higher than those at the stores in Chatham. Some Buxton's residents consequently avoided doing business with VanRankin even though he was a member of their community. This difficulty did not affect the grocer's social standing in the community, however. VanRankin was an active and respected deacon of St. Andrew's Church. Although his business suffered, many black and white settlers would also have frequented his store rather than travel to Chatham. By 1871, however, VanRankin seems to have given up his store, and the census lists his occupation as a farmer.[18]

After his 1852 visit to the community, Samuel Ward described some of the Buxtonians' abilities as mechanics and tradesmen. He referred to West's hotel as "the best country tavern in Kent" county and Thomas Stringer as one of the "most enterprising tradesmen in the county." Ward's carriage had broken down and required extensive repair, and he was quite satisfied with the service he received, noting, "I never had better repairing done to either the woodwork or the ironwork of my carriage." Ward also spoke highly of the local blacksmith, commenting that he had "never had better shoeing than was done to my horses." Ward concluded that Buxton was "blessed with able mechanics, good farmers, enterprising men and women . . . and they are training the rising generation to principles such as will give them the best places in the esteem and the service of their countrymen at some day not far distant."[19] Buxtonians seemed to be living up to King's expectations of self-improvement.

In the mid-1850s, Buxtonians gained access to a local bank, which held accounts as small as ten cents. The Buxton Savings Bank operated under the directive of the Elgin Association, with the Bank of Upper Canada as an umbrella organization. A committee consisting of three shareholders and three Buxton residents oversaw the bank's management, and only members of the Buxton community were eligible to use the institution. The settlers thus had a safe place to deposit the cash they were saving to pay the annual installments on their land and no longer had to contend with transportation challenges to make bank deposits in Chatham. Buxton residents—and particularly those newly escaped from slavery—undoubtedly lacked experience in managing money, and the presence of the Buxton Savings Bank aided them in acquiring sound financial habits. The ease of making regular deposits in a convenient location assuredly prompted Buxtonians to save more of their hard-earned cash.

In 1849 no post office existed between Chatham and Windsor, a distance of more than fifty miles, although a stage running along the Thames River carried mail through that part of the country each day. During the spring and fall, when the rains made the roads even worse than at other times, the journey to Chatham, the closest post office to Buxton, became extremely difficult, particularly for those settlers on the western side of the settlement. (Oddly, the trip became easier during the winter, when sleighs glided smoothly over the snow.) After a petition from the Buxton community, the mail route was changed slightly so that it ran directly along Middle Road (or King Street), the main road through the Elgin tract and several other rural towns. The government then established four post offices along the road, at Buxton, East and West Tilbury, and Maidstone. The establishment of the post office, with King appointed postmaster, stimulated intellectual activity throughout the community, as the inhabitants wrote and received significantly more letters and began to subscribe to newspapers, enabling residents to keep abreast of outside events. Establishment of the post office indicated the settlement's success because residents had to demonstrate a need for the service.[20]

Despite all the effort that went into the industries and service establishments, they did not prove a panacea for Buxton's financial woes. Self-sufficiency could not be attained with small-scale industries, and Buxton's industrial endeavors ironically may have made the community more dependent on outside sources. The sawmill, brickyard, gristmill, and pearl ash and potash factories depended to a considerable extent on customers—with cash—from neighboring areas. The subsistence nature of the economy may not have offered enough of an outlet for the lumber produced by the mill, in part perhaps explaining the Buxton mill's financial problems. Mills in other frontier localities were often not financially solvent and principally accommodated the community, doing little cash business. The hotel and a boardinghouse also relied heavily on outside support.

The second half of the 1850s constituted a period of acute economic stress for the settlement and surrounding environs. Significantly hampering Buxton's economy was a depression that hit both the United States and Canada and effectively curtailed the development and growth of many businesses. Currency in Buxton, always scarce, became almost nonexistent. With money tight, few people in the vicinity were building with brick or making improvements to their homes. Neither Buxtonians nor neighboring white farmers had funds with which to purchase finished lumber, and the railroad companies stopped expanding. To make ends meet and honor the obligations on their land, Buxton settlers were increasingly forced to seek employment as laborers in nearby towns and farms, something that the preceding industrial activity had sought to prevent and that the region's economic situation made difficult.

One sign of economic decline and an indication of Buxton's bleak industrial situation was that by March 1857 the sawmill had come under the management and possible ownership of Peter Straith, a Scotsman. Straith's presence and involvement with the sawmill detracted from the self-sustenance goal of Buxton's blacks. The exact circumstances of this transfer of ownership are not clear. As a white man, Straith should have been ineligible to purchase land on the Elgin reserve, but records show his owning fifty acres of land on the eleventh concession, in the center of the Elgin tract, close to the mill. Straith's arrival and management of the mill received mixed reviews. Whereas King mentioned the mill and Straith approvingly in his 1857 report to the Elgin Association, some members of the community did not concur with King's assessment. James Rapier wrote that Straith was "exceedingly unpopular with the people and [was] no business man."[21]

King worked diligently to keep the sawmill from financial collapse, even traveling to England in 1860 to solicit additional markets. King spoke to sympathetic British audiences, beseeching his listeners to buy Buxton's lumber. Besides buyers, King desired investors, hoping to raise about two thousand dollars. Banking on the mill's future success, King solicited loans with the promise of repayment plus 6 percent interest at the end of four years. King's efforts succeeded. Several influential Englishmen, including Earl Spencer, invested in the mill. Another Englishman, John Pearson, wrote to King that "having visited [Upper Canada] myself and brought some of the timber to [London and Liverpool], I can speak from experience of its quality, and the ready sale it obtains there."[22] He subsequently contributed a substantial sum for the support of the Buxton mill, as did Henry Christy from Westminster. Meanwhile, the timber merchants of the successful company of Churchill and Sim provided some encouragement and healthy criticism, providing what they described as "all the explanations and details necessary" to improve the Buxton mill's "valuable products."[23] Assistance from England temporarily helped to alleviate the mill's troubles but did not permanently cure the problems.

Much of the money King had solicited during his trip to England apparently was never repaid, implying that the mill did not sustain adequate business with London and Liverpool timber markets to produce a profit. One investor, John Jowitt, stated that he subscribed fifty pounds and for a short time received some payment toward interest but after a time heard "nothing of Mr. King or the settlement."[24] Arthur Lupton tells a similar story: "I gave Fifty Pounds to the Rev. W. King. . . . I have long ceased to expect any return of the money."[25] The unpaid monies were the subject of an accusation of impropriety against King and the Elgin Association in the early 1870s. A local white man named Stephenson reported not only that the borrowed money had never been repaid but also that King had used it for personal purposes. No action was taken against King, since it was proven that the majority of those who had loaned money for the sawmill had discharged King from any liability for the funds. Many investors looked on the money as a gift rather than a loan. Jowitt released King "from any pecuniary liability in regard" to the money he gave King, as did W. E. Forster, who gave King money "with the full understanding that it was for an object good in itself," and J. G. Barclay, who considered the money he subscribed as "being from the first a gift."[26]

Despite the growth and development of these various Buxton businesses and perhaps because of their ultimate failure to alleviate the community's financial problems, the settlement remained primarily agricultural. In this respect, Buxton resembled most rural communities, black and white. During the summer, most settlers worked the land, cared for their crops and livestock, and earned whatever wages they could doing odd jobs either in or outside Buxton. Winters were spent chopping down the bush, clearing additional acreage, and pursuing whatever other opportunities arose to acquire funds. Subsistence living predominated: Families grew or raised what they ate and made what they wore, lived in, and used.

Despite King's best hopes for the land and the praise heaped on it in proimmigration propaganda, the land on which Buxton's farmers toiled proved less than ideal, and agriculture, like industry, proved unable to meet the high expectations of the community's founders and supporters. King had apparently overlooked or ignored warnings about the land's quality, although government surveyors and others alerted him to the problems. Richard Parr, a licensed surveyor, reported that the northern section of the tract, though composed generally of good soil, was "much depreciated for want of roads, and thorough drainage."[27] The southern section likewise suffered from a lack of drainage, stated Parr, and "but little of this land could be made available unless an expensive and systematic system of drainage was resorted to."[28] Anderson Ruffin Abbott, a local black man and ardent supporter of Buxton, claimed that the site chosen . . . was . . . a most unpromising tract of land. . . . The soil was a plastic vegetable mould upon a stiff clay subsoil [and was] difficultly drained. . . . The water stood on the land till late in the spring and frequently returned in the fall before crops could be garnered."[29] Similarly, an 1848 petition by a number of respected white men of the Buxton's district stated that "the Great Marsh in Raleigh has long been a hindrance and drawback to the settlement of that section of the Township of Raleigh. . . . [I]t has also been a cause of much sickness . . . and even in some instances to loss of life."[30]

As Abbott had predicted, drainage problems plagued the community through the 1860s. Numerous drainage ditches were needed to carry water off to the creeks, but settlers were occupied with other, more urgent undertakings (including building homes and clearing land) and did not at first have time to build the ditches. Several years would pass before the ditches were built, and for at least the settlement's first decade—its most difficult years—significant portions of the area consisted of less than prime agricultural land.[31]

Once again, the similarity between Buxton and the Gist settlements in southern Ohio is striking. A local white described the land chosen for the Gist freedpeople as "covered with . . . sloughs of stagnant water," making it "almost valueless . . . for any purpose other than pasturage."[32] Local Quakers in the area informed Wickham that "the selection of their lands has not been the best, the soil being inferior."[33] They recommended that the land be sold and a more suitable site found. Unfortunately for the Gist freedmen, Wickham did not heed their advice. The Gist settlers were thus saddled with poor land that they were expected to render productive.

Black settlers elsewhere likewise faced less than ideal land conditions. Gerrit Smith admitted that the land in the wilds of the Adirondacks in New York, which he gave away to black setters, was of poor quality, being in the "colder and less fertile" parts of the state, but then, he was giving it away.[34] Although they chose their own land and the place where they settled, the settlers at the Beech settlement in Indiana had similar issues with land quality. By the time blacks began coming to Ripley Township where the Beech settlement was, most of the best lands had already been purchased. The land bought by blacks generally consisted of poorly drained soils, described by government surveyors as "third rate," the lowest possible ranking. The standing water and damp soils described sound similar to the problem at Buxton. Beech settlers' willingness to purchase such poor land underscores the importance of settling near Quakers or other sympathetic whites. The problems associated with wetlands were a trade-off for long-term comfort and safety, an exchange the settlers were willing to make.[35]

Why exactly King purchased that particular parcel of land is unclear. Several factors seem to have influenced his decision, although at base, the drainage problems may explain why he was able to secure such a large tract of virtually unsettled land in Raleigh Township. In addition, the tract boasted a relatively central location between two population centers, giving his settlers access to markets. Where others viewed the thick standing timber as a nuisance hindering cultivation, settlement, and travel, King saw a financial asset. He saw that the land was level and that part of the soil was a deep rich black loam, suitable for agricultural pursuits.

The Elgin Association attempted to capitalize on the drainage problem. In 1862 the association petitioned to have the interest it owed the Crown for the land remitted, arguing that "a considerable portion . . . is low and wet and unfit for settlement."[36] The petition went on to state that the "inability" of the already established settlers "to effect the extensive improvements necessary to reclaim these wet lands" was inhibiting the pace of further settlement.[37] The petition was rejected. Despite its claims, however, the lack of proper drainage did not seriously discourage settlement in Buxton. By 1860 a majority of the lots that the Elgin tract comprised had been subscribed, and Buxton's population had grown steadily. The southernmost and northernmost concessions were the last settled, in part because that was where the drainage problems were concentrated but also in part because they were the furthest away from the center of Buxton, where churches, schools, and businesses were being or would likely be established. In consideration of contemporary travel difficulties, logic dictated that the settlers gravitate to the center of community activity. This was especially true for early Buxtonians, who often lacked horses, carriages, or wagons; walking was the most common method of conveyance.

While the quality of the land did not greatly affect the settlement's population, the soggy condition of the land did impede its cultivation and hence the community's agricultural success. In some years the spring rains were so heavy that the water rose high in the fields, preventing Buxton farmers from properly preparing the soil for cultivation and postponing the planting of the season's crops. Standing water also wreaked havoc on crops as they grew. Both William

Parker and William Anderson, settled in the southern half of the settlement, lost all their 1860 crops to water damage. Henry Williams lost his entire potato crop to water rot the same year. Reports show further problems in 1861, when the potato crop was once again "greatly injured by the Rot."[38]

By 1856 the settlers had begun to build ditches measuring about eight feet wide and three feet deep, and the system expanded well into the next decade. These community efforts met with some success, remedying some of the flooding problems of the fourteenth and fifteenth concessions in the southernmost part of the tract. Nevertheless, although the ditches generally worked when they could be kept clear, Buxton's drainage problems were never completely solved.[39] According to Sarah Thomas, a longtime resident, "We have ditches, yet it is almost a river here in the roads some times."[40]

A farmer's most important and valuable possessions were farm tools and equipment. Several years of labor could be required to produce enough cash crops to purchase a pickax, plow, or sickle. Ox teams used for plowing were also costly, as were horses for transportation and work purposes. How many of Buxton's settlers came to the settlement with the necessary farming implements or the wherewithal to purchase them is unknown, but considering that many were fugitives, it would seem unlikely that a majority of the families did so. Free families such as the Hatters, Doos, and Thomases might have had the opportunity to prepare carefully to leave their homes in the United States and may have arrived at the Elgin tract better equipped. Those fortunate enough to have tools in all likelihood loaned them to neighbors in need, and plows undoubtedly passed from farm to farm. From land clearing to cabin raising and beyond, neighbors in a rural community such as Buxton were linked through a widespread reciprocal network.

A true test of the settlers' resourcefulness, ability, and fortitude was turning a virgin territory into a productive agricultural area regardless of the inadequacies in the land. The initial activities of the settlers would have been to clear a plot of land and plow a few acres in the crudely prepared soil. Food crops—corn and perhaps wheat—would be planted. Cash farming was out of the question at least during the first year of settlement. The farmer's primary concern during the spring and summer months was to make provisions to survive the following winter. Fences had to be built to protect the crops from livestock, and housing had to be constructed to shelter the family.

Through hard work and community efforts, the residents began the process of taming the wilderness. The settlers continually increased their agricultural production and appeared to be fairly successful in their endeavors. The first settlers had cleared 230 acres by 1851, planting 204 acres that year, including 24 of wheat, 134 of corn, 12 of tobacco, and various acreage devoted to potatoes, oats, and peas. By August 1852 the settlers were experimenting with the new crops of hemp and maple sugar and had acquired some livestock. Two years later, the community boasted 150 head of cattle, 38 horses, 25 sheep, and 700 hogs. By 1853 the number of acres under cultivation had increased to 415. The year 1856 proved to be a watershed, as Buxton farmers sowed 924 acres of various crops, the greatest acreage planted before the outbreak of the U.S. Civil War. During the war, when the southern U.S. agricultural output declined, the settlers at Buxton increased their agricultural acreage. In 1860 they planted 300 acres of wheat, 600 acres of corn, 200 acres of oats, and 400 acres of a mixture of such crops as potatoes, peas, turnips, and buckwheat. That year 14 acres were also planted with tobacco and 16 acres with flax.[41]

The 1861 Canadian agricultural census provides a snapshot of agricultural practices in Buxton, where the typical farmer planted diverse crops. Corn and potatoes were a mainstay, providing food for family and livestock. Most farms grew hay, oats, wheat, and to a lesser extent buckwheat, and fifty acres would have made most farmers modestly self-sufficient. The average Buxton farmer possessed some livestock, including hogs, oxen, cows, sheep, and assorted poultry. Families raised vegetables in their gardens and planted crops for domestic consumption and, they hoped, local sale. While Buxton families may have reached a reasonable level of subsistence, they had a much harder time generating income to pay for manufactured commodities. Pioneer farmers commonly cultivated wheat, which had strong profit potential because it stood transportation well and possessed considerable value in a relatively small bulk. Under ideal conditions, one good crop could generate a substantial segment of a Buxton farmer's land payment. Unfortunately, such conditions were never realized. Buxtonians' other main crop, corn, provided food for both humans and livestock and could be marketed. With a small amount of labor, a farmer could raise a bountiful crop of corn—under good conditions. By raising flax and keeping sheep, which provided wool, Buxtonians provided themselves with material for clothing and other household needs for cloth.[42]

A close look at two of Buxton's earliest settlers illustrates how divergent experiences and backgrounds affected the financial potential and success of a pioneer family. In 1860, after more than a decade in Buxton, Isaac Riley had cleared close to thirty of his hundred acres of land. That year, his cultivated land included five acres of corn, three acres each of wheat and oats, and one acre apiece of buckwheat and potatoes. Riley owned livestock valued at more than three hundred dollars—two oxen, seven cows, five horses, five sheep, and seventeen pigs. At the same time, Jacob King, one of William King's slaves, had only six of his fifty acres under cultivation. Half an acre was planted in oats in 1860, three were in corn, and another half acre was in potatoes. He had no livestock to supplement his family income, assist with the fieldwork, or provide additional subsistence. Many factors contributed to this disparity. Labor may have been the most crucial resource for farm production in the mid-nineteenth century, surpassing even equipment in importance. Riley could count on the assistance of three male children between the ages of thirteen and nineteen in addition to his wife's labor when necessary. Jacob King, however, could call only on his wife and their thirteen-year-old son, James. Offsetting their labor shortage, the King family would have required less in the way of foodstuffs and finances for their smaller household. Although Riley and King had both been slaves, Riley was more removed from slavery when he settled in Buxton. He and his family had had more time and opportunity to acquire some of the rudimentary household and farm equipment that the Kings lacked. The census shows Riley owning one hundred eighteen dollars' worth of farm machinery, compared to King's mere thirty dollars' worth. King's family would probably have had to struggle more, and Jacob might have had to find outside work to survive and make payments on his land. In turn, time away from his land would have slowed his progress in clearing land and cultivating crops.[43]

Another illustrative comparison is between the families of Ezekiel Cooper and Henry Thomas. Both families were free before relocating to Buxton in the early 1850s. (Thomas was technically a fugitive slave but, as previously mentioned, he had lived for years in the northern United States as a free man.) Neither family arrived in the settlement under especially straitened circumstances, and both took up land in the northern section of the Elgin tract, where agricultural conditions were more favorable. Both had cleared less than half their acreage by 1860. The census shows Cooper's 1860 crop as one acre of spring wheat, two acres of oats, two acres of buckwheat, five acres of corn, and a half acre of potatoes, while Thomas planted four acres in spring wheat, three in oats, two in buckwheat, four in corn, and one in potatoes. The two families had made comparable improvements to their land in the years since coming to Buxton and are fairly representative of the typical Buxton farmer. In a larger context, Thomas's family faced more financial pressures because the household was much larger than Cooper's. Although the families had similar labor supplies on which to draw—each had two male relatives of working age and older daughters to help care for younger siblings and household work—Thomas had more people to provide for because his household included his mother-in-law and four children under the age of eleven. Thomas's poor financial situation is evidenced by the fact that he owned only one cow, two horses, and one pig. At the same time, Cooper had two oxen, five cows, two horses, and nine pigs valued at $169, more than twice the worth of Thomas's animals. With claim to one hundred acres, Thomas also had a higher mortgage than did Cooper, who had settled on a fifty-acre plot.[44]

Milton Ragland came to Buxton under considerably better circumstances than most. Having inherited money from his brother, as discussed earlier, Ragland was able to pay in full for his fifty-acre lot. On the minus side of the ledger, however, Ragland had no children and thus lacked readily available farm labor. Perhaps as a result, in 1861 he had cleared only nine acres and had planted few crops—one acre of buckwheat, two acres of corn, and half an acre of potatoes. In addition, Ragland harvested some hay and had five acres under pasture. Ragland's harvest would not have provided fully for all his needs, but his two cows, two horses, seven sheep, and fifteen pigs would have provided him with additional money and food. Without a mortgage or children, Ragland's needs would have been few, and he may well have been able to hire other community members as laborers. Although not representative of most Buxton farmers, Ragland's agricultural record illustrates Buxtonians' ability to draw on a variety of sources for financial support.[45]

Only three farmers recorded any hemp or flax cultivation in 1860, perhaps signifying a decline or even failure in the rope-making endeavor.[46] Adam Crosswhite was by far the largest grower, with a one-hundred-pound harvest in 1860. Benjamin Richardson and Levi Simmons each produced twenty pounds on a small portion of their acreage. Simmons harvested no other crops that year, although it is not known whether he planted no other crops or whether his other crops were somehow destroyed. Simmons had additional sources of income, however, reporting raising twenty-four pounds of wool as well as owning a pair of oxen, five cows, four horses, and fourteen pigs. Barley and rye were the least common crops among Buxton farmers. In 1860 only George Taylor planted barley, using a quarter acre to produce two bushels, and Nancy Geals planted a half acre in rye, yielding seven bushels.[47]

Buxtonians never met their expected agricultural yields: acreage harvested never matched acreage planted. In 1857 the wheat crop was destroyed by the weevil and rust, and corn was planted late because of standing water in the fields and it did not mature before frost. Two subsequent successive crop failures further hurt the settlement. According to King's 1859 synod report, "The failure of the crop for two years in succession has pressed hard on the settlers. The first year was not so much felt, but last year the struggle for food has been such that very little of their scanty earnings could go for clothing."[48] The spirit of the settlers remained hopeful, as they "were neither disheartened nor discouraged, but were looking forward to the future with the hope of the coming harvest."[49]

Agricultural difficulties nevertheless continued. Marginal comments in the 1861 agricultural census state that "this District has suffered this last year from Worms and hail and early frost," which had particularly hurt corn growers.[50] The enumerator further noted that the wheat had been sown late, probably as a result of weather conditions. The community's buckwheat crop was also recorded as a failure that year.

Despite difficulties, Buxtonians spoke highly of the land. An 1852 report stated that "the land is best adapted for the culture of wheat; but it also produces Indian corn, tobacco, hemp, equal to any that is grown in the [United] States."[51] Jane Robinson, who came to Buxton from New York City, where she had been a laundress, wrote glowingly in 1854 of her family's land and crops: "I raised a fine sight of tobacco. We had turnips as big as the crown of your husband's hat, and cabbage as large as a water-pail. O, don't laugh, for it's a fact—for the ground is so rich that it raises up everything in no time. [The] land will bring you anything you plant. . . . [O]nly put in the seed and pray to the Giver of rain, and they will come up."[52] Robinson also remarked on the abundance of food: "We have all kinds of game, deer, raccoon, ground-hogs, black squirrels, hens, pheasants, quails, wild turkey, wild duck . . . wild red raspberries and plumbs, crabapples and wild gooseberries, and all kinds of nuts."[53] Even the 1861 census enumerator who noted all the crop failures remarked that the "lands are opening, roads are improving, and where they are clearing there is comfort and plenty."[54] Buxton farmers may not have always brought bountiful goods to market, but they were able to feed themselves and their families. And they took pride in their land and its products. In 1853 they established a local committee to offer "premiums for the best cloth made wholly of wool [from] the settlement, for the best houses, and the best crops."[55]

An important aspect to agricultural living was the possession of draft animals and livestock both for subsistence and labor. Twenty-four (19.8 percent) of the one hundred twenty-one black heads of households listed on the Elgin tract in the 1861 agricultural census owned at least one ox, and twenty-one owned a pair of oxen. Four of the eight female heads of household listed on this agricultural census (Mahala Hampton, Ann Jones, Rebecca Burgee, and Julie Monroe) possessed oxen. Four of the twenty-four owners of oxen owned at least one hundred acres of land, half of the eight black families on the Elgin reserve with tracts of that size.[56]

Although families who possessed oxen might be assumed to have had an advantage in clearing and cultivating their land, that is not necessarily the case. Of the twenty-four families with oxen, only nine had ten or more acres of land under cultivation in 1860. Isaac Riley, with twenty-seven of his hundred acres of land under cultivation, was the only ox owner who had more than twenty acres cultivated. With fifty-seven of his hundred acres under cultivation, Green Due had by far the most land under cultivation, with Henry K. Thomas a distant second at twenty-eight acres. Yet neither Due nor Thomas had any oxen.[57]

It is not surprising that Isaac Riley was among the more accomplished heads of household in 1860. As the first black settler to take up land on the Elgin reserve, he had had more than a decade to clear and cultivate his hundred acres. Two other early settlers, William Jackson and Andrew Harden, owned oxen but had only nine and eight acres of land under cultivation, respectively. Available labor was, of course, a factor. Harden had three children, none of whom was old enough to be of assistance on the farm; Jackson and his wife had no resident children in 1860. Riley, however, had six children, the eldest three of whom were sons between thirteen and nineteen years old in 1861. Other families with oxen in 1860 but with few acres under cultivation may have only recently acquired the animals and not yet had the opportunity to reap the benefits of their assistance in the fields. Since he owned only three acres of land, two of which were under cultivation in 1860, London Harris may have rented out his pair of oxen to other families, thus bringing in an income for himself and family as well as assisting the community.[58]

Cows provided an important source of food and dairy products for farmers as well as a source of income for some. A large majority of Buxton farmers owned at least one cow. Even those families with no other livestock possessed cows. Indeed, fewer than twenty Buxton families recorded no cows in 1861. More than half of Buxton's households owned between one and five cows, while more than twenty families owned between six and ten. Mahala Hampton, Milton Ragland, and Jesse Bass each owned more than ten cows, suggesting that the livestock represented a source of income in addition to food. It is somewhat surprising that, with Buxtonians' often tight financial circumstances, the 1861 census showed that seventy-five families (62 percent) owned at least one horse. Most of those had one or two horses, but several owned three or more. Isaac Riley, Robert Harris, William Robinson, and Mary Brown possessed five horses, while Richard Jones, George Hatter, and Levi Simmons each owned four. Green Due owned six horses, while widow Sarah Fraser owned nine, the most of any Buxtonian. That so many settlers owned horses attests to the importance of the animals in a rural environment where transportation facilities were primitive and agriculture constituted the economic base.[59]

Despite their hardships, Buxtonians were, generally speaking, able to meet their land payments, and a majority eventually came to own their land outright. In this respect, Buxton, due in large part to the Elgin Association's regulations, held an advantage over other black settlements, where landlessness was often more widespread among black settlers than it was among surrounding whites. According to the association's Fifth Annual Report, "not only have the settlers provided for their families but [they] have paid up their installments for their land regularly as they fell due."[60] One map of the settlement from some time after 1850 shows that at least thirty-four of the inhabited lots had been paid off, while about thirty other settlers owed less than one hundred dollars on their lots. The families holding full title to their lots included several of Buxton's founders, among them Henry Stockton, Alfred West, Thomas Stringer, and Joseph Liason. Others had come later, including Thomas Scott, Henry Phelps,

John Jackson, Gilbert Charles, Henry Herrington, and Isom Goodsom. Walter Toyer, Milton Ragland, John Hampton, and others had paid off hundred-acre sections. Nine other lots are not marked paid but do not have a dollar amount owed, and so they may well also have been paid off. Those were the holdings of Isaac Brodie, George Hatter, James Goodall, and the brothers Joseph and Benjamin Randall, who held adjacent acreage. King later noted that when a number of Buxtonians resolved to return to the United States after the Civil War, they were in a positive financial standing because they had paid off the balance of their land mortgage and so were entitled to the full sale price of the land.[61]

The settlers used various means to accomplish this degree of financial solvency. The residents survived by combining small-scale agriculture with occasional outside labor. As discussed earlier, many Buxtonians supplemented their incomes by working either outside the community or in community-established businesses. The rail line provided the best opportunity for settlers in the early 1850s to earn the money to pay off their lots, paying ten dollars a month, a sum that enabled a man to save his annual installment with just a couple of months of work. Additional opportunities came from established farmers in the vicinity who had need of supplemental labor at various times during the year. In their quest for subsistence, Buxtonians followed seasonal employment—working in the fields and performing nonagricultural labor. White landowners in the vicinity of Buxton would presumably have sought assistance for their agricultural needs, from plowing and harvesting to building and repairing fences and clearing land. William King undoubtedly was among those who hired black laborers to help work his farm. In fact, King may have actively cultivated his large landholdings (seventy-three acres in 1860) in order to provide employment for Buxtonians. At least forty Buxton residents were recorded by census enumerators in 1861 as "laborers." The majority of these men were—like Joseph Enos, Nathan Farmer, John Jones, Abraham Jackson, and John Goodall—young, single nonlandowners. It is probable that these men labored for local white farmers such as John Roe, Robert Slade, John Broadbent, George Thompson, and John Powell, all of whom lived on Elgin tract land and who cultivated more than fifty acres. Some of the white farmers living on the edge of the Elgin tract who may have needed supplemental labor were Timothy Dillon, John Griffin, Job Pinedecker, James Gilhula, John Finn, and Martin Drew.[62]

As in rural communities elsewhere, Buxton families were likely enmeshed in a web of financial interdependencies with other settlers. With cash scarce and needed for land payments, Buxtonians probably relied on one another for such needs as milling and blacksmithing and instituted a barter system for these and other services. The presence of skilled craftsmen and businesses would have allowed intracommunity connections that worked to lessen reliance on outsiders, particularly whites, and contributed an element of stability. Buxton was not, however, a self-contained entity. Despite the size of the Elgin tract and its exclusive nature, Buxton was less isolated than some other black settlements. Trips to Chatham and other nearby towns would not have been infrequent, and the surrounding area was fairly well settled. Black Buxtonians had widespread economic and social interaction with their neighbors of both races.

Buxton settlers augmented their incomes in other ways as well. The family constituted an economic partnership in which women and children contributed to the family economy, cementing the mutual dependency between farmer and family. They worked alongside their husbands and fathers, helping to clear the land, build homes, tend the livestock, and grow crops. Farm wives often made the difference between the success and failure of productive strategies. This would have been no less true at Buxton than elsewhere at the time. In addition to bearing and caring for a large family and performing sundry arduous domestic chores—a short list of which would include cooking, cleaning, washing, ironing, and mending—women cared for the family garden plot, preserved food, made household staples, sewed clothing, and fashioned quilts. Wives of farmers also engaged in money-making activities, using the money to buy coffee, sugar, tea, articles of clothing, and other goods not produced on the farm. Women tended flocks of chickens, collected eggs, fed and milked cows, churned butter, and sometimes made cheese. With no resident doctor in Buxton during the settlement's early years, such midwives as Julia Liason would have assisted women during childbirth.

A committee of stockholders who visited Buxton in 1855 reported finding a number of women engaged in such activities as knitting, spinning, and weaving and then selling their handiwork. The committee approvingly noted that one woman had saved a single shilling, which she used to purchase some wool; in two months' time, by knitting and selling stockings, she had made enough money to buy sufficient additional wool "to supply her husband and six children with comfortable stockings for the winter."[63] Although Buxton's overseers apparently hoped that a cottage industry would develop based on spinning the wool from sheep raised in the community, such was never the case. The census recorded only fifteen families as obtaining wool from their sheep, shearing a total of two hundred sixty-four pounds in 1860. The most productive wool-producing households were those of Milton Ragland, Isaac Riley, Henry Williams, Charles Watts, Alfred Hooper, and Levi Simmons, all of whom produced more than twenty pounds of wool. Eleven women ranging in age from thirteen to fifty listed themselves as spinsters (meaning spinners of wool). Eight of these women were single and young (six under the age of twenty). It is interesting that only two of these women, Frances Crosswhite and Hannah Scipio, lived in households that recorded wool production in 1860, implying that those families with sheep either spun the wool themselves or hired out the finishing of their wool. Buxton's spinsters, then, presumably labored for black and white farmers in the vicinity.[64]

Hog raising provided additional farm income for many Buxtonians. Among heads of household, 86 percent owned at least one pig, and twenty (17 percent) claimed ten or more pigs on the 1861 agricultural census, led by Archibald Smith, who owned twenty-one; Enos Johnson with nineteen; and Green Due, Milton Ragland, and Sarah Fraser each with fifteen. After keeping a small number of their hogs for personal consumption and breeding purposes, many Buxton farmers would have sold their excess for a modest profit.[65]

Buxton residents were for the most part marginal farmers. They generally had smaller holdings than local whites, less valuable farms, and fewer acres under cultivation. They had draft animals and livestock in smaller numbers than their white neighbors. In 1861 the average cash value of a farm located in district 3 but not part of the Elgin tract was $1,187.80, whereas the average value of a Buxton farm was just $703.90. Similarly, the average value of farm machinery owned by a family living outside of the Elgin tract was $48.46, while that of a Buxton family was $28.35. In 1861 the average Buxton farmer owned $143.77 worth of livestock (hogs, sheep, horses, and cattle), whereas the average local white farmer owned $260.92 worth of animals.[66]

The number of acres owned and cleared by individual families accounts at least in part for these differences in value. Again drawing on the 1861 census, 57 percent of the families living on the Elgin tract owned no more than fifty acres, but 74 percent of white farmers in district 3 owned between fifty-one and one hundred acres. Moreover, 74 percent of Buxton's families cultivated less than 30 percent of their land, but only 64 percent of the district's white families cultivated so little. And while 44 percent of Buxton's farmers left between 81 and 100 percent of their land "wild," only 33 percent of the white farmers left that much land untouched.[67]

Numbers in and of themselves, however, mean relatively little. Most white farmers probably had settled earlier than the blacks and would logically have had more of their acreage under cultivation than more recently arrived black families. Availability of and financial resources for laborers to assist in clearing and cultivating the land would also have aided white farmers more than blacks. Most blacks were relatively impoverished when they arrived in Buxton and focused primarily on feeding, sheltering, and clothing their families rather than on clearing excess acreage and farming products for markets. The fact that black settlers progressively cleared and planted additional acreage in itself constitutes success. The opening up of new lands for cultivation—transforming wilderness to productive farmland—progressed at an agonizingly slow pace. Even after a decade of settlement, much of the Elgin tract remained wilderness. Other demands of farm life (planting, weeding, harvesting, preparing the soil, building and repairing fences) needed their attention and slowed the progress of clearing new lands for cultivation.

Census data reveal that the agricultural yields of the black settlers on the Elgin tract compared favorably with those of local white farmers. The 1860 corn crop of black farmers Alfred West, Isaac Brodie, Henry Rann, and Alfred Washington yielded approximately thirty bushels of corn per acre planted, about the same as or slightly better than those of local whites Patrick Rann, John Black, Robert Slade, Joseph Randall, and Patrick Finland. Likewise, black and white farmers garnered similar yields for their 1860 potato crops. For reasons unknown, however, Buxton's oat production remained below that of area white farmers. West obtained fifteen bushels of oats per acre and Rann only four, while white farmers Ryan, Slade, Randall, and Finland reaped twenty-five, fifteen, thirty, and forty, respectively.[68]

Buxton's families survived in circumstances ranging from relatively comfortable to constant struggle. At one extreme lay John Thomas, whose mere half acre of crops yielded no harvest in 1860. Although he had three cows and five pigs, it is unlikely that they provided enough in the way of subsistence or cash for Thomas and his family. The situation, however, might not have been as desperate as it seems at first glance. The census lists Thomas's occupation as a laborer, and so his agricultural pursuits probably did not constitute the family's major source of financial support. Similarly, farmer Anthony Bell sought to support his wife and seven children, the oldest of whom was sixteen, with an entire 1860 agricultural yield of only fifty bushels of potatoes. Their livestock consisted of a pair of oxen, and so the Bells even lacked ready access to a supply of milk, butter, cheese, or meat. Isaac Burle was in even worse shape: He had no livestock at all and a crop consisting entirely of forty bushels of potatoes, hardly enough to support all his needs, meager as they might have been with only him and his wife, Elisa, living in the household.[69]

At the other end of the spectrum, judging by his 1860 crop, Prince Chatham led a relatively comfortable life, especially considering he supported only himself, his widowed mother, and an unrelated young child. He harvested thirty bushels each of spring wheat and oats, ten bushels of buckwheat, forty bushels of corn, and twenty bushels of potatoes. His livestock consisted of an ox, a horse, and seven pigs. Likewise, Cupid Martin, whose 1860 crop produced twelve bushels of spring wheat, ninety bushels of oats, five bushels of buckwheat, fifty bushels of corn, and sixty bushels of potatoes, would have been adequate to support himself, his wife, and their six children. The Martin family's food if not their income was also supplemented by their two cows, two horses, and three pigs. Henry Dabney and his family had twenty acres of cultivated land, fifteen of which they utilized as pasture, and on the rest they grew eighty bushels of buckwheat, four bushels of corn, and thirty bushels of potatoes. The Dabneys also had two cows, a horse, and eight pigs. Dabney's two adult daughters earned a living by spinning, further augmenting the family's income. Green Due also fared well, with ten cows, six horses, seven sheep, and fifteen pigs as well as a hundred-acre lot, nearly half of which was planted in various crops. His 1860 harvest included twenty-five bushels of spring wheat, three hundred twenty bushels of oats, one hundred fifty bushels of corn, and two hundred bushels of potatoes, amply providing for his twelve children.[70]

Most Buxtonians were humble farmers who struggled to make ends meet: to pay their mortgages, provide their families with the necessities of life, and contribute to their church and their children's education. For many, perhaps even most, Buxton settlers, even such a humble life represented an improvement over their previous lives. Those who had been slaves could now revel in their freedom; the product of their labor was now their own. Fugitives could rest easier in the security of their Canadian haven. Those who had been landless were now landowners, many of them for the first time. Despite the marginality of their farms, free blacks gained a degree of independence with their holdings. As King had hoped, landownership limited dependence on whites and assisted blacks in their attempts at subsistence.

In aspiring to true self-sufficiency, the inhabitants of Buxton sought valiantly to establish an industrial base for their economic growth. Despite moderate success, Buxton, like its surrounding environs, remained primarily an agricultural society. Buxton settlers dramatically transformed an expansive wilderness into a viable agricultural sector of the Canadian landscape. And they remained adamant in their determination to survive without reliance on outside assistance, particularly for food and clothing. Perhaps the ultimate measure of their achievements, regardless of their lack of wealth, was that they adhered throughout the community's existence to their rejection of what they called the begging system. Whatever else might happen, Buxton's blacks were determined to remain self-sufficient.

8

A Spiritual People

"It is our duty as Christians to educate [blacks] not only for time, but for eternity."[1] With this statement, William King declared a major objective for the Buxton settlement. King saw education and religious instruction as entwined. In addition to secular knowledge, the learning of a trade, and the development of civic consciousness, true education comprised religious instruction. King acknowledged that when blacks were released from bondage, their "religion is as low as [their] education."[2] The success of his effort depended on blacks being "settled permanently and placed under careful religious training. The want of this has been one of the principle reasons why the few efforts made hitherto to improve their moral condition have not been successful."[3] Thus, Buxton settlers were provided with churches, Sunday schools, and other accoutrements of a thorough religious training.

Despite King's low assessment, religion played a crucial role in the lives of antebellum blacks whether slave, fugitive, or free. They prayed for the deliverance of their race from bondage and had a deep and abiding faith in God. The church, where blacks found both spiritual comfort and opportunities for social expression, constitutes the oldest, most influential, and most stable institution of black culture. An integral part of black history, the church has been the vehicle for the rich, vital expression of blacks' culture, mores, music, songs, and lifestyle. In the black experience, "religion was the organizing principle around which . . . life was structured. [A black person's] church was his school, his forum, his political arena, his social club, his art gallery, his conservatory of music. . . . It was the peculiar sustaining force that gave him the strength to endure when endurance gave no promise."[4]

In Buxton, as in other black communities, the church provided a great many services touching on every aspect of life. Although its major function was to serve spiritual needs, the church was more than a center of religious devotion and ceremony. The church was an important vantage point for confronting the racial hostility blacks encountered in society. It also operated as a focal point for social, recreational, and educational activities, a place where they could participate with dignity, pride, and freedom. Here they could forget the drudgery and brutality of their everyday lives. Within the church they were no longer mere farmers, laborers, or domestics toiling under their masters' lash or for white employers. They were deacons, Sunday school teachers, leaders of prayer meetings, and collection officers. Each participant became someone significant. In other words, the church furnished avenues for exercising responsibility and leadership. The black church was a dynamic social institution that presented its members with "an all too rare opportunity to assemble freely, vote for officers, and express themselves spiritually, socially, and politically."[5] Prayer meetings offered opportunities for socializing and releasing pent-up emotions. Religious activities provided welcome respites from incessant labor and gave blacks hope that a better time lay ahead—either in this life or in the afterlife. In this way, blacks' religious life made their daily lives more bearable.[6]

Central to an African American sense of identity, churches formed the core of black communities, serving in part as the foundation of the social structure of communal society. Along with schools, churches served as important symbols of autonomy and achievement for the black community. Spiritual, intellectual, and economic concerns were intertwined in black communities, forming a triad of institutional support. In this trinity churches were a core component of the free black community—its institutions and organizations. In Buxton too, the church would play a role in institutional organization.[7]

Where blacks worshiped was of little consequence. If no meetinghouse was available, a personal home functioned just as well. And where no shelter was readily available, the open air served as a sanctuary. One of the first things groups of black migrants did after arriving in an area was to assemble for worship. As in the United States, the majority of blacks in Canada were either Baptists or Methodists. Blacks favored these denominations because of their appeal to the soul and emotions. Ironically, blacks' preference for passionate sermons, hymn singing, and other means of active participation in religious activities provided a rationale for segregated churches throughout Canada. Both blacks and whites maintained that blacks were unfavorably disposed toward the more formal services of the kind practiced by whites, and blacks were thus encouraged to form their own churches.[8]

And so they did. As blacks in the United States did, blacks in Canada formed separate churches. The first official black church in Canada was the First African Baptist Church of Ontario, organized by William Wilks in 1821. Escaping from Virginia in 1816, he journeyed to Colchester, Canada, where he purchased forty acres of land. As was common in backwoods areas among both blacks and whites, Wilks ministered the gospel and administered the rites of baptism to his church members even though he was at first neither ordained nor licensed to preach. In 1821, however, Wilks became the first black ordained in Canada.[9]

The founding of the First African Baptist Church of Ontario was followed by the formal organization of other black Baptist churches, leading to the October 1841 establishment of the Amherstburg Baptist Association (ABA), a joint effort with Detroit's Second Baptist Church. At its founding, the ABA included only forty-seven members from three churches. By 1861 its numbers had increased to one thousand sixty members from fourteen churches.[10]

The ABA was not the only formal religious organization for blacks in Upper Canada during the first half of the nineteenth century. In the early 1820s, the African Methodist Episcopal Church (AME), established by Richard Allen and Daniel Cocker in Philadelphia in 1816, extended its influence to the region. By 1840, when the AME organized its Upper Canadian Conference, AME churches existed in Hamilton, Toronto, Amherstburg, and Brantford. During the next fifteen years, the membership of the Upper Canadian branch of the AME increased from two hundred fifty-six members to two thousand. In 1852 Canada's AME Church sought independence from its parent body in the United States, forming the British Methodist Episcopal Church (BME). This institutional denomination was established largely by émigrés so that they could govern their own church from their new homeland. Most of but not all the Canadian churches affiliated with the AME joined the BME. By 1864 forty-two congregations with more than three thousand members were being served by sixty preachers.[11]

Religion contributed greatly to the Buxton community, providing support for community building, collective strength, and solidarity. Buxton's churches represented a focal point of community life much as they did in other black communities, although Buxton's churches do not seem to have played as large an institutional role in social and other issues as was the case with urban black churches, which served as bases for political leadership and authority roles. In and of themselves, worship services and prayer meetings provided a welcome social opportunity for people who spent most of their waking hours working.

Almost all Buxton settlers professed to be associated with one or another of the community's churches. Only three of the settlement's adult black residents declared no religious affiliation in the 1861 census. It is nevertheless unlikely that even the faithful attended church regularly under the harsh traveling conditions, especially during the winter and spring months, and the distance that many of the settlers had to traverse. One visitor to the settlement later remarked that "about one quarter of the whole number do not attend church at all, and no compulsion is used."[12] This visitor was right in that, despite the central leadership role that the Synod of the Presbyterian Church of Canada played in the creation and development of Buxton, settlers were not compelled to attend church. While the Elgin Association's constitution stated that one of the settlement's founding principles was the religious improvement of its residents, attainment of this goal was not held above personal freedom. Nonattendance does not necessarily mean nonbelief. Evidence suggests that most Buxtonians had a deep and serious love for the gospel. After his visit to Buxton in the mid-1850s, Samuel Ringgold Ward commented that Buxton's inhabitants were exemplary in their religious faith: "I know of no community . . . where stricter, better attention is paid to religion, than in Buxton." Their "deep, serious interest, their intelligent love of the gospel" and the "lives they exhibit in daily transactions render them a most agreeable congregation."[13]

The initial sermon of the Buxton Mission Church (later formally constituted as St. Andrew's) was convened by Rev. King on the first Sabbath in December 1849. Lacking a formal church building, this first service, conducted before twenty-four worshipers, was held in a log schoolhouse near the settlement but not on the official Elgin tract. Thereafter, King's house served as the official meeting place for St. Andrew's congregation until a proper church building was completed in the mid-1850s, whereupon the congregation moved its services into this new house of God.[14]

Unlike most other churches in Canada, interracial services were the norm at Buxton, at least at St. Andrew's. The Sabbath school and weekly prayer meetings were open to all area residents, regardless of race. During that first winter, 1849–1850, when few blacks had joined the settlement, whites from outside Buxton formed most of St. Andrew's congregation. Local whites displayed little antipathy toward the black settlers in religious matters. Whereas black worshipers elsewhere were often relegated to rear pews or galley seating, blacks and whites sat beside each other at St. Andrew's. This is not to say that Buxton was entirely devoid of racial differences in spiritual matters. The experiment in interracial spirituality had an inauspicious beginning: When King arrived at the schoolhouse on that Sunday morning in December, he found a "very respectable congregation" of black and white worshipers gathered outside. He also discovered that the former white trustees for the building had locked the door.[15] When those assembled suggested that the door be broken open in protest, King refused. He was prepared to return home without having preached when one of the women in the crowd stepped forward, took a key out of her pocket, and opened the door. King and his worshipers then went inside and held their services. Whether the door had been locked explicitly to keep King and his congregation out or simply by accident is uncertain, but the incident was resolved and no other difficulties associated with interracial church services ensued. Such interracial contact and association in religious matters helped pave the way for amiable relations between the races in other matters, if only in that, as King noted, many local whites became acquainted with the black settlers and discovered that they were "not the vicious and indolent persons they had been represented in the petitions sent to Lord Elgin and to the Synod of the Presbyterian Church."[16]

King's congregation grew steadily as new residents arrived in the settlement. The Lord's Supper was celebrated in Buxton for the first time in September 1851, with the Reverend Dr. Michael Willis from Toronto performing the service. Nine new communicants were entered on the roll as full members of the Presbyterian Church of Canada, the mother church. The event was occasioned with a celebration attended by Buxton's church members as well as visitors from Presbyterian congregations in nearby Tilbury and Chatham. By 1855 the St. Andrew's Church communion rolls contained forty full members. Three years later, the number of communicants was fifty-six, and the average Sunday attendance reached one hundred. Through the early 1860s, most congregants added to the communion rolls were black, including Ezekiel Cooper and several members of his family; Joshua Steel; James Rolls; Lucy Day; Joseph Elliss; Aron Johnston; Lydia Bond; Ann Riley; and Minella and Margaret Ford. At Buxton's zenith on the eve of the Civil War, St. Andrew's membership peaked at seventy official communicants and approximately one hundred fifty weekly attendees. Since freedom of worship led to the establishment of several rival churches in the community, St. Andrew's never had a majority of Buxton residents either attending services or as members.[17]

Sunday church services were accompanied by other religious activities. At the first service, King sent out a call to young people interested in initiating a Sabbath school. Ten children, some black and some white, came forward and enrolled. By March 1850, these students were well on their way to learning the short catechism. One black girl about ten years old had already committed it to memory. By July 1851, weekly attendance at the Buxton Sabbath School ranged between thirty and forty, and official enrollment had grown to more than fifty. This number steadily increased until 1856, when one hundred twelve students were on the roll. Actual attendance rarely reached that number: Various circumstances, including poor roads and traveling conditions, inadequate clothing, and the need to work in the fields and on the farms even on the holy day prevented children from attending. Nonetheless, weekly attendance averaged fifty-two. Evidence that the concept of a Sabbath school was welcomed is found in the 1857 opening of an additional Sunday school in the northern section of Buxton to accommodate those who lived at a distance from St. Andrew's. Two years later, twenty-five pupils were attending this Sunday school.[18]

In conjunction with the Sunday school, a children's library was established, supported largely by donations from "ladies' church" organizations in the United States, Great Britain, and Canada. The Ladies of Knox Church in Hamilton presented the Sunday school with a pulpit Bible and psalmbook in 1852. Friends in Glasgow, Scotland, donated a valuable collection of books in 1856. By 1859 the Sunday school library had reached two hundred fifty volumes. This availability of books no doubt encouraged both spirituality and literacy among the settlers.[19]

The pecuniary difficulties that Buxton inhabitants experienced, especially during the early years, did not prevent congregants from doing what they could to aid others. The scholars of the Sabbath school organized the Juvenile Missionary Society and regularly took up collections. In February 1856 the missionary box was opened and found to contain eighteen dollars, a sizable sum, considering the financial stress of the families who contributed. The children decided to send that money to the Calabar Mission in an effort to assist their brethren on the coast of Africa. In the years to come, the Juvenile Missionary Society continued sending what aid it could to foreign missions in Africa, showing their connection to their ancestral homeland. St. Andrew's further endeavored to train a generation of blacks whose voices would be heard throughout not only Canada and the United States but also the rest of the world. The American Baptist Association, the Presbyterian Church, and the Buxton community at large espoused similar ideas. The community yearned to send missionaries from Buxton to "carry the lamp of eternal truth, and plant the cross on the remotest shores of Africa."[20] Although at least two Buxtonians became ministers, none would personally carry the Word of God to Africa. King was particularly involved in the prospect of sending missionaries to Africa, during the late 1850s developing a plan in conjunction with the Social Science League in London. King was present when black abolitionist and reformer Martin Delany reported to the league in 1859 that he had obtained permission to settle on land on Africa's west coast. This meeting resulted in the formation of the African Aid Society, which had the goal of sending out black missionaries to Africa. King was to furnish the young men and the Social Science League was to provide the financial backing. By the spring of 1861, King reportedly had several volunteers, but the outbreak of the U.S. Civil War interrupted the plans.[21]

Despite white participation and again in contrast to churches elsewhere (with the obvious exception of independent black congregations), St. Andrew's leadership was predominantly black. Whites were not excluded from office holding, but St. Andrew's elders and deacons were, with only a few exceptions, black. In 1858 only two whites plus Reverend King were appointed as leaders of the St. Andrew's congregation: Peter Straith served as a deacon, and schoolteacher George Thomson was an elder. St. Andrew's six other deacons and elders were black men. Moreover, Robert VanRankin was selected that year to represent the congregation, along with Rev. King, at the next synod meeting. VanRankin received this honor in future years as well. From 1858 until 1865 VanRankin served as the commissioner to the synod and representative to the Presbytery of

London all but one year when, for reasons unknown, Thomson served in that role. In 1865, VanRankin relinquished his position to Ezekiel Cooper, who had recently been installed as a deacon. Over the years, the congregation elected other black officers, among them Cooper and George Charleston. After Thomson's death in 1862, Cooper took over Thomson's position as the secretary for the St. Andrew's congregation.[22]

St. Andrew's leadership represented Buxton's most upstanding citizens. The church was an arena for developing leadership skills. VanRankin, Abraham Brodie, and Edward Thompson were long-standing elders of the congregation. Isaac Riley, Alfred Hooper, and Joseph Liason were deacons. At least four of these men owned more than fifty acres of land. Likewise, Cooper and Charleston, who later held considerable influence in the Presbyterian Church, were part of the upper ranks of Buxton society. Although the 1861 census recorded Cooper as a Methodist, by 1865 he had become a member of the Presbyterian congregation.[23]

Despite the prominence of the Presbyterian Church of Canada in Buxton's planning, founding, and growth, the synod chose not to limit residents' religious freedom. Just as church attendance was not mandated by the establishment at Buxton, residents were free to choose other denominations. As Buxton's population grew, so too did its religious diversity. Throughout the 1850s, an increasing number of Buxton families devoted themselves to Baptist and Methodist denominations that allowed worshipers more freedom to express their emotions. The more informal, simpler, and warmer worship style of Methodism appealed to blacks, as did the sect's advocacy of lay preachers, its personal and emotionally engaging religious experience, and its message of humble living, self-discipline, and mutual support. One of the attractions of the Baptist denomination was the greater independence allowed to individual churches, which could maintain local control of their congregations while remaining part of the loosely constituted Baptist Association.[24]

The presence of numerous congregations suggests a source of fragmentation within the settlement. Evidence does not, however, elicit any deep divisions in the community based on different religious affiliations. Religious differences do not appear to have separated neighbors from each other. The various churches may be more reflective of the difficulties associated with traveling through the wilderness and of the diverse origins of Buxton residents and their religious backgrounds. The majority of black families who reported affiliation with the Free Church (Presbyterian) in the 1861 census lived on the tenth concession. The remainder were clustered on the eleventh and twelfth concessions, which were close to St. Andrew's Church. Only a few Free Church members lived on the edge of the settlement, farthest from St. Andrew's. Baptist congregants were located primarily on the eighth and A concessions, the northernmost sections of the

Elgin tract. The Second Baptist Church, on the seventh concession, would have been centrally located for the majority of Buxton Baptists. Whether those settlers living in the northern part of the Elgin tract tended to be Baptist because of their spiritual beliefs or because of the convenience of the Baptist church cannot be determined. The First Baptist Church, on the twelfth concession, just to the south of the village center, was relatively small, but it does signal a dedication to their faith because those Baptist families struggled with their small congregation rather than attending the distant Second Baptist Church or the closer St. Andrew's Presbyterian Church. A plurality of Buxtonians were Methodists, most of them settled in the northern section of the Elgin tract: forty-five families on concessions A, 8, 9, and 10 professed Methodism, as did only ten families on the eleventh, twelfth, and thirteenth concessions. Residential clustering of religious adherents evidently existed in the Buxton community.[25]

Economic class sometimes played a role in determining religious affiliation. The Presbyterian denomination in particular was usually associated with the elite, although Buxton did have somewhat of a mix between status and church membership. Landownership is a major indicator of economic status in a rural setting such as Buxton. Seven of the sixteen families with more than fifty acres of land were Methodists, while another seven were members of the Free Church. The other two were Baptist. Racial distinctions also went along with religious affiliations in some cases: 10 percent of Buxton's black population was Presbyterian, as was 25 percent of the mulatto population.[26]

A number of Buxton families had members in different religious sects, thus splitting the family. According to the 1861 census, at least nineteen families divided their religious loyalties. Abraham Crabtree, for example, was a Baptist, while his wife and children were Methodist. The Steal, Brodie, Scott, Stockton, Duncan, Thompson, and Roper families, among others, were likewise split in their religious affiliations. In most cases in which the head of the household professed a different religion from the mother, the children followed the mother's religious beliefs. Henry K. Thomas's family was uncommon in that his wife was a Methodist while Henry and the children were members of the Free Church. The census records do not reveal whether these family members attended different church services or otherwise practiced separate religious beliefs, making the extent of such religious differences within families difficult to determine. Nonetheless, if families could withstand such religious differences, it seems likely that the settlement too could do so.[27]

As the community grew and different congregations emerged, a majority of Buxtonians eventually became adherents of Baptist and Methodist sects, tangible evidence of Buxtonians' desire for control of their religious lives. An unnamed visitor to the settlement around 1855 noted that although "Mr. King's personal influence has brought a full attendance to his own little church, many

... maintain their former religious connections."[28] An 1859 report to the Presbyterian synod revealed that thirty-two families living in or near the settlement belonged to the Presbyterian Church, whereas about sixty families had joined Methodist and Baptist churches. Two years later, census reports confirm this trend, showing approximately sixty-five families or parts of families adhering to Methodism, thirty-five Baptist families or parts of families, and twenty-eight Presbyterian families or parts thereof living on the official Elgin tract. At the height of Buxton's success, the settlement had almost twice as many Methodists as Baptists and nearly three times as many Methodists as Presbyterians. Methodist and Baptist denominations continued to gain adherents. By 1871 Methodists totaled 65 percent of the populace. This popularity of Methodism mirrors that among the black population elsewhere. Indeed, the strength of the Presbyterian denomination distinguished Buxton among most black communities. For example, Methodism was the leading sect of Brooklyn and both the Beech and Roberts settlements, although Beech also had a Baptist presence.[29]

In 1850 a handful of Baptists living on or near the twelfth concession began holding services in individual houses. Three years later, this First Baptist Church of Buxton, with a membership of seven, applied for admission to the ABA. Deacon L. Harris was recorded as the congregation's first representative to the ABA. On September 14, 1854, the church officially received confirmation of its ABA membership. Some of the First Baptist Church's early lay leaders were George Hatter, Alfred West, William Jackson, and Isaac Washington, all prominent members of the Buxton community. Four years after this congregation had been meeting regularly, it had no fixed place of worship and no resident minister and apparently constituted more of an informal gathering of worshipers than an established church. Official membership remained small, perhaps because the congregation lacked a church building, a situation they eagerly sought to change. In 1854 congregation members appealed to the ABA for financial assistance in the quest for a real church: Without a pastor, they had not had the Lord's Supper administered to them during the past year. Under such desperate conditions, they asked for "sympathy concerning a place of worship"—specifically, a minimum of twelve dollars to purchase a site on which they could put up some kind of house of worship.[30] The ABA's member churches subsequently took up a special collection to aid their fellow Baptists at Buxton. Funds were also solicited from the black population at large through an advertisement placed in the *Provincial Freeman* seeking subscriptions "for the purpose of building a house . . . for the worship of God."[31] Buxton's Baptists also received aid from one of their own when George Hatter sold the church a piece of land for the nominal fee of five shillings. Not until 1856, however, was the First Baptist Church of Buxton prepared to start building on the site. By this time, the church had grown substantially in membership, and the congregation had appointed a pastor, the Reverend Francis Lacey. In 1857 the ABA minutes recorded the Buxton church membership at fifty-six. The First Baptist Church maintained its association with the ABA, but with a relatively small congregation and small finances, it is likely that its role in the parent organization was minor. Similarly, St. Andrew's remained a mission station under the Presbytery of London until 1858, when its congregation had finally grown enough to be duly constituted on its own in the Presbyterian Church of Canada.[32]

Finding the first church too distant and inconvenient to regularly attend services, a group of Baptists in the northern part of the settlement established a new congregation sometime between 1850 and 1856. It met in a schoolhouse on the seventh concession. In the late 1850s, this second group of Baptists received a gift from William and Catherine Moorehead, a plot of land in the seventh concession on which to build a church. A log church was later erected on the site, and a small cemetery stands as mute historical evidence of this little congregation. Around 1856 these two Baptist congregations united in principle; because of transportation difficulties, however, the groups continued to meet separately. From at least 1866 to 1883, the two congregations had individual listings in the ABA records, illustrating their continual separation. Second Baptist had fifteen members in 1866 but had grown to fifty-two members in 1882. ABA records show Anthony Binga and Samuel H. Davis as early ministers at Buxton as well as other places; they were probably itinerant ministers, traveling among several small congregations. Not until 1883, when Enos Johnson willed two lots to the Baptist congregations with the stipulation that they jointly build a church on the site, was a church erected. A complete and lasting union finally took place. Frances Lacey was the first minister of the combined Baptist church. Other early preachers, some of whom were not ordained, were Samuel Jones, William Moorehead, Isaac Washington, Benjamin Ferris (Phares, one of King's former slaves), and Elizabeth Shreve, who was one of the few nineteenth-century women, black or white, to stand behind a pulpit.[33]

Buxton's Baptists established a third church organization, about which considerably less is known. Known as the Macedonian Church of Elgin or the Anti-slavery Baptist Church, it had eight members in 1854. The church existed for only a short time and was built on the corner of the seventh concession and Center Road. Leaders of this fledgling group were Charles Johnson and Alfred Lewis. Its plight was presented to the Canadian Anti-Slavery Baptist Association in 1854.[34] Despite a lack of a pastor, the group kept "regular meetings, and have preaching sometimes." Its members declared their commitment to God, stating that "we still trust in the Lord. He will help us." They concluded their plea with an appeal for prayer: "Brethren, we send you the true Macedonian cry—Come over and help us."[35]

Ironically, although the Methodist denomination was the most popular religious sect in Buxton, less is known about the settlement's Methodist congregation than about either the Presbyterian church or the Baptist churches. Proof that the spirit of community cooperation and religious toleration was strong in Buxton is evidenced by Presbyterian and Baptist assistance when the Methodist group constructed its church. Thomas Stringer, the chief organizer of the first Methodist congregation in Buxton, preached the first service. Stringer was joined by the Reverend Walter Toyer, who came to Buxton from Maryland in 1851. Another early Methodist minister in Buxton was the Reverend Benjamin Stewart, who presented a resolution to the 1854 AME Church conference in Chatham to set the Canadian churches aside to form the British Methodist Episcopal Church. This change came about two years later. Buxton's Methodist congregation started with thirty members and grew to almost three hundred by the time of the Civil War. Sometime between 1866 and 1872, the little log church was replaced with a more substantial building on land previously owned by Jacob and Hannah Gunn on the seventh concession. Initially, the Bethel Methodist Church, as it was called, consisted of only a shell. It took several years for plaster, pews, a pulpit, and a choir loft to be added. A small graveyard accompanied the church. Again in testament to the community nature of the settlement, Buxtonians of all denominations were buried in this cemetery.[36]

Spirituality is often associated with morality, and church records allow a glimpse of the moral expectations in Buxton. Beyond matters of religious instruction and worship, church leaders addressed moral problems in the community. Certainly, not all Buxtonians were strict religious adherents. Many were not official members of any of the congregations. Some did not even regularly attend church services. Others, though professing to have religion, did not lead exemplary lives. St. Andrew's provides the only extant record of moral expectations and violations, particularly those of a sexual nature. Several members of St. Andrew's were admonished for adultery or fornication. In 1860 James Straith and his wife appeared before the session of St. Andrew's Church and confessed themselves to be guilty of prenuptial fornication. Having earlier spoken to the parties privately, King reported in their favor, and the session gave them "a serious rebuke and solemn admonition" but subsequently allowed them to receive church privileges.[37] Shortly thereafter, the couple became full members of the church and participated in communion. Senneth Burns also came before the session and confessed that she had been guilty of fornication. Appearing penitent and promising to change her ways, she received a rebuke but then had her church privileges restored. Before his conversion experience, James Rapier claimed to have had relations with Senneth and implied in a letter to his brother that she was not alone in her willingness to engage in premarital sex; referring to her sister as "the one which you told me you had one night against a tree."[38] Other instances of extramarital sexual relations occurred: By 1863, at least four illegitimate children had been born in Buxton, one of whom was borne by Senneth Burns.[39]

Such instances do not necessarily reflect a preponderance of immoral activity in the community at large. It is certainly plausible that, given the nature of the residents in Buxton, many of the settlers, particularly those who had been slaves, were simply continuing the moral habits they had observed in slavery. Some women may have followed a practice whereby they married after the birth of their first child and did not perceive this as immoral activity on their part. The existence of illegitimate children in no way reflects a tolerance of immorality among most Buxtonians. Viewing acts perceived as immoral as a disgrace to the entire settlement, Buxton churches censured mothers of children born out of wedlock. Another indication of the general moral quality of Buxton was the apparent lack of adulterous relations. King noted that although he suspected the conduct of three or four women, few cases of adultery had occurred. The infrequency of this type of behavior lends weight to King's assertion that the settlers paid "a very great respect to chastity and to the marriage relation."[40] The infrequency of such immoral activity further implies that the churches exerted considerable influence on settlers' behavior.

All Buxton churches were in general agreement about what constituted moral conduct, principles that may have been violated to one degree or another by individuals. James Rapier, for one, saw no inconsistency in living in Buxton and disregarding the community's religious and social scruples against drinking, fighting, and entertaining women. In letters to family members, he admitted to having altercations with several settlers, drinking hard liquor, and engaging in sexual activity with women. Other violations of the ban on liquor by black settlers no doubt went unrecorded, although not necessarily unnoticed by the community. As a whole, however, Buxtonians observed temperance, and visitors often commented favorably on the settlers' moral character: said one observer, "No intoxicating liquor is made or sold within the settlement; drunkenness is unknown, and . . . the general moral standard of the community is high."[41]

Another problem experienced by Buxton's churches was irregular attendance at worship services. Church officials were sometimes instructed to call on congregation members to discuss absences. For example, members of the St. Andrew's session visited both William Scott and Abraham Brodie to ascertain their reasons for irregular attendance at Sabbath meetings. Settlers typically pled illness or some other acceptable excuse, although the session records do not always record those reasons. In most cases, the session received the excuse as satisfactory and asked only for a promise that the offender would attend more regularly in the future.[42]

Nonattendance did not necessarily signal nonbelief. An incident during the first winter of the settlement's existence showed the religious character of some of those who stayed home on the Sabbath. It seems to have been common when Buxton first opened for curious local white men to go through the settlement on the Sabbath, when the settlers were less likely to be at home, to examine the dwellings and farms. One Sabbath, several white men were engaged in this snooping when they came upon Riley's cabin. Looking in at the window, they discovered that while Isaac and the two eldest Riley children were at church, Catherine Riley was reading from the Bible to the two youngest Rileys. As the story has since been told, after finishing reading, she "knelt down with her children and offered up a fervent prayer thanking God for the deliverance of herself and family from bondage and asking God's blessing on the settlement and on the people in the neighbourhood."[43] This particular incident apparently alleviated local whites' concerns that "coloured riff-raff," devoid of morality, would deluge their neighborhood.

As was the case elsewhere in Canada and in the United States, Buxton experienced periodic religious revivals. One of these awakenings occurred during the late 1850s. According to King, an increase in spiritual activity was first observed in the Sunday school during the winter of 1856. From there, it extended to the mission church and eventually to the settlement at large. A marked increase occurred in the attendance at the Presbyterian church, including its Sabbath and weekday meetings and especially at its Bible classes and prayer meetings. Buxton's other churches may well have experienced similar increases in attendance at their worship services.[44]

James Rapier's 1857 letters provide further evidence of this religious revival, in that they often refer to spiritual matters. On April 21 of that year, Rapier wrote at length about the increase in religious activity throughout Buxton, to which he attributed "some 70 odd" new converts, including his cousin, Sarah. As a result of the intensity and influence of this spiritual awakening, Rapier, by his own admission a drinker and womanizer, became a self-proclaimed religious enthusiast and "transformed" into a noticeably more moral person. His religious enthusiasm seems to have continued for at least several years. Nearly two years after his conversion he reported that he had not played cards, smoked, drank any liquor, or "touched a woman." In 1860 he was listed as a member and vice president of the newly founded Buxton Bible Society.[45]

As expected in light of the community's financial circumstances, Buxton's churches were relatively poor. Even so, the desired separation between the civil and religious spheres was maintained in that Elgin Association funds were never used for any religious expenses. Other sources, primarily contributions from mother church organizations (the Synod of the Presbyterian Church of Canada, the ABA, the AME, and later the BME associations), covered congregational expenses. Further aid for the spiritual advancement of Buxton's residents came from fund-raising missions conducted by King and others. Numerous organizations sought to do what they could—and what the settlers would permit—to help. Collections from various other religiously affiliated philanthropic societies, such as ladies' benefit societies, contributed to the financial stability of Buxton's churches. Such financial aid was multinational, coming from Canada, the northern United States, and Great Britain.

The financial history of the Buxton Mission (St. Andrew's Church and its associated school) serves as a window on the plight of the settlement's other religious denominations. Much of the record is bleak. The Presbyterian synod's repeated attempts failed to ease fully the mission's financial situation. In 1851 the annual meeting of the Presbyterian Church of Canada placed the Buxton Mission under the charge of the Home Mission Committee in an attempt to bring some financial stability. The committee sought assistance from the various presbyteries throughout Upper Canada and distributed the money to the Buxton Mission, hoping to raise sufficient funds to support adequately the Buxton Mission's congregation. Nevertheless, the Buxton Mission remained in dire financial straits and the synod took additional steps to defray Buxton's growing debt, designating a special collection day exclusively to benefit the mission in 1852. A special committee recommended steps to liquidate the mission's debt in 1853, and Buxton's residents appealed directly to Presbyterians nationwide. Throughout the 1850s, the Presbyterian Church of Canada continued to appeal to its members to contribute to the support of the Buxton Mission Fund. These appeals were often accompanied by fund-raising missions conducted by King and others in Ohio, Michigan, Illinois, and Pennsylvania. All these efforts were insufficient to completely relieve the Buxton Mission.[46]

In several respects, however, these fund-raising efforts succeeded. First, they spread word about the community at Buxton and they did accumulate money for Buxton residents' spiritual advancement. During a monthlong visit to western Pennsylvania that included stops at Allegheny, Pittsburgh, Mercer, and Erie, King collected more than four hundred dollars plus a handsome assortment of books. The Female Association at Pittsburgh, a white women's group, donated five missionary maps for the Sabbath school so that "God may bless your efforts in training up a native ministry to preach the gospel to their own people both here and in Africa."[47] The most touching gift was a church bell presented to Buxton by a group of black Pittsburgh inhabitants. Known as the Liberty Bell, it was placed in the steeple of St. Andrew's Church, and its ringing became a regular part of the settlers' lives.[48]

An issue of especial concern was the building and proper maintenance of the Buxton Mission's church and schoolhouse. As late as 1858, the mission had only temporary buildings, much in need of replacement. The structures had deteriorated so extensively that neither the school nor the church would be usable during the following winter without considerable repair because "every heavy shower that comes passes through the roof and walls, and the snow drifts through in all directions."[49] The situation remained virtually unchanged a year later, when a settler noted that "the church and school house [were] quite open in the sides and roof."[50] The Presbyterian synod hoped that the establishment of a Mission Building Fund would secure the necessary financing to build permanent structures. For more than a year, the treasurer of the Presbyterian synod made appeals in the *Ecclesiastical and Missionary Record* for members to pay their subscriptions to this fund. Such pleas proved futile, and the Presbyterian synod adopted yet another, more successful approach.[51]

In 1859 King visited the British Isles to solicit contributions, collecting $6,000 to be used exclusively for the Buxton Mission Building Fund. In addition, the Presbyterian Church of Ireland pledged an annual grant of $730 for the general support of the mission buildings. After deducting King's expenses, $4,180 was placed in the Buxton Building Fund, managed by the Reverend William Reid, clerk of the Presbyterian synod, to be distributed as needed to erect the buildings in Buxton. The Civil War interrupted these plans, however, straining Buxton's population and almost completely ending the arrival of new settlers. Concerned about the declining size of Buxton and its Presbyterian congregation, the synod decided not to construct new buildings at that time. Instead, it arranged with Buxton residents to prepare three hundred twenty-five dollars' worth of timber from the community's sawmill and sanctioned the building of the new facilities in 1862. In the interim, the roofs and floors of the present church and schoolhouse were repaired. The uncertainty that accompanied the Civil War and its aftermath further postponed building plans. In 1868 the committee overseeing the Buxton Building Fund purchased five acres and arranged for the erection of a new church and manse. The two buildings, completed in 1869, cost the fund three thousand dollars. The remaining money was presented to William King in recognition of the energy and devotion he had extended to the Buxton settlement and its residents.[52]

Despite their often financially precarious existence, Buxtonians were not comfortable relying on the Presbyterian synod to provide fully for their religious maintenance. As early as 1855, the members of St. Andrew's decided to make an effort to be self-supporting in spiritual matters and began taking up a collection every Sabbath for congregational expenses. Parishioners also resolved to contribute—or at least to make an effort to contribute—to all the synod's ventures. From that point on, the Mission Church at Buxton annually donated to such synod funds as the Knox College Fund, the Home Missionary Fund, the Foreign Mission Fund, and the Widows' Fund. The amount that Buxtonians tendered, though small, showed their commitment to spiritual matters.

Buxtonians' good intentions did not always translate into monetary contributions. Church leaders decided in January 1863 that congregational members should pay fifty cents to the treasurer to defray local expenses. By May, however, only a small portion of the members had paid the money. Church leaders then agreed that elders and deacons should visit individual families to collect the unpaid contributions. This manner of collection met with some success. Nonetheless, the Buxton congregation failed to sustain itself. During its first two decades, the Presbyterian church at Buxton relied primarily on outside resources to finance its daily expenses. Not until 1869 were Buxtonians able to contribute to their minister's stipend, and even then their contribution varied between a mere forty-five and one hundred fifty dollars of the minister's six-hundred-dollar annual stipend over the next four years.[53]

Some members of the Presbyterian synod believed that the failure of the Buxton congregation to achieve financial independence or even stability rested on its members' attitudes. Late in 1858, a committee from the London Presbytery, under whose direct care the St. Andrew's Church at Buxton had been placed, remarked "that from the amount of the contributions reported there seems to be a want of interest on the part of the people."[54] The presbytery requested that its findings be read to the congregation, presumably to make the fault public and perhaps shame the worshipers into contributing more. The presbytery looked to growth in the future and hoped that the Buxton congregation would become self-sustaining as soon as circumstances made it possible to do so. King later noted that the message was duly delivered from the pulpit. Although King contended that the small collections gathered at Buxton resulted from the settlers' moral attitudes, he also acknowledged that other financial demands competed with the desire to support religious endeavors. King qualified his belief that "the moral principle is so low that it has little or no power to compel them to give to Christ, with a few honourable exceptions" by stating that "all . . . have to struggle . . . and can afford to pay but little for the support of the Gospel."[55]

In spite of the inability to sufficiently provide for their church expenses, Buxtonians did what they could, with both Presbyterians and members of other religious denominations providing for the physical upkeep of their churches. In keeping with its community spirit, congregation members united in efforts to carry out as best they could the work necessary to maintain church building. In 1858 the deacons of St. Andrew's decided to plaster the church inside and out. Isaac Riley, Abraham Brodie, George Thompson, Edward Thompson, Joseph Liason, and Peter Straith completed the work, and a group of Buxton women provided dinner for the workers. A year later, the deacons undertook to shingle the church, drawing on church funds only for nails and shingles. Again without drawing on church funds, settlers whitewashed and cleaned the church sometime before August 1, 1859.[56]

When the deacons resolved that blinds should be supplied for the church windows, VanRankin, Riley, and Straith supplied the cloth free of charge; school-teacher John Rennie paid for the necessary needlework; and George Thompson hung the finished curtains. In 1861, when the choir chairs needed a new coat of paint, church members performed the work. Likewise, the building of the new church in 1863 involved the settlers, who cut the trees needed for the timber and sent the timber to the sawmill. Such community spirit was also evident when the congregation agreed to fence the church lot. Under Riley's supervision, posts were made and placed in the ground during the spring of 1865. VanRankin, Riley, Edward Thompson, George Charleston, and two other male members of the church agreed to supply at least three elm logs each for the fencing.[57]

Buxton settlers did not build splendid chapels or cathedrals with exquisite stained-glass windows or beautiful sculptures. They did not send missionaries the world over. They did not make substantial financial contributions to their coreligionists in other areas of the world. Nevertheless, religion played a central role in their lives and in the settlement at large, helping to bind the residents together in a true community.

9

In Pursuit of an Education

The first Monday in April 1850 was a typical damp spring day—typical, that is, except for the small group of children waiting in the morning light for their new school to open. Fourteen children were gathered outside the rough-looking little building that was to serve as the Buxton Mission School. Included in this group of anxious yet eager young scholars were two whites, the children of Joshua Shepley, who owned land on the outskirts of the Elgin reserve. Shepley had decided that the Buxton Mission School, more convenient to his land than the district common school, would offer his children the same quality of education. Shepley apparently was unconcerned about the prospect of his children learning alongside black children. An interracial student body, begun that first day, was only one of the characteristics that set the Buxton Mission School apart from schools in other communities of its kind.[1]

A strong symbol of the developing community at Buxton appeared in the creation of social institutions, particularly schools. Along with churches, schools were the focal points of community life in free black communities throughout the United States and Canada, a "source of triumph amidst the overall tragedy of . . . race relations."[2] Often founded in response to racial discrimination and proscription, schools for free black children became vehicles for community and cultural identity. William King and other white reformers and black leaders contended that education was one of the primary means by which blacks could achieve complete independence and self-reliance. The transformation of blacks, particularly the children of former slaves, into productive citizens hinged on education.

Black society in the United States and Canada had long recognized the vital importance of education, most significantly in its connection to "the destiny of [their] race."[3] Perhaps because they lacked other instruments of advancement such as family influence and access to capital, blacks placed greater faith in the benefits of education than did many whites. Largely denied education as slaves, blacks who had gained their freedom viewed schooling as bridging the gap between their former status and genuine freedom, both an avenue to economic opportunity and success and symbolic of racial achievement. Education was a key to moral improvement and a foundation of community progress.[4]

Black leaders almost universally promoted education as the means by which to advance equality on a number of levels. Education was central to the environmentalist view that if the circumstances of life were altered, blacks would perform as capably as any other people—that their inferior status resulted from their degradation under slavery rather than any innate inability on their part. Educational efforts could counter that degradation. As involuntary illiteracy under slavery was tied to racial oppression, education was hailed as an important tool of freedom, accomplishment, and self-determination. Martin Delany contended that self-improvement was impossible without the availability of an education to provide blacks with productive employment, while Samuel Cornish emphasized education as a socializing device for imparting moral virtues to the young.[5] Henry Bibb, editor of the *Voice of the Fugitive*, summed up black attitudes about education: "By it we can be strengthened and elevated—without it we shall be ignorant, weak, and degraded. By it we shall be clothed with a power which will enable us to arise from degradation and command respect from the whole civilized world: without it, we shall ever be imposed upon, oppressed and enslaved."[6]

Reality, however, did not necessarily mirror desire. Before the Civil War, legal constraints severely restricted black education in the United States. With the exception of Kentucky, all the southern states passed legislation prohibiting the education of blacks. Some southern blacks nevertheless acquired a rudimentary education, but southern whites in general believed that education not only was wasted on blacks but also promoted excessive independence, creating a heightened desire for freedom, and thereby endangering the slave system and orderly society. All the same, some southern whites ran the risk of legal prosecution and social disapprobation, teaching their "favorite, most trusted" slaves, typically their domestic servants or those with whom they shared an illicit blood relationship. In other cases, the children of masters clandestinely shared their school lessons with selected family slaves, usually their playmates. Some free southern blacks received private instruction from whites. And, despite legal prohibitions, a few schools for free blacks existed in cities such as Charleston and New Orleans. And in turn, those blacks, slave or free, fortunate enough to have learned the rudiments of reading and writing would often, despite the dangers involved, impart such knowledge to those otherwise lacking such an opportunity. Still, it has been estimated that only 5 percent of the black population in the U.S. South was literate in 1860.[7]

White northerners generally opposed education for blacks out of fear that educational opportunity would encourage black migration to the region, an influx that would harm northern white society. Such fears led many northern states to prohibit blacks from obtaining any education or from obtaining an education equal to that of whites. Negative public opinion further served to discourage integrated schooling throughout the antebellum North. Whites strongly objected to integrated education because of the social mixing that would result from the inevitable contact between white and black children in integrated schools. Whites feared that black and white children being together on equal terms on one level would lead to additional actions or perceptions of equality. Further protests against integrated education arose because of fervent beliefs about blacks' supposed mental inferiority. Hence, in the few places where public education existed for blacks, it was usually separate, took place only for short periods of time, and was unequal. When New York City implemented a public school system, for example, it did so with segregated classrooms. Meanwhile, numerous blacks, children and adults, were educated at the African Free School and others that received some city funds, albeit less than the amounts allocated to the white public schools.[8]

Because of such proscriptions on black education in the United States, most blacks who fled to Canada were illiterate and arrived with a hope of finding equal access to education. Nevertheless, many immigrants found this dream elusive. Although destitution played some role in preventing blacks from attaining an education in Canada, a further and more pervasive deterrent to black education was inaccessibility caused by prejudice and discrimination. In this regard, education for blacks in Canada closely resembled the U.S. racial environment that blacks had hoped to escape. A few white Canadians, such as John Scoble, an abolitionist and political activist for racial equality, advocated that "one mode of breaking down the prejudice which exists against colour, will be educating children of all complexions together."[9] White Canadians' opposition to integrated schooling soared after 1830; in Amherstburg, for example, white citizens emphatically stated that they would rather "cut their children's heads off and throw them into the road" than have their children taught with black children.[10] Even in areas where schools were supposedly integrated, prejudice was evident, for black students were forced to sit on separate benches from white students and given inferior materials and attention. As in the northern United States, most blacks who received an education in Canada did so in separate, usually unequal and inadequate, schools. In other cases, blacks themselves provided for their and their children's education through community efforts.

Black Canadians were not unified on the issue of segregated schooling. Some blacks ardently disagreed with the focus on integrated education, preferring to concentrate on simply getting some kind of schooling for their children, whatever its quality, duration, or circumstances. This issue was part of a larger debate within black society over segregation versus integration: Was it in blacks' best interest to integrate their lives with those of whites or to be separated from an essentially hostile white society? This debate over integration and segregation reflected the most fundamental dilemma facing black activists. Should they strive for acceptance in white America or struggle to achieve a distinctive and separate culture? Should segregated facilities be viewed as an end in themselves or as a transition stratagem and so be shaped as to bridge white and black communities? An integral part of community life, education was enmeshed in this controversy. Debate over schools split the black community.[11]

Numerous black leaders vocally advocated integration in educational facilities, chastising those blacks who seemed docilely to accept separate schools. Those who favored integration argued that separate schools were and always would be of an inferior quality that prevented blacks from reaching their full potential. In language that would be repeated through the next century, integrationists argued that separate schools were inherently unjust and received unequal resources. Mary Ann Shadd Cary, editor of a black newspaper, the *Provincial Freeman,* and Henry Bibb, editor of the *Voice of the Fugitive,* stressed the necessity of a proper, thorough, and racially mixed education as the primary means of advancement for blacks and of lessening white prejudice. The pages of Cary's and Bibb's newspapers provided an effective forum for their relentless support of integrated schools. Other Canadian blacks agreed. In the late 1850s, the Association for the Education and Elevation of the Coloured People, a black organization dedicated to improving the educational opportunities available to blacks in Canada, was established. Led by Alexander Augusta, Isaac Cary, and Wilson Abbott, the association opposed separate education and worked continuously through the early 1860s to end the practice.[12]

On the other side of the debate lay those blacks who contended that racially separate schools were vital for black advancement. Proponents of this view insisted that in so-called integrated schools black children did not receive the necessary quality or character of education, that prejudicial attitudes in such schools prevented truly equal education, and that separate schools better served black children. The idea of separate schools provided many blacks comfort by offering security from white prejudice and opportunities for black children to grow intellectually under the guidance of black teachers. Another component of this argument was the contention that separate schools were necessary to negate slavery's detrimental effects. Because of their lack of prior educational opportunities, children raised in slavery commonly needed to enroll in the first grade, regardless of their age. In an integrated school, such children would be taught with younger white children and would be subjected to teasing and other forms of harassment that would harm their intellectual advancement. Placed in a separate school, young blacks would be more comfortable and happier and would receive training more suitable to their backgrounds and needs.[13] Others viewed it as advantageous for blacks to maintain their own schools because separate facilities "would train up those who would afterwards instruct others; and [blacks would] thus become independent of the white man for [their] intellectual progress."[14]

As elsewhere, Buxton's leaders and residents confronted this issue. Although the settlement itself was residentially segregated, its primary social institutions, St. Andrew's Church and the Buxton Mission, were not. With the presence of the two Shepley children on that opening day, the Buxton Mission facility functioned as an integrated school without any openly hostile reactions by neighboring whites. The opening day of the Buxton Mission School passed without incident, and the institution continued its integration unchallenged.

The integrated nature of the Buxton Mission School was furthered in January 1851 when the trustees of the local district school, unable to procure a qualified teacher for the upcoming term, decided to close the common school. Many local whites subsequently chose to enroll their children in the Buxton Mission School, probably for at least two reasons: First, the Buxton Mission School represented the closest facility; second, Buxton's reputation for high-quality education had already been established, even though the school had been open for less than a year. When discussing the feasibility of sending some of the displaced white children in and around the Elgin tract to the Buxton school, John Broadbent, a member of the local white community, communicated the satisfaction of those parents of white children already attending the Buxton Mission School with the education their children were receiving. Either those white families who chose to send their children to a school located in an all-black community had little concern about integrated schooling, or the convenient location and superior education offered at Buxton effectively countered any prejudice.[15] Whatever the reason, by 1854 half the students at the Buxton Mission School were white, and, according to a leading educator in the area, "the black school [was] the fashionable academy of that region."[16]

Although one scholar's claim that the Buxton Mission School was "the first integrated public school established in North America" is inaccurate, Buxton nonetheless did have one of the few fully integrated schools prior to the Civil War.[17] Unlike some of the ostensibly integrated schools in Canada and the United States, the Buxton Mission School went beyond merely bringing black and white children together in the same building. It offered equal facilities and equal education to all its pupils. Few if any racial problems developed among the student body. One visitor to Buxton commented that he "had the pleasure of seeing [black and white students] distributed through the various classes, without distinction, and found that they studied harmoniously together."[18] As King later noted, the relationship between black and white students at the Buxton Mission School was equal and amicable, as they "mingled freely in the playground and sat together in the school room, and stood up in the same class."[19]

Interesting parallels exist between the educational opportunities afforded to blacks at Buxton and Oberlin Collegiate Institute in northern Ohio. Founded in 1833, this small college gained a national reputation for being the first coeducational college in the country and its willingness to accept black students. The two evangelical missionaries who established Oberlin, John Jay Shipherd and Philo Penfield Steward, envisioned, much like William King did, a utopian community centered on an institution of Christian learning.

Oberlin was not initially intended to educate blacks. Financial needs, an evangelical commitment to humanitarian principles, a willingness to experiment with equal access to education regardless of class and gender, and a spirit of liberal reform were among the forces that brought about the institution's integration. When abolitionist students and faculty at Lane Theological Seminary in Cincinnati withdrew from the school in 1834 after confrontation with the administration over their antislavery activity, they were courted by Shipherd to attend Oberlin, in part because Shipherd needed the financial aid that would accrue to Oberlin if the Lane rebels, as they were dubbed, came to Oberlin. Among the conditions demanded by the Lane rebels was that students be admitted to Oberlin without regard to color. After heated discussions, Oberlin's board accepted the principle of equal access to education. Between 1835 and 1865, Oberlin's black students represented between 2 and 5 percent of Oberlin's overall population. The goals of the Buxton Mission School and Oberlin were similar in that they stressed religious training, future missionary work, and training teachers. They were both open to blacks and whites, males and females. A subsidiary of Oberlin was a preparatory department that enrolled students in need of precollege training. The Buxton Mission School likewise engaged in such preparatory schooling for male and female students, some of whom went on to college. It is rather surprising that only one of Buxton's youth is known to have attended Oberlin, Anderson Ruffin Abbott. Certainly the training they received at the Buxton Mission School would have adequately prepared them for study there. Oberlin, located not far from Cleveland, was situated within a reasonable distance from Buxton.[20]

Despite its success in integrated schooling and the high quality of education it provided its students, the Buxton Mission School was not without problems, especially during its early years. It is not surprising that the most severe threat was financial. As part of the Buxton Mission, the school was connected with the Presbyterian Church of Canada. Education, rather than being considered secular and thus under the realm of the Elgin Association, was entwined with religious training. Education was the exception to the separation between the settlement's civic and ecclesiastical elements. The leaders of the Elgin Association and the Presbyterian Church synod deemed the merging of religious and civil spheres of influence acceptable in matters of intellectual development because of their belief, commonly held among nineteenth-century blacks as well as white abolitionists, that religion and education were the factors that would allow blacks to rise above slavery's detrimental effects. The Buxton school relied heavily on monies bestowed by the church. As the school's sponsor, the Presbyterian synod was expected to bear the responsibility for teachers' salaries, instructional materials, and the school's other financial commitments. Because these monies were collected from congregations throughout Canada and constituted but one of the many activities the synod supported, these contributions failed fully to cover the Buxton Mission School's expenditures.

In its effort to secure additional finances, the synod repeatedly beseeched its constituents to donate money expressly for the Buxton Mission Fund. The results of these efforts did not meet the school's financial needs, and King continually solicited aid from a variety of outside sources, traveling repeatedly throughout the northern United States and Great Britain with the approval and perhaps even at the instigation of the Presbyterian synod. The precise effectiveness of King's trips remains unclear, but at least enough money was raised to allow the Buxton Mission School to remain open, albeit with continued financial hardships.[21]

While King's reservations about charity obviously did not extend to assistance for intellectual development, in keeping with his ideology that the road to independence went through self-reliance, he conscientiously requested monies expressly for educational purposes rather than for the settlers' material support. At the same time, since the Buxton Mission School and the St. Andrew's congregation were associated with one another, King probably combined religious and educational financial needs. King rationalized these contradictions by contending that only through education (and spiritual guidance) could blacks achieve complete independence and self-reliance, thereby providing a justification for the soliciting of financial contributions for educational purposes. As was the case with industrial development, the ends justified the means.

Money for the Buxton Mission School came from other sources, including individual contributions made without the inducement of fund-raising. The mission school received books, maps, and other educational materials from various benevolent associations. In November 1851, several distinguished Chicagoans presented the school with "a complete set of Mitchell's Outline Maps, together with a map of Palestine."[22] A combination of such means kept the mission school continually open, although it never completely escaped its financial woes.

Despite the Presbyterian Church's difficulty in securing adequate financial support, the synod did not waiver on its commitment or require monetary contributions from the settlers. Of course, the impoverished circumstances of most of the black families (and many local white families) whose children attended the school presented serious difficulty for contributing financially to their children's education. Like frontier settlers in other areas, Buxton residents may well have offered what nonmonetary aid they could to support the education of their children—firewood to heat the schoolroom, labor for cleaning and building purposes, and perhaps food and board for the teachers.

Beginning in 1856, it was decided, presumably by King and the Presbyterian synod but possibly by the settlers themselves or by King and the synod in consultation with the settlers, that the parents of students attending the mission school should pay a "small sum" toward the institution's support. This tuition was not mandatory in that children could still attend if their families were unable to contribute. The move nonetheless represented a symbolic step on the road to true independence and self-reliance. It is unknown, and perhaps undeterminable, how many families, black or white, managed to contribute. This development did not mean that the Buxton Mission School was prepared or able to sustain itself in full. The school still relied heavily on funds bestowed by the Presbyterian Church of Canada and collected by various other means. In this, and other respects, Buxton was typical of many frontier areas, especially those in the early-nineteenth-century midwestern United States, that relied on subscription schools, organized and paid for by associations of parents who were then in charge of all the various aspects of their schools from the building of a schoolhouse to the hiring of a teacher and provisions of supplies.[23]

In time, the school's most severe financial difficulties were alleviated. Using a variety of donated materials, the settlers built a log schoolhouse during the winter of 1850–1851. King reported to the Elgin Association in 1866 that the school was "self-supporting: the settlers have subscribed this year one thousand dollars for educational purposes, besides four hundred dollars which has been raised towards the erection of a brick school house in the village of Buxton."[24] Through fund-raising efforts, the settlers continued to contribute approximately one thousand dollars annually to help maintain their educational facilities. A new schoolhouse, built by local residents, was completed in the early 1860s. A sign of the community's success, this one-room schoolhouse boasted a fourteen-foot-high ceiling, eight tall windows, whitewashed stamped-tin walls, and a pine floor. After the Civil War, the schools in the Elgin tract were incorporated into Kent County's public school system and consequently received government assistance, which made them solvent.[25]

A second major difficulty encountered by the Buxton Mission School during its early years was the lack of a stable teaching staff. A community of its nature and with its financial woes was bound to experience difficulties procuring a competent teacher over the long term. Buxton mirrors, albeit for different reasons, a problem experienced by midwestern frontier schools, where, for the most part, country schoolteachers taught only two or three years and then married, so that untrained teachers continually replaced those with even the smallest amount of experience. These difficulties were particularly acute in Canada, where teachers were in chronically short supply because of the small number of training facilities. Fortunately for the Buxton settlement, its affiliation with the Presbyterian Church of Canada provided a ready supply of teachers. Beginning with John Rennie, the school's first teacher, and continuing through much of the 1850s, the young scholars at the mission school were instructed by persons training to be teachers. Knox College, the Presbyterian Church of Canada's institution for learning and its theological school, provided these student teachers—predominantly white males.[26]

Buxton's reputation as a place to receive a first-rate education supports the assertion made by King and other representatives of the Presbyterian Church that despite being student teachers, these teachers were of prime quality and imparted more than a marginal level of education to the pupils at Buxton. The quality of these teachers was not the issue. Rather, the school suffered from the instability, unavoidable with student teaching, that accompanies the constant rotation of teachers. Student instructors typically came to Buxton for an academic term and then returned to Knox College to complete their studies. This meant a change in teachers approximately every six months. In the first five years after the Buxton Mission School opened, ten teachers passed through its doors, not counting King, who substituted between instructors. The numerous teachers forced students to adjust to a variety of teaching styles, disciplinary methods, personalities, and curricula, a situation that undoubtedly affected student learning and advancement. This instability was detrimental to Buxton students and to the settlement in general. King described the lack of a permanent teacher as having "a paralyzing effect on the efficiency of the School." Success depended heavily on placing the mission school "on a permanent and efficient basis," and that required an end to the parade of teachers.[27]

The termination of the student teaching program with Knox College in 1857 achieved this goal. George Thompson, a white man, was then appointed the full-time teacher of the Buxton Mission School. The imposition of a tuition occurred less than a year prior to Thompson's hiring and may well have represented the first step toward achieving the financial stability that would better attract a more permanent teaching staff. Thompson had taught previously at the Free Church School of Kintore, Aberdeenshire, Scotland, and remained at the

Buxton School until his death in 1862. When the school became part of the local public school system and its teachers were supplied by the government, many of the teachers remained homegrown, including Eunice Shadd and Harriet Rhue. Being taught by one of their own undoubtedly created a tremendous source of pride among Buxtonians, symbolizing their accomplishment, self-sufficiency, and autonomy.[28]

Few organized black communities had as fruitful an educational experience as did Buxton. The Roberts settlement, which turned out a proportionally similar number of college graduates and future black professionals, is a notable exception. Other black communities were not as successful. Free Frank actively promoted the development of a private school at New Philadelphia, which he hoped would provide more advanced educational instruction for black children in the area. It was to be called Free Will Baptist Seminary. In 1848 Free Frank donated two full blocks in the town and arranged for the building's construction. To Free Frank's great disappointment, construction of the Free Will Baptist Seminary was never completed because of contractual difficulties and a series of legal issues. Black residents at Brooklyn had no school of their own and few black children attended the district school. Other black communities likewise suffered from a lack of educational facilities. In the 1830s Hiram Wilson lamented the lack of schools in black communities like Wilberforce. He strove to correct this deficiency, helping to establish educational facilities in many areas of black settlement in Upper Canada. By the late 1830s schools had been opened in Colchester, Amherstburg, Brantford, Niagara, St. Catharines, and Toronto, all locations with significant black populations.[29]

Unlike the educational facilities of experimental communities elsewhere, particularly Wilberforce and Dawn, the Buxton Mission School was not a manual or industrial institution. Rather than teaching skilled trades for economic advancement, the Buxton Mission School imparted a common school education for intellectual betterment that would in turn lead to economic improvement. The curriculum encompassed the basics of academic education. Students were trained in reading, writing, and arithmetic. In addition, the mission school offered the rudiments of both a classical and humanist curriculum to those capable and desirous of advancing beyond a common education. In November 1850 the first Latin instruction began with a class of six boys. A year later, Greek was added. James Rapier, who underwent this classical education at the mission school, studied "Latin, Greek, Spanish, history, shorthand, phrenology, Old Testament scriptures, classical literature, and higher mathematics."[30] The school also endeavored to hone students' rhetorical skills by conducting debates on germane issues. Once such debate centered on the question of "who suffered the most from the hands of the white man the Indians or the colored men."[31] By offering such advanced subjects, the school hoped to prepare young black men for admission to higher education. Females attended the mission school but generally received only a common education. Like most of his male contemporaries, King believed that girls should receive schooling that would assist them in their future lives, by which he meant in their traditional role as homemakers. By 1855 a semi-separate female school had been established as part of the Buxton Mission. A female teacher instructed the girls in reading and domestic sciences, including sewing, cooking, and cleaning.[32]

As might be expected, all Buxton Mission School students received religious instruction. Reverend King, serving as both the Presbyterian Church of Canada's missionary to the Buxton settlement and supervisor of the school, implemented the school's curriculum. In his teaching and supervisory experiences before the founding of the Buxton settlement, King had fostered a close connection between education and religion, and he followed this pattern at Buxton. King ardently contended that literacy and religious schooling not only complemented each other but were inseparable. Like teachers elsewhere, those at Buxton felt that freedmen needed to be taught in values such as thrift, industry, cleanliness, and civic responsibility.

King's ideology of Christian education remained in place from the school's inception. On opening day, he began class with prayer and a reading from the Scriptures, establishing a tradition that would continue beyond the 1850s. According to his account of that day, King then explained to the students that "the school would be conducted on religious principles."[33] Following this introduction, each child received a Bible in which King had written the child's name, and the students were told that they would regularly be assigned lessons from the Scriptures.[34]

The Buxton Mission School's noteworthy success largely resulted from its broad curriculum and quality education. Within two years of its establishment, the school's accomplishments were recognized locally as well as in the broader circles of the Elgin Association and the Presbyterian Church of Canada. Semi-annual examinations of the students determined and recorded their progress, with the results forwarded to Elgin stockholders and members of the Presbyterian Church, presumably to illustrate the experiment's success and to encourage continuation of support. One such examination, with fifty-two students participating, was held on October 21, 1852. According to the subsequent report, the scholars' improvement from the last examination "was manifest; the Latin, Geography, English Grammar, and History classes displayed a degree of acquirement which plainly demonstrated that the intellectual facilities of the colored race are by no means of an inferior order."[35] The report's authors saw Buxtonians as instrumental in disproving the widespread belief that blacks were inferior to whites, incapable of learning and sustaining themselves outside of slavery. The students must have faced immense pressure: Not only were they asked to meet the expectations of their parents, teachers, and King, but they were further displayed as representatives of their race.

The education provided at the Buxton Mission School played a key role in the community's success and acclaim. Buxton provided the intellectual and social focus for the Raleigh Township black community. A number of black patriarchs, including Isaac Riley, Henry Johnson, and Wilson R. Abbott, uprooted their families and resettled them in Buxton for the express purpose of obtaining a quality education for their children. With a certain degree of optimism, Riley and his family trekked to Buxton specifically to secure a lot near the proposed school even before the school and its reputation had been established. Riley's goal was fulfilled: The Riley children completed their schooling at Buxton, and two of them went on to pursue higher educational training. Johnson, a free man originally from Pennsylvania, had been the proprietor of a successful business in Massillon, Ohio. When the local school turned out his children because of their color, he gave up his business and brought his family to Canada, living in various places before moving to Buxton, where the Johnson children got the education they and their father desired. As Johnson recalled, "I came to Canada for rights, freedom and liberty. But most of all I came to Buxton so my children could have a good education."[36] Abbott, a freedman in the U.S. South, had come north seeking better conditions, first in the northern United States and then in Canada, where he first settled in Toronto. Abbott prospered and became a prominent black leader and activist. By 1841 he owned five frame houses, which he rented out, and engaged in other business ventures that had an estimated accumulated capital value of thirty thousand dollars. Later that decade, Abbott moved himself and his family temporarily to Buxton to advance his children's education.[37]

Rather than relocating their entire families, some fathers chose to send their children to Buxton for their education. John H. Rapier Sr. was one such parent. Born a slave, he gained his freedom through self-purchase. Because his first wife was free, four of Rapier's children had been born free. Earning a living as a barber in Alabama, Rapier used much of his savings to educate his free children. He sent two of his sons, John Jr. and James, to Buxton to receive their education under the care of their uncle, Henry Thomas. The decisions of men such as Riley, Johnson, Abbott, and Rapier attest not only to the impressive reputation of the Buxton Mission School but also to the high regard in which blacks held education.[38]

Another sign of the Buxton Mission School's accomplishments was that by 1856 two students had gained entrance to Knox College in Toronto, although neither man could afford to enroll. A third Buxton scholar preparing to enter Knox College in fall 1857 was ultimately turned away because his family lacked the funds to support his academic ambition. The plight of these young men brought talk of remedies. Buxton residents were especially concerned because this situation could reflect negatively on the settlement and impede progress toward training "young men of piety and talents, for further usefulness in the Church."[39] This goal could hardly be achieved if scholars were denied higher education because of a lack of money.

King suggested the establishment of a bursary fund to support two or three students during their first and second years at college. Although the exact means remain unclear, the students and their families apparently would shoulder further financial responsibility for their education. King suggested incorporating the fund as part of the Presbyterian Church of Canada's missionary schemes, with a nucleus of one thousand dollars bequeathed to church missions by James Thompson, a philanthropic church member. The church ultimately divided the money among several of its missions so that, in the end, Buxton received only four hundred dollars. A year later, King was still requesting that the reluctant synod execute his plan. The synod's reasons for resisting the creation of the fund are unknown but may have included the fact that the church's funds were already stretched to capacity. The synod may also have believed that it was already assisting the settlement as much as the constituents would support. Lack of interest among church members may also have been a factor, although contributions did come from some local and foreign sources, including a Canadian philanthropist who contributed five pounds toward the formation of the fund and a Scottish benefactor who donated ten pounds. The Ladies Society of Edinburgh for Emancipation contributed twenty-two pounds, while the Dundee Ladies Anti-Slavery Society donated ten pounds "to assist a scholarship for any promising pupil . . . that may wish to prosecute his studies at college with a view to the ministry."[40] King undoubtedly was particularly proud of a one pound, ten pence sterling contribution from the children of the Sabbath School of the West Port Church in Edinburgh. Despite such donations, the bursary fund was never officially established, although some of Buxton's most promising scholars attended Knox and other colleges, in part with financial assistance from the Presbyterian Church of Canada; philanthropists from Canada, Great Britain, and the northern United States; and the Buxton community.[41]

As Buxton grew and the mission school's reputation spread, the number of scholars enrolled rose. The settlement eventually outgrew its original one-room schoolhouse. As more black families took up residence in and surrounding the Elgin tract, many children found themselves living at some distance from the mission school, located on King's lot just outside Buxton Square. With poor roads and no transportation facilities, the trek to the school could become prohibitive, especially with winter cold and ice and spring rains and mud. Children in the northernmost and southernmost, less developed parts of the settlement had the additional hazard of making the daily journey through heavily forested areas that still harbored wild animals. Lucy, Ellen, and Margaret Bell; Adelia and Solomon Williams; and Josephine Stewart were among those who daily traipsed more than four miles to and from school.

To respond to this need, a second school, school section thirteen, was built in 1855 at the northern end of the settlement. A third school was completed two years later in another area of the Elgin tract. Once again, Buxton was typical of the times, when the schools were brought to the children rather than taking children to the schools. Little is known about Buxton's ancillary schools. Neither seems to have been connected with the Presbyterian Church or other religious denominations. They apparently were supported by members of the Buxton community, presumably those families whose children benefited from the facilities. Evidence suggests that the teachers for these schools, at least from the early 1860s, were men and women who had been educated at the Buxton Mission School. After receiving his college degree, James Rapier, for example, returned to Buxton for a short time in 1863 and taught in one of the schools briefly before resettling in the United States.[42]

The Elgin Association's Third Annual Report, dated September 1852, recorded seventy-three pupils at the Buxton Mission School. The following year, the annual report noted one hundred twelve students. The number of scholars peaked in 1855 at one hundred fifty, twice the enrollment of only three years earlier. By 1857, however, this number had decreased to one hundred, presumably a result of the opening of the two additional schools. During the 1850s, school enrollment throughout the settlement fluctuated between 18 and 21 percent of the population. Between 1850 and 1873, more than five hundred students received some portion of their education at one of the settlement's schools.[43]

Despite their limitations, census returns are useful in obtaining a composite picture of Buxton.[44] In 1861 60 percent of Buxtonians twenty years of age or older were recorded as literate. It is somewhat surprising that 49 percent of Buxton residents forty years of age or older—those most likely to have grown up as either slaves or in areas of the United States where formal education for blacks was uncommon—were literate. Since this age group consisted of adults who presumably did not benefit from Buxton's schools with the exception of those who attended the adult night school or those young adults who had come to Buxton early in the 1850s and may have learned to read and write as teenagers, this statistic may say more about the nature of Buxton's settlers than about its educational system. Buxton recorded a higher number of literate adults than other organized black communities. At the Beech and Roberts settlements in 1850, only one-fifth of the residents forty years of age and older could read and write. The lower literacy rates at the Beech and Roberts settlements are reflective of laws discouraging the education of free blacks in Virginia and North Carolina, for many of the settlers in those communities during the first decade of settlement were freeborn blacks from those states.[45]

According to the census records and somewhat contradictory to the Buxton Mission School's attendance rolls and annual reports, school attendance at Buxton was lower than what might be expected in a community that professed great dedication to the intellectual improvement of its residents. As table 9.1 shows, the 1861 census recorded only 33 percent of Buxton residents between the ages of five and twenty attending school.[46] Several factors, alone or in conjunction with one another, may have contributed to this lower-than-expected school attendance record. Despite the emphasis on education as a means of racial improvement, neither King nor the Elgin Association mandated school attendance. Whereas deprived backgrounds may have led many parents to a strong commitment to provide their children with schooling, others undoubtedly believed schooling to be futile and saw their children's futures as agricultural laborers in a white-dominated society unaltered by education. Moreover, limited resources would have prevented other children from going to school: No direct evidence suggests that Buxton's ancillary schools charged tuition; however, since they were not formally supported by the Elgin Association, the Presbyterian synod, or any other religious institution, it seems unlikely that they could have functioned without financial support from the pupils' families, which would have been beyond the means of some families. Furthermore, despite the fact that the Buxton Mission School allowed children to attend free of charge even after the institution of a nominal tuition in 1858, some parents would have been reluctant to accept what they perceived as charity, a concern that may have had added importance because of the value Buxtonians placed on self-sufficiency.

The harsh demands of farming further worked against even the desire of those families who stressed education. School often became of minor importance in comparison with economic necessity—subsistence was an immediate concern, whereas education was a future ideal. Buxton families necessarily depended

Table 9.1 School Attendance among Buxton Residents 5–20 Years of Age, 1861

	Number	In School	Percentage in School
Male	157	48	31%
Female	138	49	36%
Total	295	97	33%

Source: Canadian Population Census, 1861

on their children to supply labor, and children significantly contributed to the household economy. As elsewhere in nineteenth-century rural communities, Buxton children served various capacities in the house and on the farm and could be spared for schooling only for about four months out of the year, particularly in the case of boys. Sons labored in the fields alongside their fathers, plowing and hoeing; they built and repaired fences, cleared land, mucked out the barns, and assisted in all the other chores of a farm. Daughters assisted with the domestic chores, helped care for the livestock, learned the skill of preparing yarn and cloth, needlework, and constantly performed other chores. They also helped care for younger siblings. Such demands at home in part explain why the percentage of children in school varied considerably by age group, as table 9.2 shows. Widower Louis Carter's sons, William (sixteen) and Robert (fifteen) did not attend school during the 1860 academic year. Neither did sixteen-year-old James West, although his four siblings between the ages of eight and fourteen did. George and Nancy Hatter's three youngest children—Mahilda, thirteen, Barbara, ten, and Pricilla, six—attended school, but their older brothers, sixteen and fourteen years old, did not.[47]

John and Rebecca Carter's family can serve as a microcosm of what other families may have done. According to the 1861 figures, the Carters had fifteen children between the ages of two and twenty-four, seven of them sixteen or older and not attending school that year. Four children between ten and fifteen were enrolled, while none of those under age ten did so. The census records that the Carter children over the age of twenty were literate. Thus, it can be concluded that the Carter family held education to be of value and wanted their children to receive some level of instruction, although they clearly did not or could not send their children to school before the age of ten. Furthermore, in some cases, girls were sent to school while their brothers were not because the girls' labor could be more easily spared. In the common school era, before compulsory attendance, people were less age-conscious, and years of attendance in common schools were more variable. A ten-year-old boy might not be attending school because of farming demands while his seven-year-old sister might because her labor domestically was more expendable.[48]

Other factors prevented older children from attending school. Some, such as Catherine Riley and Mary Moore, were married by the age of nineteen, and

Table 9.2 School Attendance among Buxton Residents, 1861

Age	Number	In School	Percentage in School
5–10 years	119	28	24%
11–16 years	128	54	42%
17–20 years	48	15	31%

Source: Canadian Population Census, 1861

establishing and running households took precedence over education. Regardless of gender, marriage commonly marked the end of schooling. Jerome Riley, seventeen, was not attending school because he had completed his education at the Buxton Mission School and was ready to pursue higher education. Children may have attended school only for a few years or so in order to learn the rudiments of reading and writing rather than entering school with the intention of staying until age eighteen, as is the case today. The census listed most children in their late teens not attending school as having occupations, although the records do not indicate whether they worked for their family or outside the household. Twenty-year-old Henry Goodall had not attended school in 1860, presumably because he assisted his family as a laborer, his trade as the census recorded it. Nineteen-year-old Isaac Williams worked as a laborer rather than attending school, as did Benjamin Matthews, eighteen. Sixteen-year-old Edward Thompson and his eleven-year-old brother, Joseph, were both listed as laborers, as were Henry (thirteen) and William Johnson (sixteen) and John Overton (fifteen). Immanuel Roper, age thirteen, was a laborer, as was fourteen-year-old Henry Dabney. The children of Jacob and Ann Matthews were contributing to the family income by the age of ten, when young William and his brothers, twelve-year-old Daniel and fourteen-year-old Isaiah, were laborers. Their sister, sixteen-year-old Levina, worked as a spinster. Other young women contributed to the family income at a young age. Sixteen-year-old Lucy Bell, eighteen-year-old Frances Crosswhite, and fifteen-year-old Hannah Scipio were also spinsters. Several young boys labored rather than attending school, including ten-year-old Daniel Matthews, twelve-year-old Joseph Bell, and nine-year-old John Scipio. It is understandable that none of the Cronan children attended school when the eldest children, Richard, eleven; John, ten; Catherine, nine; and even seven-year-old William were working as laborers. Combined with their need to assist the family and their lives as farmers, both parents and children may have been reluctant or realistically unable to view education as a means to achieve a better career path.[49]

Meanwhile, other families maintained a strong dedication to education despite economic necessity. According to the 1861 census, nineteen-year-old John Jones worked as a laborer and attended school, as did Abraham Jackson, seventeen. Both Mark Peterson and Cathrine Micham balanced their educational pursuits with work as servants.

Only 24 percent of children between the ages of five and ten attended school, making them the least likely group to enroll. In the absence of regulations or statutes mandating school attendance at a certain age, parents determined for themselves when their children were mature enough for an academic environment and capable of traversing the distance to school, and most children did not start attendance until they neared age ten. In the Rann family, twelve-year-old

Rachel and nine-year-old George went to school, but eight-year-old Elisa and five-year-old William did not. Fourteen-year-old Emeline and eleven-year-old Elizabeth Washington attended school, but their seven-year-old sister Clarissa did not. Likewise, seven-year-old Margaret Hooper enrolled, but her brother Dempsy, a year younger, did not. Maria and William Harris, eleven and eight, respectively, were in school in 1861, but their five-year-old brother, John, was not. In William Parker's family, John and Cassanda, ages eleven and ten, attended school while their younger siblings, William and Charleat, eight and six, stayed at home. Archibald and Susan Smith's three children above the age of seven went to school, while their two children between five and seven did not.[50]

Not attending school did not necessarily mean illiteracy. The 1861 census does not record nineteen-year-old Samuel Lightfoot attending school, yet two years later, he signed his enlistment papers when he volunteered for the Union army, clearly indicating at least some level of literacy, and he had probably completed his education by the time of the census. Some literate parents may have chosen, for whatever reason, not to send their children to school but rather to provide the rudiments of literacy at home. Unlike her husband, Addia Bailey was literate, and she may have taught her children, five of whom were school age in 1861, to read and write. The same may have been true in the Watts household, where Ann (seven) and Sarah (five) did not attend school, although they may have done so in later years. The Wattses lived fairly distant from the Buxton Mission School and may not have felt comfortable sending their young daughters off to school. Literate themselves, Charles and Nancy Watts would have been capable of imparting their knowledge to their children at home.[51]

Some gender differences are apparent, particularly when looking at individual families, but considerable discrepancies did not exist overall, and age may explain the difference more than gender. Fifteen-year-old Isaac Brodie was in school, but his sister Ann, age eight, was not. Eighteen-year-old William Brooks and his ten-year-old brother, Augustus, attended school, but their eight-year-old sister, Ester, remained at home. Richard and Emily Jones's two sons, John (nineteen) and James (twelve) attended school, while their sister, Martha (eight), did not. In 1861 31 percent of Buxton boys between the ages of five and twenty attended school, while 36 percent of Buxton girls in the same age group did so. For those between eleven and sixteen years old, 56 percent of females attended school, compared to only 32 percent of males. In contrast, only 21 percent of young women between the ages of seventeen and twenty attended school, compared to 42 percent of males in the same group, a finding that may reflect the pattern of earlier age at marriage for women. Alternatively, boys may have delayed education because their labor was needed at home, returning to school at later ages, when the family's prospects had improved and the sons could be spared.[52]

Despite the educational opportunities available in Buxton, some parents chose, for whatever reason, not to educate their children in the community's facilities. Cupid and Rebecca Martin's four children did not attend school. None of Hampton and Addia Bailey's five school-age children were recorded in the 1861 census as attending school. Likewise, the census data do not show David and Maria Stuart or Edward and Sarah Thompson as sending any of their children to school. No direct correlation between illiterate parents and school attendance exists. Roughly half the households in which one or both parents were illiterate sent at least one child to school.[53]

Improvement continued during the second decade of Buxton's existence despite the uncertainty the settlement faced. The 1871 census shows that 67 percent of Buxton residents age twenty or older were literate, as compared to 60 percent in 1861. The rate for women in that age group, however, declined from 63 percent to 59 percent over that period, as table 9.3 shows.[54]

Additional improvement could be expected in the future as the number of children attending school in 1871 had grown considerably higher than the numbers from ten years earlier. Seventy-one percent of children between eight and fourteen attended school, compared to 41 percent in 1861. The number of children between the ages of five and twenty attending school grew from 33 percent in 1861 to 61 percent, as shown in table 9.4.[55]

The future activities of the graduates of the Buxton Mission School furthered Buxton's educational reputation. Buxton graduates went on to become teachers, ministers, lawyers, and doctors, and by 1860, Buxton was sending educated blacks to other parts of Canada and the United States. Anderson Ruffin Abbott,

Table 9.3 Percentage of Literate Buxton Adults

		1861	1871
Age 20–24		94%	87%
	Male	96%	87%
	Female	92%	88%
Age 25–29		85%	89%
	Male	100%	90%
	Female	76%	88%
Age 30–39		52%	70%
	Male	43%	60%
	Female	62%	80%
Aged 40 and over		49%	53%
	Male	48%	69%
	Female	52%	34%
Total (20+)		60%	67%
	Male	58%	74%
	Female	63%	59%

Source: Canadian Population Census, 1861, 1871

Table 9.4 School Attendance among Buxton Residents

		5–20 Years of Age	
	Number	In School	Percentage in School
1861	295	97	33%
1871	125	76	61%
		8–14 Years of Age	
	Number	In School	Percentage in School
1861	151	62	41%
1871	56	40	· 71%

Source: Canadian Population Census, 1861, 1871

son of Wilson R. Abbott, was one of the first Buxton students to go on to higher education. Anderson then attended the Oberlin College Preparatory Department and then studied for three years at the Toronto Academy, completing all his classes with honors. He then studied medicine at the University of Toronto and received a license from the Medical Board of Upper Canada in 1861. He subsequently served as a U.S. Army surgeon during the Civil War, reaching the rank of lieutenant colonel. Two of Isaac Riley's sons completed their studies at the Buxton Mission School and went on to receive degrees from Knox College, with the older one becoming a Presbyterian minister and the younger one choosing a medical career and serving as a surgeon during the Civil War. Alfred Lafferty, another Buxton scholar, attended Trinity College in Upper Canada, graduating with highest honors. Henry Johnson's son, Richard, studied medicine in Edinburgh after a short stay at the University of Toronto and eventually became a medical missionary serving in Africa. Abraham Shadd, son of a prominent Buxton resident whose family emigrated from Pennsylvania, became a lawyer.[56]

The Rapier family produced several scholars. After graduating from the mission school, John Rapier Jr. became the first black to gain admittance to the medical school at the University of Michigan.[57] He later transferred to the school of medicine at the State University of Iowa in Keokuk, receiving his degree in 1864. He then traveled to Washington, D.C., where he became an assistant army surgeon, working at the Freedmen's Hospital, which cared for indigent former slaves. His brother, James, returned to Florence, Alabama, and became a successful landowner and politician. A broader benefit of the educational system at Buxton can been seen in the articulateness of Buxton settlers' letters, resolutions, and memorials published in various Canadian and U.S. outlets, including the *Toronto Globe,* the *Voice of the Fugitive,* and the *Liberator.*[58]

King's hopes for the elevation of blacks' moral, social, spiritual, and intellectual condition did not rest on the adult black population but rather on the young. King contended that "little [could] be done by way of improving an adult population that has been raised in slavery beyond supplying them with the means of grace."[59] He believed that primary concentration should be placed on the next generation of blacks, who could be taught and trained. Black leaders elsewhere echoed this emphasis on the maturing generation rather than those who had grown up under the constraints of slavery. Despite his emphasis on education for Buxton's children, King opened a night school for adults in the early 1850s. According to King, "it was interesting to see men and women from 25 to 30 years of age and some even older who had never tryed to learn before, begin with the A, B, C[s], and try to learn the names of the letter[s], and put them together in [words]."[60] Attendance records at the night school illustrate that many of Buxton's adults were eager to learn to read and write and applied themselves with diligence. Such dedication acquires added value considering that those adults invested precious time in night school at the end of a long day of labor. Assuming their probable future as farmers, it was unlikely that such knowledge would gain them financial benefit. One graduate of the Buxton adult school, Thomas Stringer, later assisted in founding several local British Methodist Episcopal churches before returning to his birth state of Mississippi after the Civil War. William Parker also learned to read and write at the Buxton adult school. Joshua Shepley and his two eldest daughters were among the first adults to participate in King's night school. Other whites joined as well, adding to the depth of the integration of education in Buxton.

The education available to Buxtonians stood among the settlement's most notable achievements. White and black students learned side by side in a condition of equality. In a time when racially segregated schooling was accepted—indeed, often imposed on blacks or sought by them—Buxton proved that integrated education was not destructive; rather, it could offer strong benefits, both educational and social, to all involved. Those black children who attended Buxton's schools received an education equal if not superior to what most of their contemporaries could obtain either in Canada or in the United States. Their success in education was certainly not unique. Many pioneer children of the early-nineteenth-century Midwest received little formal education yet put that instruction to use in becoming doctors, lawyers, ministers, teachers, and other professionals. Buxton's scholars carried the knowledge they received throughout their lives, imparting that knowledge in various ways to others and in this way improving their own lives and the lives of those around them. The Buxton school system went far in proving blacks to be capable, motivated, and promising scholars. In this way the Buxton settlement was further influential in countering the contemporary opinion that blacks were incapable of improvement outside bondage. These students uplifted the expectations and aspirations of freedpeople in Canada and the United States. Besides making possible the schooling of countless children who otherwise would have gone uneducated, the schools at Buxton brought families together in a common effort, provided a sense of community, and gave Buxtonians a sense of belonging.

10

A Community Transformed

Within a decade of its founding, the experimental settlement at Buxton had become a true community, with agricultural, industrial, spiritual, and intellectual ties between its members. Its most difficult period lay just ahead. A barrage of issues faced the young community. What would happen to the settlement when the initial ten-year period ended? Would blacks become a "foreign" element in their own community after white settlement was allowed? Would the community withstand the disruption and dislocation accompanying the U.S. Civil War? Would Buxton survive the ultimate test, that of time? As Buxton entered its second decade, outside forces would produce marked changes. The United States, which a majority of Buxton's residents viewed as their homeland by virtue of their birth, was on the verge of a civil war that would affect blacks in Buxton in numerous ways.

When war broke out in the United States, most blacks in Canada, including Buxtonians, rejoiced, believing that the conflict would inevitably bring to an end the long, difficult battle against slavery. Shortly after the United States opened its armies to blacks in 1863, Buxton's young men began to show their loyalty to and support for both the United States and their brethren in bondage by enlisting. In fall 1863 a group of Buxton men left their families behind, traveled together across the border, and volunteered their services to the Union army. Most were mustered into duty in Detroit, Michigan, to serve in various companies of that state's First Colored Infantry, later reorganized as the 102d U.S. Colored Troops (USCT). Solomon King, William King's former slave, was one of the enlistees, serving with Company A of the 102d from his enlistment in October 1863 until he was mustered out with the rest of his regiment in September 1865. He rose to the rank of corporal but was later reduced to the rank of private for reasons that remain unknown. One of Solomon King's friends, Elijah Doo, enlisted in

1864, serving as a substitute for John Humphreys, a white man. Doo was part of a second group of Buxtonians who traveled together and enlisted early that year. Other Buxton men who served in the 102d included Samuel Lightfoot, Kincheon Brooks, Isaac Brodie, Johnson Dabney, Lorenzo Rann, Abraham Jackson, John Alfred, Peter Scipio, and Ezekiel Cooper.[1]

While attached to the Department of the South, King, Doo, and the other soldiers of the 102d engaged primarily in garrison and picket duty but saw action in two major engagements (Honey Hill, South Carolina, on November 30, 1864, and Deveaux Neck, South Carolina, on December 7–9, 1864). At Honey Hill a detail from Companies A and D drew off a disabled section of the 3d New York Artillery, an act conducted in the "coolest and most gallant manner."[2] Several Buxton men, including Solomon King, were assigned to Companies A and D and may have been a part of this dangerous mission. That evening, the 102d, with one section of artillery, remained at the front, providing cover while the rest of the Union Army moved out. The regiment then helped to remove wounded men to the rear. The 102d also participated in a number of skirmishes, including those at Salkehatchie, South Carolina, on February 9, 1865; Bradford Springs, South Carolina, on April 18, 1865; and Swifts Creek, South Carolina, the following day.[3]

Buxtonians also served in other units. William Hooper, originally from Kentucky, enlisted as a substitute for one year in November 1864 in Toledo, Ohio. He served with the 14th USCT. James Harlin Newby enlisted in the 3d USCT, a heavy artillery unit. The Newby family were free blacks who sold their eighty-acre farm in Orange County, Indiana, to come to Buxton, settling there only about a year before James enlisted. Newby served for three years as a sergeant in Company I, participating in the siege of Fort Wagner and Battery Gregg, Morris Island, South Carolina, and helped to capture several forts in and around Charleston. Anderson Abbott and Jerome Riley, both surgeons, arrived in Washington, D.C., in the summer of 1863 to become part of the founding staff of the Freedmen's Hospital. During the winter of 1863 Abbott was honored with an invitation to attend a reception at the White House, where he was received by President Abraham Lincoln, an event newsworthy enough to appear in the *Washington Star*.[4]

Buxton was fortunate in that none of its young men were killed in action during the course of the war. At least one Buxtonian did, however, die while in the service. Benjamin Matthews, who mustered into the 102d USCT in September 1863 as a corporal in Company A, fell seriously ill before the regiment left for the theater of war. "In consequence of severe cold contracted in their temporary quarters," Matthews was hospitalized in December.[5] In early January his father arrived from Buxton and obtained a furlough for Benjamin, conveying him to Buxton to recover, but he died of consumption in January 1864 and never returned to his regiment. Another Buxton soldier, William Richardson, died in 1865 of consumption contracted while in the service.[6]

Pension records reveal that many former soldiers suffered ailments related to their time in the military. For example, William Hooper's application for an invalid pension notes "chronic rheumatism of service origin" from exposure and hardship. Likewise, Lorenzo Rann applied for invalid benefits in 1891, claiming permanent disability caused by chronic diarrhea, rheumatism, and back pain. Rann had been discharged from service at Beaufort, South Carolina, in June 1865 for disability after an extended hospital stay. From his return to Buxton after the war until his death in 1928, James Newby suffered from injuries and poor eyesight, both a result of his wartime service. Solomon King left the army in "very delicate health, with a persistent cough, haggard looking, not able to work much after the war."[7] From the time of his mustering out until his death sixteen years later, he was weak and sickly, never recovering his health.[8]

The Civil War's impact on the community at Buxton ranged far beyond the battlefield. The war years did not provide Buxton with growth or prosperity. The absence of men serving the Union cause resulted in hardships for their families. Emigration of blacks from the United States virtually ceased, depriving Buxton of new settlers to replace those who were departing. The Raleigh Township Assessment Rolls for the years between 1861 and 1866 reveal an increase in the number of absentee landowners and abandoned properties, signs of a community under stress. Despite such deprivations during the war years, community life persevered. Buxton's churches and schools remained open and continued to provide unifying points for the community; crops were planted and harvested; family members cared for each other; and neighbors helped those in need. A core of landholding families remained in Buxton, providing continuity and stability that signified an ongoing sense of permanence and place that helped see Buxton through those difficult years. Although the community struggled, it did not collapse.[9]

The Buxton community suffered other hardships during the 1860s and 1870s. An 1865 fire took the lives of four of the Grice children. Typhoid and consumption outbreaks resulted in the deaths of three Cronan children in 1866 and two more from the same family in 1870. An outbreak of smallpox occurred in 1866 when a Union soldier returned to Buxton with the disease. The settlers successfully fought a full-fledged smallpox epidemic, suffering eighteen cases but only one fatality, a fourteen-year-old boy. In 1882 fourteen people, mostly teenagers, succumbed to a typhus outbreak. Buxton was no stranger to tragedy, but its residents survived these and other calamities.[10]

Buxton was not the only black community transformed over the course of the Civil War era. Brooklyn, New Philadelphia, and the Beech and Roberts settlements experienced change during the 1860s and 1870s, each in its own way. In contrast to Buxton, the black population of Brooklyn grew from one hundred nineteen in 1870 to two hundred eighteen in 1880 as newly freed persons who wished to leave the South streamed into the area. Unlike pre–Civil War years, blacks fleeing slavery did not have to leave the nation of their birth. Likewise, New Philadelphia experienced its period of greatest growth during the war years. Black migration, not only from the South but also from the West, principally Missouri, contributed, although only briefly, to an increase in the town's population. Unfortunately, New Philadelphia as a town did not survive. In 1869, when the railroad came through Pike County, it bypassed New Philadelphia by a mile, and other towns springing up along the line killed the black town. New Philadelphia was not strong enough to withstand the postwar changes. Meanwhile, as in Buxton, both the size and population of the Beech community grew progressively smaller after 1870. The situation was direr at the Beech settlement, where fewer than half a dozen families remained by the mid-1920s. Other black communities experienced outmigration of young men and women seeking opportunities in surrounding towns and cities.[11]

Contact between Buxton residents and other blacks increased during the Civil War as service in the military exposed Buxtonians to new places and new people. For those born and raised in Canada, the war provided a more intimate acquaintance with the United States. Some lasting ties developed. These influences did not necessarily affect Buxton positively. Not all the men who left Buxton to enlist in the Union army returned after the war. Solomon King, for one, chose not to return to the community where he had been raised, remaining instead in Charleston, South Carolina, after his discharge. He met and married Sarah Richardson in 1867 and lived there until his death in 1881. Many other Buxton men who had gone off to assist the Union in its fight against the South returned to Buxton after their service was completed. James Newby returned shortly after his discharge at Jacksonville, Florida. He later married Eliza Rann, and the couple raised six children and lived in Buxton until James and Eliza died in 1928 and 1932, respectively.[12]

Buxton did not endure a continuing downward spiral during the 1860s. Some additions to the community did occur during the war years. Unlike the 1850s, when many of its residents came from the United States, more families relocated to Buxton from other parts of Canada. George Cromwell and his family came from Huron County. The Zebbs, Travises, Hardings, and Mooreheads, all related, journeyed from Wellington. The Morrises and Smiths came from nearby West Tilbury, and the Emmanuels arrived from Gray County. William Robbins and his family left the Dawn settlement to resettle in Buxton. Ohio-born William Parker Walker came to live in Buxton after the Civil War. His mother Ann, a runaway slave, had sought haven in Ohio before moving to Buxton with her husband, George Walker, a few years before William joined them. Abel Cockfield came to Buxton in 1872 from British Guyana. Cockfield studied Latin under William King and later became the village teacher. Arrival rates had dropped precipitously from the previous decade, however, and did not offset those who left. Nonetheless, some of the newly arrived families became longtime residents of Buxton and did much to shape its postwar identity. The Cromwell, Harding, Robbins, Zebb, and Travis families maintained their presences at Buxton well into the twentieth century.[13]

Newer arrivals established relationships that furthered the interlocking community that characterized Buxton. James Tyson Robbins, who came to Buxton during the 1870s from the Dresden area, married Elizabeth Travis, the oldest daughter of John and Mary Travis, who had settled in Buxton during the 1860s. James's brothers Joseph, Archibald, and John came to Buxton during the 1870s and were subsequently joined by their parents and at least one of their sisters.[14] The infusion of energy from these and other newcomers over the years helped Buxton survive, if only in that younger residents might have been more inclined to remain in the area than would have been the case without the arrival of new blood. A decline in black newcomers would understandably have contributed to a social and economic malaise in the community.

The foundations established in the 1850s were firm enough to keep the community at Buxton going in the face of outside challenges and opportunities during the ensuing two decades. As the Civil War drew to a close, stories of cheap available land in the U.S. South reached Buxton, enticing many of its residents to consider returning to the land they had previously fled. Buxtonians conceived the idea of transplanting their settlement in its entirety to the southern United States. After several community meetings and much discussion, Buxtonians drew up a plan in which they proposed to purchase a large block of land somewhere in the South and then to re-create Buxton there, just as in Canada, with small individual farms and a village centered on a school, church, and various businesses. Buxton residents asked William King to serve as their representative and travel to Washington, D.C., to approach the federal government with the plan and to inquire about its feasibility.[15]

The settlers' proposal received mixed reactions. Several considerations recommended the idea. First, many Buxton residents had paid for their land in its entirety during the preceding decade and now had clear title to it, with equity estimated at between one thousand and twelve hundred dollars per fifty-acre lot. Second, Buxtonians were experienced in the problems of community building and would be prepared for many of the inevitable difficulties such a scheme would encounter. Finally, one of the settlement's initial goals had been to have Buxton settlers impart their moral, spiritual, and intellectual growth to other blacks. Their plan to go south would be a step toward fulfilling that goal.

Other factors worked against the proposed move. The end of the Civil War brought peace, the end of slavery, and the downfall of the plantation South. It also brought political and social turmoil. In numerous ways, the postbellum U.S. South was unstable. Slavery had been abolished, but the freedpeople's political, economic, and social future remained ambiguous. A great many issues lay unresolved in 1865. Had the Union victory really toppled the aristocracy of the planting, slaveholding elite? If so, who would rule the postbellum South, and what would be the new rulers' objectives? What benefits could be offered by a South devastated physically, agriculturally, and economically? Armed with such questions, King took the Buxtonians' proposal to Washington in fall 1865. After meeting with Secretary of State William Seward and Major General O. O. Howard, head of the Freedman's Bureau, men who had good knowledge of the current situation in the South, King returned to Buxton with a recommendation against relocating the settlement. After listening to the arguments, which included the unavailability of large blocks of land, the prevalence of white prejudice, and the uncertainty of the former slaves' legal status, Buxton residents decided not to pursue the matter any further. King did, however, encourage Buxtonians, especially young adults, to go south, arguing that those now educated could go and give instruction to "their brethren in ignorance."[16]

Though not specifically presented as a reason, another explanation for Howard's and other Washington officials' reluctance to endorse the idea of perhaps hundreds of blacks resettling en masse in the South may have been the experience of contraband camps in the District of Columbia and elsewhere during and after the war. Freedman's Village, located on the Arlington Estate, formerly the home of Robert E. Lee, was the largest and longest-lasting of these camps. Established as a temporary camp in May 1863 for black war refugees, Freedman's Village lasted for almost thirty years. What began as merely a tent camp quickly grew into a community, complete with wooden homes housing two to four families each, churches, schools enrolling as many as nine hundred students, an industrial training center teaching blacksmithing, carpentry, shoemaking, and tailoring skills, a hospital, and homes for the aged and infirm.[17]

Initially run by the War Department, the Freedman's Village later fell under the jurisdiction of the Freedman's Bureau. The camp community was intended to create a climate of order, sobriety, and industry with the goal of helping freedmen on their journey from slavery and dependency to freedom and self-sufficiency. Refugees were expected to learn a vocation, receive a basic education, and then leave to find work and lead a productive life elsewhere. The American Tract Society, a charitable religious organization based in Boston, helped to run the village. The society erected a chapel by the end of 1863 and opened the first school there. Assistance was also provided from various other relief organizations. Residents of the Freedman's Village were under military rule. In exchange for military protection, often from their former owners, residents gave up some of their independence. Social order, in the eyes of the military authorities who controlled the village, demanded strict oversight. In comparison with the military rule at Freedman's Village, the Elgin Association rules regulating settlement and housing appear benign. Freedman's Village residents chafed under military discipline to the point where some residents felt that life in the village was little different than slavery. Unlike Buxton, the residents of Freedman's Village had no legal claim to the land they lived on.[18]

Washington officials may have feared that the Buxtonians' resettlement proposal would result in nothing more than another camp for blacks. Some viewed the contraband camps as a failed experiment and may have feared the resettlement plan of perhaps hundreds of blacks as doomed to failure with the settlers ultimately seeking protection and assistance from the government. On the other hand, many whites may have felt threatened by a proposal such as that of the Buxtonians, fearing perhaps the potential power a group of black landowners could garner if provided such an opportunity.

Although the proposed resettlement plan came to naught, a number of Buxton residents decided to return to the United States on their own or with their families. Various motivations—including personal ambition, homesickness, and the chance to do something positive for newly liberated blacks—played a role in individual decisions to relocate. Many Buxtonians were caught up in the widespread belief that the United States had, in the war's immediate aftermath, crossed a new threshold, with improved race relations on the horizon. They excitedly joined others in returning to the land they or their parents had fled out of frustration, fear, or disillusionment. They may have embraced James Rapier's exaltation "the year of jubilee has come, return you exiles, home."[19] Little direct evidence exists of why specific individuals chose to remain in Buxton or seek their future elsewhere, but a number of reasons may be suggested. Economic motivations presumably loomed large, as did family ties and bonds of kinship and community. Leaving Buxton for distant places meant severance from the familial, communal way of life of the community, a lifestyle that would not easily be found elsewhere. The lure of city life entranced those seeking adventure but was countered by a reluctance to abandon the distinct way of life that had developed in Buxton's agricultural community.[20]

Many of the men and women who left Buxton contributed positively to Reconstruction as ministers, teachers, lawyers, doctors, and politicians. Among them were John Riley, who served as a minister in Louisville, and his brother, Jerome, who worked as a doctor at the Freedmen's Hospital in Washington. Jerome would later settle in Pine Bluff, Arkansas, where he practiced medicine and served as the county coroner. Anderson Abbott also took a position at the Freedmen's Hospital in Washington, but he resigned in April 1866 to return to

Canada.[21] John Rapier Jr. continued working as a surgeon at the Freedmen's Hospital until his sudden death in May 1866. Abraham Shadd practiced law in New Orleans, and Sarah Thomas held a teaching position in a Mississippi school for former slaves. Thomas Stringer became general superintendent of the African Methodist Episcopal Church in Mississippi and established thirty-five churches in that state as well as a Masonic Lodge in Vicksburg. The 1869 Home Mission report, presented to the Presbyterian Church of Canada Synod, detailed the activity of some former Buxton residents: "one . . . is now preaching in Kansas and superintending a large Sabbath school of freedmen. . . . [A]nother writes from Missouri and states that he is teaching a large school of freedmen. . . . [A] female is teaching in Louisville, Kentucky . . . and another was lately conducting a large school for freedmen in Washington."[22] Others who chose to leave Buxton journeyed to Indiana, Michigan, Kansas, and Nebraska and established new homesteads. Equity from land in Buxton provided mobility for those who eventually went elsewhere.[23]

Of Buxton residents, James Rapier reaped the most success in the aftermath of the Civil War. Rapier returned to the South in 1864, finding temporary employment in Union-occupied Nashville as a reporter for a northern-based newspaper. After the war, he moved to Maury, Tennessee, where he rented two hundred acres of land. Discouraged by the direction of Reconstruction in Tennessee, Rapier returned to his native Alabama, where he rented more than five hundred acres of land from William Coffee, a former planter and slave owner. While in Alabama, Rapier became active in politics, serving as a delegate to a black convention held in Nashville where, in an address to the delegation, he called for equal rights and the vote. His ideas were later published in the *Nashville Daily Press and Times.* Rapier served as one of eighteen black members of Alabama's 1867 state constitutional convention. As chair of the platform committee, he helped to draft a document that called for free speech, free press, free schools, and equal rights for all men. Two years later, Rapier traveled to Washington as the lone Alabama representative to the National Negro Labor Union Convention. He was elected vice president of the union, and in his new role he received the twin honors of addressing Congress and meeting with President Ulysses S. Grant.[24]

In April 1871 Grant appointed Rapier assessor for the Second Alabama Revenue District, making him the first black man in the state to obtain such a high patronage position. The height of Rapier's political career came in 1873, when he was elected to the Forty-third U.S. Congress. Congressman Rapier helped push through legislation making Montgomery, Alabama, a port of delivery, proposed a bill to improve public education in the South, and delivered an eloquent address in support of what became the 1875 Civil Rights Law.[25]

As Reconstruction waned, so too did Rapier's political career. He was defeated in his 1874 and 1876 bids to retain his congressional seat. His defeat did not, however, signal an end to his political career. Rapier was appointed collector of internal revenue for the U.S. Treasury Department in 1878, a position he held until his death from pulmonary tuberculosis in May 1883. Remaining a political activist, Rapier supported the former slaves' struggle for political rights, economic opportunity, and social equality. He retained title to his family's Buxton lands until the mid-1870s, perhaps signaling his reluctance to sever the last ties with the community of which he had once been a part.[26]

Not all those residents who left the Elgin tract went to the United States. Some, including the Cooper family, departed for other areas of Canada, many in the nearby vicinity. The Cooper patriarch and matriarch, Ezekiel and Louisa Cooper, settled in Buxton in 1852 after having left Maryland with their three children, Ezekiel C., Elizabeth, and Thomas. While Ezekiel and Louisa lived out the rest of their lives on their fifty acres in the northern section of the Elgin tract, by 1871 the younger Ezekiel had moved with his wife, Lydia, to Chatham, where he ran a grocery. The couple remained in Chatham for approximately fifteen years before heading to San Francisco, where Ezekiel died in 1910. Henry K. Thomas gave up farming three years after the war and moved to Windsor, Ontario, where, returning to his previous profession, he opened a barbershop. In 1870 he, his wife Maria, and at least one of their children, Richard, headed back to the United States. They settled in Bovina, Mississippi, about ten miles outside Vicksburg where they opened a boardinghouse. In 1873 Henry became a justice of the peace and was the postmaster by 1880. His wife worked as a cook and Richard taught in a local school.[27]

After resigning his position at the Freedmen's Hospital in Washington, Anderson Abbott returned to Canada and married Mary Ann Casey. They set up residence in Chatham, and he opened a medical practice. Abbott became a pillar of the black community, serving on numerous boards, including those of the Chatham Collegiate Institute and the Wilberforce Educational Institute, of which he was president from 1873 to 1880. He served as president of the Kent County Medical Society in 1878 and became the first president of the Chatham Literary and Debating Society. He also served as the associate editor of the *Missionary Messenger,* published by the British Methodist Episcopal Church, and became one of Kent County's first coroners. Alfred Lafferty returned to the Buxton area as well. Living in Chatham, he held the post of principal of the Wilberforce Educational Institute from 1875 to 1882. He too was an active member of the Literary and Debating Society and a member of the Masonic lodge. He became a lawyer in 1886 and practiced in Chatham, which came to attract Buxtonians who elected not to farm but wanted to remain in the area. Alfred Shadd became a doctor and settled in Saskatchewan, later teaching school in Kinistino and breeding cattle before his death in 1915 in Winnipeg.[28]

The movement out of Buxton of which these, and other, individuals were a part did not constitute a mass exodus. Between 1861 and 1871, the settlement's black population declined only slightly from seven hundred to just under six hundred fifty, certainly not a devastating or unrecoverable loss. Census records show many antebellum surnames persisting well past 1861, including Brodie, Cooper, Cronan, Dabney, Due [Doo], Freeman, Hatter, Hooper, Jacobs, Lightfoot, Newby, Parker, Prince, Riley, Robinson, Rue, Scipio, Shadd, Shrieves, Thomas, Thompson, Toyer, and Washington. As with Canada's black population as a whole, the Civil War shook but did not destroy the Buxton settlement. Rather than an exodus, a slow, steady decline in population occurred through the 1880s; by the end of that decade, only a minority, albeit a significant one, of Buxton's original families remained on the Elgin tract. In a broader context, Buxton's experiences formed part of a larger postbellum pattern when black Canadians, by birth or as fugitives, moved to reclaim ancestral soil, to rebuild their families, and to assist in the work of reconstructing the lives of the ex-slaves. This phenomenon constituted a reversal of the pattern evidenced over the previous half-century.[29]

Many Buxtonians who left the community did not leave until the mid- to late 1870s. Isaac and Catherine Riley moved to Nebraska, but not until after their daughter, Ann, married William J. Robinson in 1876. Kincheon Brooks resided in Richmond, Indiana, by 1890. Edward Kersey had likewise left Buxton by 1890, resettling in Kalamazoo, Michigan. William Richardson moved to Cass County, Michigan. Some gave up rural life and chose to settle in urban areas: Benjamin Brooks resided in Detroit during at least part of the 1880s and was living in Chicago by 1896. Lorenzo Rann returned to Buxton after his discharge from the army in 1865 and married his first wife, Lucinda, who died of consumption in Buxton in 1869. Lorenzo Rann remained in Buxton at least through 1872, when records show that he married Dorothy Ward at the local British Methodist Episcopal Church. His request for an invalid pension in 1890 shows that he was then living in Michigan; within a few years, he was placed in an Old Soldiers' Home, where he remained until his death in 1922. Another veteran, Kincheon Brooks, was living in the U.S. National Military Home in Dayton, Ohio, by 1901.[30]

Other Buxtonians, some long-standing members of the community and others newer arrivals, left the area in the 1870s. This suggests that the "exodus" often portrayed by previous scholars was not necessarily triggered by the Civil War and emancipation in the United States or at least that Buxtonians did not become eager to leave Buxton and Canada until the tumult of the Civil War and Reconstruction had settled. Alternatively, it may suggest that the outmigration had to do with Buxton's economic and social situation. Men such as Richardson and Kersey may have been seeking out more fertile farmlands. Civil War veterans such as Rann and Brooks may have had physical needs that could only be supplied by the U.S. government in soldiers' homes.

Some Buxtonians who left the community during or after the Civil War later returned. William Hooper came back to Buxton after his discharge from the army, married Senneth Burns in August 1866, and resided in Buxton until at least 1867, when the couple's son, James, was born. For unknown reasons, they subsequently moved to Detroit for a time, but the family was back in Buxton by 1874, when James was baptized by Rev. King at St. Andrew's Church. They remained in Buxton for the rest of their lives, and both William and Senneth are buried in the Methodist church cemetery in North Buxton. Harriet Rhue, daughter of fugitive slaves William Isaac Rhue and Serena Lewis, left Buxton to teach at a school in Kentucky, returning to Buxton ten years later and marrying Millard Hatchett. She taught school at Buxton for many years and lived there until her death.[31]

Some residents moved away but maintained connections to Buxton. Ezekiel C. and Lydia Cooper had at least two children born to them while living in Chatham, one in 1869 and the other in 1870. Both children were baptized in Buxton by Rev. King. Although John and Rebecca Carter lived outside Buxton by 1870, their son, James, married Catherine Morris at St. Andrew's Church in 1873. Another indication of community ties continuing can be seen in the register of marriages officiated at Buxton. Anderson Abbott, then residing in Toronto, returned to Buxton in fall 1871 to serve as a witness to the marriage of William Carter and Pricilla Hatter, both of whose families were longtime residents of the settlement.[32]

Outmigration did not decimate Buxton but did alter it significantly. One of the transformations was the nature of the residents. Buxton had been founded and developed as an all-black community with an emphasis on fugitives, but emancipation ended the need for a haven from slavery. Many members of Buxton's postwar population had been slaves, but they were no longer fugitives in need of a haven from their masters or others. A major change in Buxton's population that began in the 1860s was an influx of white settlers as land in the Elgin tract became available to them when the ten-year ban on white land purchases expired. At the end of the decade, blacks still constituted the bulk of Buxton's population and controlled most of the land, but white numbers were increasing. Whites were also acquiring larger individual plots of land than their black neighbors owned. Local tax assessment rolls reveal that in 1872, 50 percent of the blacks owned fewer than fifty acres of land, whereas only 33 percent of white residents owned such small plots. This marks a notable distinction from the previous decade. At least some of this decline in the amount of land held by individual blacks was the result of subdivision of property within a family. Many of Buxton's pre–Civil War residents had taken up the fifty-acre minimum required by the Elgin Association, dividing it among family members as needed when children came of age. As is typical in maturing communities, the first-generation farms were transformed into smaller holdings through inheritance and sale to create farming operations for younger family members. Furthermore, the phenomenon of renting increased in Buxton, particularly among its black residents. Almost one-fifth of Buxton's 1872 black population were renters, a dramatic change from the 1850s, when renting land had been prohibited. Farm tenancy rates rose in part because some young farmers were unable to purchase land either because they lacked funds or because land for purchase was unavailable, and they chose to rent rather than abandon Buxton.[33]

Other related changes, damaging but not necessarily devastating, took place in Buxton during the 1860s and 1870s. One was religious life. The population decline curtailed the strength of local churches. Buxton's ministers found it increasingly difficult to earn a comfortable salary, and church property depreciated in value. By 1874 the Union Baptist Church on the twelfth concession and the Anti-Slavery Baptist Church on the corner of the seventh concession had closed. Also hard hit was St. Andrew's Church, still headed by the Reverend King, now in his seventies. As early as 1876 the elders of St. Andrew's reported that Sabbath service attendance had profoundly declined and that prayer meetings were not well attended. The problem became acute by the 1880s. The settlement's population loss does not provide the only reason for this drop. One alternative explanation for the deterioration of St. Andrew's popularity among black Buxtonians is that, with the end of Buxton's settlement status and with more residents less beholden to King, blacks felt freer to express religious choice by leaving the Presbyterian Church in favor of other denominations. It is surprising that St. Andrew's apparently did not benefit significantly from the influx of white settlers to the area. According to the 1881 census, whites residing on division 3 of Raleigh Township (the same division as the Elgin tract) were fairly evenly split between the Church of England, the Methodist Church, and the Presbyterian Church.[34]

The 1881 census provides evidence supporting the shift away from the Presbyterian Church by black residents of the Buxton area. Only twenty-two families or individuals were recorded as Presbyterians. The Baptist congregations had declined as well, with only thirty-four families or individuals affiliated with this denomination. A noticeable shift toward Methodism had occurred, with ninety-eight families or individuals claiming that affiliation. Methodism thus increased its popularity among black residents primarily at the expense of the Presbyterian faith. Incidentally, at least one black family was Roman Catholic, with seven others listed as "R. Papt." another possible indicator of Roman Catholicism.[35]

Another sign of the decline was that in 1880 the Presbyterian Church of Canada discontinued the Buxton Mission Fund, which no longer seemed necessary as a consequence of Buxton's demographic shifts, the increased popularity of the Methodist and Baptist denominations, and the merging of the Buxton Mission School with the district public schools. The perception that Buxton residents were no longer a people in need of special treatment also played a role in the fund's termination. William King retired as the minister of St. Andrew's soon thereafter. The Presbytery of Chatham initially provided a replacement, the Reverend John Cairns, but after 1883 no permanent minister was available to the congregation of St. Andrew's. Instead, theological students were sent to Buxton, creating problems similar in nature to those that earlier plagued the mission school. By 1888 St. Andrew's was at the brink of dissolution. Although it would survive, it never regained its earlier prominence.[36]

After the death of his second wife, Jemima, in 1887, King moved to Chatham. He may have wanted to retire completely—from farming, preaching and ministry work, and his work with blacks—although his move did not result in a complete end to his work or social schedule. King continued to make missionary calls throughout the settlement and regularly visited old friends, especially Robin Phares. King's move to Chatham may also have resulted from a personal need to remove himself from the church and settlement to which he had dedicated so much of his life. He apparently refused to move from his home in Buxton while Jemima, who was mentally unstable, was alive, and her death may have served as a catalyst for change in King's life.[37] After his move, King sometimes preached at the First Presbyterian Church in Chatham. He remained active in the church in other ways, attending his last conference in 1893, when he traveled to Toronto for the Pan-Presbyterian Council. He even returned to Ohio in 1893 for a King family reunion, during which he delivered what was to be his last sermon. Bedridden for more than a year, William King died on January 5, 1895. His death was mourned throughout the Buxton area. Hailed as a hero to the black people to whom he dedicated so much of his adult life, most people had forgotten that he was once a master of slaves. Perhaps a telling testament to his impact was the fact that several Buxtonians honored him by naming their children after him or his family. Senneth and William Hooper named their firstborn Theophilus, presumably in honor of King's deceased child. Isaac and Catherine Riley named one of their sons, born in Buxton in the mid-1850s, William King Riley. One of their sons, John Riley, also had a son whom he named William K.[38]

The community at Buxton underwent other transformations over the years. A change that had begun during the early 1860s and that continued afterward was a shift of settlers to the northern end of the settlement. Numerous families relocated as land opened up, either from people moving out of the area or because the Elgin Association's stipulation of a fifty-acre minimum land purchase had been lifted and subdivisions of lots now occurred. Various factors motivated this population shift. The northern part of the Elgin Tract was closer to Chatham and additional employment opportunities. The land was of better quality, not as prone to water damage and better drained than the southern section. The Canada Southern Railroad passed through the northern part of the Elgin tract by 1872, bringing many jobs with it, first in its building and then in its maintenance. This population shift resulted in the creation of North Buxton. In 1874 Enos and Sarah Johnson, longtime Buxtonians, set aside a portion of their land on the eighth concession, consisting of lots 9 and 10, for the hamlet of North Buxton. White families in turn began to settle in the now open southern sections of the former Elgin reserve.

North Buxton soon took on the characteristics of a village center, incorporating existing structures and businesses while attracting new ones. The oldest building in North Buxton, predating the hamlet's incorporation, is School #13, built between 1861 and 1863. It still stands today and is currently undergoing restoration. Bethel Methodist Church, also in existence before North Buxton was officially formed, is an example of old and new Buxtonians coming together. A church building was constructed on land formerly owned by Jacob and Hannah Gunn, longtime Buxton residents, with the labor of older residents such as old-timer John Kersey and newer arrivals such as John Travis and Joshua Emmanuel. The new structure replaced the little log church where Thomas Stringer had first preached. Mount Carmel #10 Lodge Hall, a Prince Hall Freemason lodge, had been established in 1866 on Green Doo's land; some of its early trustees were Abraham D. Shadd, his son Garrison, William Parker, and Green Doo. After North Buxton's incorporation, a post office and other businesses joined the businesses already there: a tavern/hotel, blacksmith shops, sawmill and gristmill, carpenters, shoemakers, and a barbershop.[39]

When the Canada Southern Railroad opened a station, jobs opened for many of Buxton's men, who became section hands in charge of inspecting and maintaining the railroad bed. Millard Hatchett became the railroad's first black foreman. The railroad and the station also were responsible for the growth of several small businesses in North Buxton, including coal sales; grain, pig, and cattle shipping; and passenger service.[40]

North Buxton had a notably higher level of white involvement than the older Buxton settlement. Whereas most white businessmen had been mainly excluded before the 1860s, they would play an integral but not dominant role in the development of North Buxton. Alongside black artisans John Kersey, who ran a sawmill, blacksmith James Miller, miller Isaac Shadd, barber Archibald Smith, and Prince Chase, a stonecutter, worked with such white tradesmen as blacksmith John Watkins and carpenters William Moore and Governor McSpaden. North Buxton's interracial collaboration can further be seen in the town's early merchants and storekeepers. Some black merchants were Frederick Griffin, Robert Allen, Elbert Dyke, George Charleston, James Dabney, George Shreve, and

William Shadd and his son, Ira, while merchants David Taylor, Richard Cole-
man, and Angus McPhee were white. Elbert Dyke opened the first post office
in North Buxton in 1875, and most of North Buxton's subsequent postmasters
were black, including William Parker Walker, Charleston, and Shreve. As time
passed, the once unified Buxton community became divided into North and
South Buxton, with blacks dominating North Buxton and more whites residing
in South Buxton, a pattern that continued through the twentieth century.[41]

The St. Andrew's Church marriage register provides another indication of ongoing interracial cooperation in the larger Buxton community. During the 1860s
and 1870s, blacks and whites served as witnesses to each other's marriages. When
King Bruce and Rose Black, both white members of St. Andrew's congregation,
married in January 1865, Ezekiel Cooper stood up for the couple. Cooper also
served as a witness to the exchange of marital vows between Harvey Wilkison
and Ellen Smith, both black residents of Buxton, as did Archibald McKellar,
a long-standing white supporter of the settlement. Robert VanRankin served
as a witness to the January 1872 wedding of a white couple, Samuel Smith and
Margaret McNeil.[42]

Furthermore, in 1881 at least nine interracial couples lived in Buxton or in the
immediate vicinity, indicating the community's continued acceptance of such
relationships. Only two of those couples, Isaac and Elizabeth Washington and
Charles and Nancy Watts, had been living in Buxton since before 1861. William
and Catherine Moorehead, William and Frances Wright, and possibly John and
Catherine Morris had settled in the area by the time of the 1871 census.[43] Several
of these biracial families likely lived somewhere in Canada before coming to
Buxton. Peter Pool, a black, was born in the United States, while his wife, Ann,
was born in Ireland, and they probably relocated to the Buxton area between
1871 and 1881. Charles Muhan, an Irishman, was born in the United States, but
his African-descended wife, Hester, and their two children were born in Ontario, and so the couple had resided in Canada at least since 1877. The remaining
two families—those of Abraham and Jannett Sage and John and Ametta Willson—also seem to have roots in Canada predating 1881, when they are known
to have been living in Buxton. Abraham Sage was a black from the West Indies,
while Jannett was born in Scotland; however, their son, Robert, age twelve in
1881, was born in Ontario. African American John Willson married the English-
born Ametta, and then had five children born in Ontario, the earliest in about
1865.[44]

Yet another change facing the settlement was the demise of the Elgin Association. In 1873, the stockholders closed the business's books and dissolved the
corporation. Many factors played a role in this decision, most prominent among
them that the initial objectives for the establishment of the settlement and hence
the association had either been accomplished or were no longer relevant. In

short, the association's leaders reasoned that the settlement no longer needed to be a separate entity. Its twenty-three years of existence had given the Elgin Association a much longer lifespan than King had originally intended—he had thought that the association would be needed for no longer than ten years, the time required to settle the lands. The association's demise did not mean the end of Buxton. In a way, Buxton's survival symbolized the ultimate fulfillment of the experiment's objectives. The settlement had metamorphosed into a community, no longer needing the association's artificial support. Buxton residents had completed the process of community formation. They had carved out a common space, formed key social networks, and built core institutions.

The closure of the Elgin Association signaled the beginning of reflection on the settlement's achievements and failures, first by contemporaries and later by historians. Few observers, then or now, refer to Buxton as an unqualified success. Buxton's inhabitants did not gain great material wealth. Nor did the land live up to King's and others' initial lofty expectations. The settlement certainly did not achieve agricultural prosperity, as continual crop failures and drainage problems show. And Buxton's industrial sector failed to bring affluence to the community. The sawmill and gristmill ended up managed by outsiders and ultimately failed; the pearl ash and potash ventures closed amid financial stress; neither the store nor the hotel made its owners prosperous; and other businesses (such as the brick making, shoemaking, coopering, and blacksmithing enterprises) remained small and localized.

Lackluster economic performance should not necessarily signal failure on a general level, however. The settlement's objectives did not, after all, include wealth but encompassed improvement and self-reliance. And, in most cases, Buxton's residents were better off than they had previously been, whether in slavery or freedom. Though poor, the residents prided themselves on their community history and their hard-won relative economic independence. Buxtonians did not rely on outside assistance for their material support. They maintained an independent lifestyle, sustaining themselves and their families. They cleared their land, built houses for their families, and planted and harvested crops for sustenance. The settlers generally achieved self-sufficiency, "supporting themselves in all material circumstances."[45] One contemporary observer noted that in the community there were "signs of industry and thrift and comfort everywhere; signs of intemperance, of idleness, of want nowhere."[46]

In contrast to its economic aspects, the settlement's spiritual and intellectual life flourished. Buxtonians' religious life was vibrant and extensive, with four churches of different denominations organized during the settlement's first decade. Regardless of their religious affiliations, Buxton residents were active spiritually, maintaining their churches and ministering to the local community. Religion contributed greatly to the community as a whole in that religious activity provided support for community building and collective strength. Likewise, the settlement's educational component was dynamic: A majority of the community's school-age children learned basic educational skills, and many undertook classical studies in preparation for a college education. Perhaps the crowning glory was that local whites thought highly enough of Buxton's schools—specifically the Buxton Mission School—to send their children to learn side by side with blacks. Generally speaking, then, those blacks who settled in Buxton improved themselves spiritually and educationally. Buxton achieved its goal of enabling blacks to elevate their moral, religious, and educational condition. Buxton fulfilled another of its missions by serving as a haven for both fugitive slaves and oppressed free blacks. Buxtonians successfully carved out a secure place for themselves. In an era of slavery, prejudice, social discrimination, and economic hardship, Buxton's residents proved their determination and implicitly that of other blacks to rise above the adversities and become independent and self-reliant.

One manner of assessing Buxton is to consider contemporaries' opinions. It is no surprise that King viewed Buxton as an unqualified success in that the settlement provided the "children of Africa" with the opportunity to improve the condition of their race. Buxton "demonstrated by actual experiment that the coloured men when placed in favourable circumstances were capable of supporting themselves and improving socially and morally the same as the white race."[47] In King's eyes, the Buxton experiment had been "a perfect success; there is no doubt about that."[48] King noted that by the late 1850s, the land had been settled and nearly paid for, families were living comfortably, and the settlers had cleared and drained the roads. Of course, King was biased toward the settlement to which he had devoted most of his adult life. Nevertheless, his observations were supported in fact. Members of the Presbyterian Church of Canada, similarly biased although with greater motivation for being skeptical, also believed that "the results of the experiment made by the Elgin Association proved satisfactory" and that "the coloured man . . . for thrift, sobriety, and the capacity of acquiring knowledge . . . is not behind the white population."[49]

Contemporaries not directly associated with the settlement itself or with the Presbyterian Church of Canada also had occasion to observe Buxton's development. During the 1850s, knowledge of and interest in Buxton spread through North American and British antislavery circles, bringing visitors to see how the settlement was faring. Their observations were in many cases published, primarily in antislavery periodicals, a phenomenon that may in itself indicate bias. Nevertheless, these visitors' reports help draw a clearer picture of Buxton's achievements and their meaning for the time. In its role as a proving ground for abolitionists who maintained that educating and Christianizing blacks would enable them to succeed, the Buxton settlement held significance beyond its immediate assistance to fugitives. Buxton attained an importance in the antislavery movement that was perhaps greater than its numbers warranted.

One such visitor was Samuel J. May, a Unitarian minister and abolitionist from Syracuse, New York, who traveled to Buxton during summer 1852, not quite three years after the settlement's founding. May's glowing report was published in the *National Anti-Slavery Society Standard,* the organ of the American Anti-Slavery Society. According to May, Buxton residents lived in "comfortable" log houses, and each family had "one to two acres of ground cleared [and] planted with potatoes, corn, and a variety of vegetables."[50] He commented on the community nature of the settlement, noting that in the advent of illness or other calamity, neighbors came together to plant crops, tend gardens, and feed families. May also wrote approvingly of the settlers' intellectual development, stating that the children were doing well in their schooling. He concluded that Buxton's blacks accepted the responsibilities of freedom and abided by the principle that able-bodied men must provide for themselves and their families These settlers' achievements gave him a "much deeper respect for this whole people than before."[51]

Thomas Henning, a onetime schoolteacher who became a journalist for the *Toronto Globe,* was "highly gratified" by what he saw during his 1855 tour of Buxton, particularly the "encouraging character" of the settlement and its development.[52] Yet he perhaps unintentionally qualified his estimate of the achievements of Buxton's blacks by stating that they proved that "under proper management, the black man is [as] capable of success . . . as the white one."[53] Henning continued to express his belief "that the social and moral habits of the Ethiopian, when properly directed, are not inferior in any respect to those of the European."[54] With such wording, Henning underscored his belief that blacks required white assistance to rise above the degradation that slavery had imposed. Such an attitude was common among contemporary whites. Both May's and Henning's judgments may have been influenced by their strong abolitionist sentiment and, in Henning's case, by the fact that he was a stockholder in the Elgin Association.

Perhaps a more objective visitor, in that he had no direct relation to the settlement and was not officially associated with an abolitionist society, was a representative from the *New York Tribune* who toured the settlement in 1857 and reported his impressions, which agreed substantially with those of May and Henning. The reporter wrote that the "general moral standard of the community is high," with drunkenness, bastardy, and crime virtually unknown.[55] The *Tribune* correspondent noted that those settlers who arrived in Buxton "accustomed to farming" and with some capital did "remarkably well."[56] Many had succeeded in clearing more land and making greater improvements than the "great majority" of local white settlers in similar circumstances. But, he contended, "those who . . . brought neither skill nor capital . . . had a much harder time."[57] Yet even those less fortunate were paying the annual installments on their lots. On the whole, the *Tribune* correspondent had gained a positive impression of the settlers at Buxton and, by extension, of the abilities of blacks once freed from bondage. Of course, if whites' opinion of blacks and their abilities were low—as they were in the mid-nineteenth century—then it stands to reason that any improvement would be taken as a marked rise.

Buxton received visitors from abroad as well. Three prominent Englishmen— Earl Spencer, Henry Christy, and John W. Probyn—toured the community in 1857. Returning to their homeland, the men wrote jointly to William King, praising him and the residents of Buxton for showing that by "practical demonstration . . . the coloured man, when placed in favourable circumstances, is able and willing to support himself."[58] Christy further noted that he believed that Buxton's blacks had made rapid progress "without assistance" from white people. In 1857 the Presbyterian Church of Ireland sent a deputation who visited the settlement and dined at the home of longtime Buxtonian Joseph Liason, leaving "well pleased with what they had seen."[59] Frederick Monod, a prominent French Reformed minister who came to Buxton with his son, Theodore, declared that the community gave "proof positive that all the oppressed coloured race required to raise them from degradation was a fair chance."[60]

The U.S. government was also interested in Buxton—in fact, officially interested. After President Abraham Lincoln's Emancipation Proclamation, Congress appointed a commission to investigate strategies to help former slaves in the South make the transition to freedom and self-reliance. One of the assignments of this American Freedmen's Inquiry Commission was to observe the condition of those American blacks who had sought asylum in Canada, had become British subjects, and were enjoying the rights and privileges of British citizens. Three members of the commission—Robert Delowe, James McKay, and Samuel G. Howe—visited Buxton in September 1863. After touring the settlement and conversing with many of its residents, they reported favorably to the U.S. government about the accomplishments of Buxton's fugitive and free blacks. In comparing Buxton to a colonization scheme that attempted to relocate blacks in Africa, the commission reported that "there is a most striking contrast between these exiles [in Buxton],—penniless, unaided, in a cold climate . . . and those who were sent, at great expense . . . to an African climate, then supported entirely for six months, and afterwards aided and bolstered up by a powerful society, which still expend a large sum for the support of the Colony. The first have succeeded; the latter have virtually failed."[61]

While acknowledging that Buxton and other such communities had met the goal of providing security, members of the Freedmen's Inquiry Commission questioned whether the ideal of self-determination had been equally met. Speaking in broad terms and not specifically referencing Buxton, the commission reported that "the discipline of the colonies, though it only subjects the Negroes to what is considered useful apprenticeship, does prolong a dependence which amounts to servitude; and does not convert them so surely into hardy, self-reliant men, as [does] the rude struggle with actual difficulties, which they have to face and to overcome, instead of doing so through an agent."[62] The committee may have been seeking to garner opposition to government assistance for former slaves. How much Buxton contributed to this statement, unfortunately, is not clear. Elsewhere in the report, however, Howe spoke highly of Buxton and its accomplishments. "Twenty years ago most of [the settlers] were slaves, who owned nothing, not even their children. Now they own themselves; they own their houses and farms; and they have their wives and children about them. They are enfranchised citizens of a government which protects their rights. . . . The present condition of all these colonists as compared with their former one is remarkable."[63]

Historians have generally been relatively critical of Buxton, particularly its post–Civil War years, which are usually described as a period of unrecoverable decline. William and Jane Pease present a somewhat mixed report on Buxton's success, calling it a success, but only in the short run: "In the long run Elgin failed; failed because it was an experiment in a vacuum. It trained no Negro to live among white men, but only to live a full and productive life among other Negroes."[64] This observation, however, fails to consider the totality of the Buxton experiment. Despite the settlement's residential segregation, extensive interracial interaction occurred in religious and educational institutions and social and business contexts. Buxton residents were protected from the abuse of whites during the first decade of settlement, when they were most vulnerable, but they were never entirely set apart from the world around them. The Buxton area of the postsettlement period proved blacks' ability to live within an interracial setting. Dr. Anderson R. Abbott, writing a report of the Buxton area in 1894, testified to the continued interracial nature of the town: "A large number of white settlers now occupy the land, but that makes no difference. The two classes work together on each other's farms, go to the same churches, their children attend the same schools, the teachers are white and coloured, and the pupils fraternize without any friction. . . . The various offices of the municipality . . . are fairly distributed among both classes."[65] Even if Abbott overstated the goodwill between the two races, a good working and living arrangement clearly existed. And so perhaps Buxton was more of a success than many have considered it.

Not all black communities could make such statements. Like Buxton, the Beech and Roberts settlements met the expectations of most of its residents, the majority of whom experienced economic self-sufficiency, access to schools and churches, and community stability. Meanwhile, other experiments in black community formation did not succeed. The Randolph experiment failed inasmuch as John Randolph's former slaves could not even settle as a unified community. A thriving black community of pioneers never developed at Timbucto as its creator, Gerrit Smith, had hoped. By 1848, two years after Smith offered deeds to more than two thousand blacks, fewer than thirty families had settled on the land. Eventually, about a hundred families managed to make the move to Timbucto, but a host of additional difficulties faced the settlers and plagued Smith's utopian dream. The wild state and generally poor quality of the land as well as the harsh climate of New York's Adirondacks prevented most settlers from raising enough crops to feed themselves and their families and generate enough money to pay their taxes, and consequently they faced foreclosure. Others fell prey to unscrupulous whites, who swindled the settlers of their land. Many such obstacles faced Buxton's pioneers, but they were more successful in conquering them—perhaps because of the presence and leadership of William King, the oversight and support of both the Elgin Association and the Presbyterian Church of Canada, or the strength of the community, which helped overcome individual difficulties.

The Gist settlers too failed to achieve true success, although that experiment was more successful than Timbucto. These failures were not necessarily the fault of the freedmen. In the Gist case, a great deal of money meant for Gist's slaves went to creditors and was drained by several lawsuits. The lack of adequate finances greatly contributed to the settlement's overall failure in that a viable, independent community did not develop. An 1883 history negatively summed up the experiment: "As a matter of course, they did not prosper. Some who were able returned to Virginia; others built rude huts and began to clear away the forest. What little money they had was soon spent. Scheming white men planned to get their personal property . . . and from various causes, they were reduced almost to pauperism. In later years their lands have been sold so that at present but few families remain as relics of this once large settlement."[66] Similar statements could be made about Dawn and Wilberforce.

Buxton and Brooklyn are among the handful of freedom villages organized by fugitive slaves and free blacks to survive into the twentieth and twenty-first centuries. And therein marks the success and strength of Buxton. Buxton has withstood the ultimate test of time, and the community has, to a large extent, preserved the cooperative way of life with which it began. Neither the Beech nor the Roberts settlement remains an active African American community, with fewer than half a dozen black farming families remaining at the Beech settlement by the 1920s, the last one departing in 1955. In the Roberts neighborhood, several hundred acres of land remained in the hands of families through the end of the twentieth century, but by the early 1930s the number of owners actively working the land dwindled to around half a dozen. They remained more or less stable for a generation and then dwindled further in the 1960s. This is not to say that the decline of these and other black settlements has meant an end to the black agricultural presence in areas where nineteenth-century black communities bloomed.[67]

At Buxton, the end of the nineteenth century saw a return of a practice William King had hoped to end. Many area residents, particularly those living outside the village, were farmers who sought employment elsewhere to enable them to either buy land or add to their existing property. One of these men was Arnold Watts, who worked as a Pullman porter in Detroit for a few years to save the necessary funds to buy a farm. He finally purchased a plot on the eighth concession of the old Elgin tract, living in a log cabin left over from the settlement days until he could afford to build a house of his own. In another reversal of the settlement days, many of Buxton's children were denied a high-school education because of lack of funds. Almost a complete generation of Buxton children were handicapped by this lack of a secondary education.[68]

Buxton men fought for Canada in World War I. Like their ancestors, they initially faced rejection because of their race, but the acute need for soldiers led to their acceptance by 1916. Some of Buxton's World War I soldiers were Harvey Travis, Charles and Arnold Black, Fred Parker, Robert Crosby, George Shreve, and Edward and Thomas Robbins (the last two died in the 1918 influenza epidemic). Like the rest of Canada and the world, the Buxton area suffered through the Great Depression during the 1930s, experiencing ruined crops, bank failures, and lost farms. In 1932–1933, prolonged drought and resulting dust storms caused massive crop failures in Buxton, in some cases causing longtime members of the community to lose their farms. The depression years were not entirely bleak ones nor devoid of community events. Many of Buxton's departed children returned home, for the community's rural setting helped it suffer less than urban areas did. In 1930 the young people of North Buxton formed the Dramatic Club to provide recreation and entertainment for the community. They put on plays and held dances throughout the depression. In 1933 club members built a hall that would be the center of many of the village's future social activities.[69]

Farm prices made a comeback during World War II, when farm labor was of equal importance with factory work and military service. Buxton men also found employment opportunities on the railroad during the war, since the increase in rail traffic necessitated more maintenance crews. Buxton also again contributed men as soldiers—in this case, roughly thirty during the war. Two men, Arthur Alexander Jr. and Lester Brown, were wounded on D-Day. Lawrence Brooks and Shirley Rhue lost their lives, and Edgar Shreve was captured and spent part of the war as a prisoner. The 1960s brought political advancement and sadness. In 1965 Garrison Shadd was elected as a Raleigh Township councillor and Earl Prince won a seat on the Raleigh Township School Board, but in December 1968, School #13, the last remaining school from the settlement years, closed its doors for the last time after 107 years of service to the community.[70]

Although the community today is still rural and agricultural, it experienced a dramatic change in the 1970s when many of the younger generation ventured beyond farming. As the rise of big farms took hold, the fifty-acre farms of the settlement years—many of which survived past World War II—became a thing of the past. Residents sought jobs elsewhere, many of them in the public service. As previously, many Buxtonians pursued a career in education. Buxton teachers found positions in both public and private high schools throughout Canada. Other young adults serviced the community in various ways. At least four medical secretaries worked in Chatham's hospitals, and other secretaries and technicians found positions all around Canada. And, for the first time since the settlement days, two Buxton residents received medical degrees. Dr. Violet Shadd graduated from the University of Toronto in 1972 and Dr. Bryan Bowles graduated from the University of Pittsburgh two years later. Both were descendants of Dr. Alfred Shadd.[71]

Long ago, some way distant from the road, sat a log building with a front gallery "shaded by luxuriant grape vines [and] a belfry rising high above the house."[72] Tasteful white fences enclosed the premises, and a long avenue of shade trees led up from the road. These features "contributed to give to the whole, when seen against the brilliant blue sky and embosomed in the rich green foliage of a Canadian summer, a picturesque and charming aspect."[73] Once inhabited by the Reverend William King, this house was later called the Clayton House after it became widely believed that Edward Clayton, the hero of Harriet Beecher Stowe's novel, *Dred: A Tale of the Great Dismal Swamp,* had been modeled on King. King's house stood for many years as testimony to all that he and Buxton's black settlers had accomplished. Today a simple monument in front of St. Andrew's Church in Buxton serves as a memorial to the community's founder.[74] This monument reads:

> 1949
> In Memory of
> REV. Wm. King who founded
> BUXTON SETTLEMENT 1849
> And Built
> ST. ANDREWS CHURCH 1858

Driving south from Chatham, still the closest town to Buxton, a traveler passes through a densely agricultural sector. During harvest time, crops of corn and wheat dominate the surrounding countryside, and farm equipment dots the fields. At frequent intervals, farmhouses rise among the crops. Many of these houses reveal their age with a distinctly weathered look. Others are clearly more recent additions to the landscape. More than one hundred years have passed since this tamed and fruitful land was a virgin wilderness. Oak, ash, and elm have been replaced by cultivated crops. Standing water from the Great Marsh that once hampered travel, settlement, and development has given way to modern drainage and irrigation. Yet this land and those who inhabit it have not forgotten the past.

Indications that blacks successfully developed a community with a strong sense of interconnectedness abound in the annals of Buxton's history since 1883. Bereft of the Elgin Association and the assistance of the Presbyterian Church, the neighborhood at Buxton did not become a mere shadow of its former self. The centers of its community life—schools and churches—continued in Buxton. Various efforts have been undertaken to maintain, preserve, and cultivate the memory of the Buxton settlement. As in other areas, events in Buxton shadow those at other black communities. Annual homecoming events or reunions became popular at many former all-black communities during the first half of the twentieth century. The popularity of such events evokes a sense of tradition and accomplishment among descendants and current residents and speaks to the strong sense of identity and place they offer to the community. Descendants of these areas often collect information about their families and the communities' histories. Preservation of material culture is a mainstay of this effort as well. Such activities speak to the strong sense of tradition, values, and identity fostered by these communities.

Descendants of the original settlers farm the same land as their forbears. A glance at a local directory shows some familiar names, including the Shadds, Shreves, Rhues, Chases, Princes, and Alexanders. Every year, descendants of families who left Buxton long ago return to the land tamed by their ancestors for an annual Labour Day weekend celebration, a tradition now more than three-quarters of a century old. Returnees talk with those who have chosen to remain, hearing stories handed down for generations. Even today, someone knowing the history of the area who stops alongside City Road 6 (still commonly referred to as Center Road) can picture William King traveling through the countryside astride his favorite horse; roughly clad children walking the long distance to the mission school, clutching their textbooks and yearning for the education that had been denied their parents; or men and women laboring in the fields and woods yet basking in the knowledge that their hard work was for their own benefit rather than for a master's. A sobering walk through Buxton's cemeteries testifies to the hardships suffered by the early settlers.

In 1967 the Buxton National Historic Site and Museum opened, memorializing the community's rich heritage. Fittingly, the museum was built through a community effort. William Newby sold seven acres of land to the museum for just over two thousand dollars, with the money donated by numerous groups, including the Maple Leaf Band, Dramatic Club, and the Community Club. The museum was the first in Canada dedicated to preserving the artifacts and documents of a black settlement. The museum's prime concern is the preservation of material and artifacts of Buxton. Among other things, it houses William King's bed, dresser, and diary, along with farm implements and tools of the times, household goods and furnishings, clothing, jewelry, and personal belongings of some of the original settlers. In addition to the restoration of School #13, plans are moving forward to move an 1850s-era log cabin, known as the Henderson House, from its original site on the tenth concession to the museum grounds, where the structure will be restored. Today's residents have an expansive collective memory of the Buxton settlement to impart to scholars and other interested parties. Visitors are invited to listen to a presentation of the community's history, interested families are encouraged and assisted in discovering their genealogy, and scholars are welcome to use the available resources. Members of the community periodically stop in and converse with those who lend an ear, recalling the memories of bygone days. Descendants of the original Buxtonians are a proud people; indeed, they should be. The dedication of these descendants in celebrating the history of the settlement's humble beginnings testifies to the significance of Buxton in Afro-American and Afro-Canadian history. Through these descendants, the Buxton community remains alive.

Notes

Introduction

1. William King, "Autobiography," January 6, 1892, 285.

2. Buxton is also commonly referred to as the Elgin Settlement, so named after the incorporated entity that sponsored the settlement.

3. Unless specified otherwise, the terms *Canada* and *Canadians* refer to Upper Canada (Canada West) and Upper Canadians.

4. Cha-Jua, *America's First Black Town*, ix, 1–3, 48; Pease and Pease, "Organized Negro Communities," 19–34.

5. Lapsansky, "Since They Got Those Separate Churches," 54–78; Vincent, *Southern Seed, Northern Soil*, 27, 44.

6. Winks, *Blacks in Canada*; Pease and Pease, *Black Utopia*; Walton, "Blacks in Buxton and Chatham."

7. Kusmer, "Black Urban Experience," 91–122.

8. Canadian Population Census, 1861, National Archives of Canada, Ottawa, Ont. Robbins, *Legacy to Buxton*, 39; Schweninger, *James T. Rapier and Reconstruction*, 1–14; Schweninger, "Slave Family in the Ante-Bellum South," 34; H. K. Thomas to John H. Rapier, Jan. 1859; Faragher, *Sugar Creek*, xiii.

9. Robinson, "Difference Freedom Made," 63.

Chapter 1. Canada: Canaan or "A Freezing Sort of Hell"

1. King, "Autobiography," 355–60; *Detroit Tribune*, June 12, 1892; Register for Sale of Land, Elgin Association, October 21, 1851, King Papers.

2. Finkelman, *Imperfect Union*, 4.

3. Ibid., 3–6, 11, 136, 144.

4. Hill, *Freedom Seekers*, Wayne, "Black Population of Canada West," 465–85.

5. Winks, *Blacks in Canada*, 28–32; Quarles, *Negro in the American Revolution*, 173; McDonnell, "Other Loyalists," 9–18.

6. Simpson, "Negroes in Ontario," 11; Walker, *History of Blacks,* 47.

7. Coffin, *Reminiscences,* 264.

8. Lewis, *Religious Life of Fugitive Slaves,* 19, 21.

9. Sampson, "Away to Canada," as printed in the *Liberator,* December 10, 1852.

10. Robert Ellett, interviewed by Claude W. Anderson, in *Weevils in the Wheat: Interviews with Virginia Ex-Slaves,* edited by Charles L. Perdue (Charlottesville: University Press of Virginia, 1976), 83–86; *London Anti-Slavery Reporter,* February 1, 1853.

11. Howe, *Report to the Freedmen's Inquiry Commission,* 11.

12. Ward, *Autobiography,* 161.

13. Drew, *North-side View of Slavery,* 335, 364.

14. An Act to Regulate Black and Mulatto Persons (approved 1804, *Laws of Ohio*). Middleton, *Black Laws.*

15. An Act to Repeal the Act Entitled "An Act for the Introduction of Negroes and Mulattoes into This Territory, and for Other Purposes" (approved 1810, *Laws of Indiana*). Middleton, *Black Laws.*

16. An Act to Prevent the Migration of Free Negroes and Mulattoes into This Territory and for Other Purposes (approved 1813, *Laws of Illinois*). Middleton, *Black Laws.*

17. An Act to Amend the Last Named Act, "An Act to Regulate Black and Mulatto Persons" (approved, 1807, *Laws of Ohio); * Negroes and Mulattoes (approved March 3, 1845, *Revised Statutes of Illinois); * An Act to Prevent the Migration of Free Negroes and Mulattoes into This Territory and for Other Purposes (approved 1813, *Laws of Illinois); * Indiana Constitution (1851), Article 13. All in Middleton, *Black Laws.*

18. *Cincinnati Advertiser,* March 29, 1829, n.p.

19. U.S. Census, 1830, 1840, 1850, 1860; Wade, "Negro in Cincinnati," 49–51; Pease and Pease, *Black Utopia,* 1–63; Winks, *Black in Canada,* 154–56.

20. Hodges, *Root and Branch,* 192.

21. Ohio Constitution (1802), Article 1; Ohio Constitution (1850), Article 5; An Act to Prescribe the Duties of Elections in Certain Cases, and Preserve the Purity of Elections (approved 1859, *Laws of Ohio); * Census, March 3, 1845, *Revised Statutes* (Illinois); Illinois Constitution (1848), Article 6; Indiana Constitution (1816), Article 6; Indiana Constitution (1851), Article 2. All in Middleton, *Black Laws.*

22. Indiana Constitution (1816), Article 7; Indiana Constitution (1851), Article 12; Illinois Constitution (1818), Article 5; Illinois Constitution (1848), Article 8. All in Middleton, *Black Laws.*

23. An Act to Organize and Discipline the Militia (approved 1803, *Laws of Ohio*). Middleton, *Black Laws.*

24. Ohio Constitution (1802); Michigan Constitution (1850) Article 17; Ohio Constitution (1850), Article 9, Section 1. All in Middleton, *Black Laws.*

25. An Act to Provide for the Support and Better Regulation of Common Schools (approved 1829, *Laws of Ohio*). Middleton, *Black Laws.*

26. An Act to Provide for the Support and Better Regulation of Common Schools (approved 1831, *Laws of Ohio); * An Act to Authorize the Establishment of Separate Schools for the Education of Colored Children, and for Other Purposes (approved 1849, *Laws of Ohio*). An Act to Provide for a General System of Common Schools, the Officers Thereof,

and Their Respective Powers and Duties, and Matters Properly Connected Therewith, and to Establish Township Libraries, and for the Regulation Thereof (approved 1855, *Revised Statutes, Laws of Indiana*). All in Middleton, *Black Laws*.

27. An Act to Regulate Black and Mulatto Persons (approved 1807, *Laws of Ohio*); An Act Relating to Juries (approved 1831, *Laws of Ohio*). All in Middleton, *Black Laws*; Cooper Guasco, "Confronting Democracy," 144.

28. Hodges, *Root and Branch*, 227–228; Litwack, *North of Slavery*, 75–93, 263; Lapsansky, "Since They Got Those Separate Churches," 54–78; Curry, *Free Black*, 100–103.

29. "A Voice from Columbia," in Garrison, *Thoughts*, 33.

30. "Voice from the West," *Liberator*, September 17, 1831.

31. Hodges, *Root and Branch*, 241 (first quotation); George Putnam, "Meeting of Colored Inhabitants of Boston," *Liberator*, March 23, 1833 (second quotation).

32. "Colored Philadelphian to the Editor," letter to the editor, *Liberator*, February 3, 1831.

33. Du Bois, *Souls of Black Folk*, 2.

34. Horton, *Free People of Color*, 146.

35. "The Fugitive Slave Act of 1850," *Statutes at Large of the United States of America 1789–1873*, vol. 9 (1851), 462.

36. *Pennsylvania Freeman*, October 31, 1850.

37. Proceedings of the Colored National Convention, held in Rochester, July 6th–8th, 1853 (Rochester, 1853).

38. Parker, "Freedman's Story," 162.

39. *Pennsylvania Freeman*, October 31, 1850.

40. Drew, *North-side View of Slavery*, 153.

41. Ibid., 333.

42. Douglass, *Life and Times*, 279.

43. *Pennsylvania Telegraph*, October 2, 1850.

44. *Liberator*, October 4, 1850.

45. Landon, "Negro Migration," 22–36.

46. Dorn, "History of the Antislavery Movement"; Hodges, *Root and Branch*, 256; Williams, *History of the Twelfth Baptist Church*, 15–17 (quotation); Horton and Horton, *Black Bostonians*, 103.

47. Ezekiel C. Cooper to Henry Bibb and James Theodore Holly, printed in the *Sandwich Voice of the Fugitive*, July 15, 1852.

48. Wayne, "Black Population of Canada West," 470–72; Wilson, *Freedom at Risk*, 50–51; Torrey, *Portraiture of Domestic Slavery*, 97.

49. Wayne, "Black Population of Canada West."

50. Stouffer, *Light of Nature*, 110–13.

51. Ibid., 52; Howe, *Report to the Freedmen's Inquiry Commission*, 1, 5, 11, 14, 101.

52. Murray, "Canada and the Anglo-American Anti-Slavery Movement," 117.

53. John Q. Adams to G. C. Antrobus, June 11, 1819, in Manning, *Diplomatic Correspondence*, vol. 1, 294.

54. Murray, "Extradition of Fugitive Slaves," 300.

55. Parker, "Freedman's Story."

56. Ibid.; Katz, *Resistance at Christiana*, 262–64.

57. Hill, *Freedom Seekers*, 93; Farrell, "History of the Negro Community in Chatham," 147.

58. Drew, *North-side View of Slavery*, 141.

59. Ibid., 174.

60. Colonial Church and School Society, *Occasional Paper*, No. 1, February 1854, 8–10.

61. Howe, *Report to the Freedmen's Inquiry Commission*, 1, 5, 11, 101 (quotation).

62. "Constitution of the American Society of Free Persons of Colour" (Philadelphia, 1831).

63. *Provincial Freeman*, November 11, 1854.

64. Howe, *Report to the Freedmen's Inquiry Commission*, 46.

65. *Provincial Freeman*, November 11, 1854.

66. *Provincial Freeman*, March 25, 1854; *Toronto Globe*, July 31, 1852; Ripley, *Black Abolitionist Papers*, vol. 2, 7; Walker, *A History of Blacks in Canada*, 88.

67. *Liberator*, August 25, 1854; Ripley, *Black Abolitionist Papers*, vol. 2, 297–99; *Provincial Freeman*, August 12, 1854; *Sandwich Voice of the Fugitive*, October 21, 1852.

68. *Sandwich Voice of the Fugitive*, July 2, 1851, October 21, 1852; *Frederick Douglass Paper*, July 16, 1852.

69. Knight, "Black Parents Speak," 269–84.

70. Hill, *Freedom Seekers*, 102; Knight, "Black Parents Speak," 277 (quotation).

71. Silverman and Gillie, "Pursuit of Knowledge," 179; Hill, *Freedom Seekers*, 102; Winks, "History of Negro School Segregation," 164–91; Spencer, "To Nestle in the Mane," 113.

72. Jehu Jones to Charles B. Ray, Toronto, August 8, 1839, in the *Coloured American*, September 14, 1839.

73. Jones, *Experience of Thomas Jones*.

74. S. R. Ward to Henry Bibb, Beauharnois, Canada, October 16, 1851, in the *Sandwich Voice of the Fugitive*, November 5, 1851.

75. Drew, *North-side View of Slavery*, 159–60; Ward, *Autobiography*, 144–45; Colonial Church and School Society, *Occasional Paper*, no. 1, February 1854, 8–10.

76. The published census of 1871 records the black population as close to 13,500. A cursory examination of the Index to 1871 Census of Ontario, which lists heads of households, substantiates that claim: 4,311 heads of households (or individuals with a different surname living in the household), listed "Africa," "African," or "Negro" as their ethnic origin. According just three people per household (probably a low estimate; average birthrates per family were generally higher) brings the number to the reported 13,500.

77. Wayne, "Black Population of Canada West," 470.

78. Drew, *North-side View of Slavery*, 130.

Chapter 2. The Reverend William King

1. King, *History of the King Family*, 1; King, "Autobiography," 1; Jamieson, *Friend and Champion*, 18.

2. King, "Autobiography," 2.

3. Ibid., 8; Ullman, *Look to the North Star*, 12–13.

4. King, "Autobiography," 24–27; Jamieson, *Friend and Champion*, 32–33.

5. King, "Autobiography," 32, 36, 38, 40–41.

6. Ibid., 93.

7. Ibid., 95.

8. King, *King Family,* n.p.; King, "Autobiography," 198; Gregg, "African in North America"; Pease and Pease, *Black Utopia,* 84; Simpson, "Negroes in Ontario," 67; Ullman, *Look to the North Star,* 23.

9. King, "Autobiography," 115–18; Ullman, *Look to the North Star,* 49.

10. King, "Autobiography," 153; Bill of Sale, King Papers.

11. King, "Autobiography," 129.

12. Ibid.

13. Ibid., 11–20; Stouffer, *The Light of Nature,* 21, 83–84; Ullman, *Look to the North Star,* 11, 26; Stauffer, *Black Hearts of Men,* 123–24; Blight, "In Search of Learning, Liberty, and Self-Definition," 7–25.

14. King, "Autobiography," 142–43.

15. Ibid., 123.

16. Ibid., 124.

17. Tise, *Proslavery,* 113, 115, 118; Smith, *In His Image,* 41–42, 152.

18. William King to Rev. Dr. Cunningham, Toronto, April 6, 1847, King Papers.

19. King, "Autobiography," 125.

20. Ibid.

21. Ibid., 126–28.

22. Ibid., 127; King, *King Family,* 5; Ullman, *Look to the North Star,* 55.

23. In May 1843 a conflict occurred between the established Church of Scotland and the British Parliament. Known as the Disruption, this dispute resulted in the formation of the Free Church of Scotland when Thomas Chalmers and his evangelical supporters walked out of the General Assembly and withdrew from the Established Church. More than one-third of the twelve hundred ministers and perhaps one-half of the lay members of the established Church of Scotland subsequently declared allegiance to the new body. Watt, *Thomas Chalmers and the Disruption*; Rice, *Scots Abolitionists, 1833–1861.*

24. King, "Autobiography," 153; Bill of Sale, King Papers; Ullman, *Look to the North Star,* 74.

25. King, "Autobiography," 153; Jamieson, *Friend and Champion,* 63; Ullman, *Look to the North Star,* 66–67.

26. King, "Autobiography," 181–82, 193–97; King to Rev. Dr. Cunningham, Toronto, April 6, 1847, King Papers; Ullman, *Look to the North Star,* 74; Jamieson, *Friend and Champion,* 65, 68–70.

27. Ullman, *Look to the North Star,* 74.

28. After it separated from the established Church of Scotland in 1843, the Free Church embarked on a fundraising program during which a deputation traveled to the United States and raised approximately £9,000, primarily from the slave states. The American and Foreign Anti-Slavery Society and later the Glasgow Emancipation Society, spurred on by Garrisonian abolitionists including Frederick Douglass, condemned the fundraising effort and began a "send back the money" campaign demanding that the Free Church return all funds garnered from southern churches. These abolitionist attacks

culminated in a full-scale onslaught against the Free Church. In the end, Douglass and the others failed to persuade the Free Church to return the money. Pettinger, "Send Back the Money," 32; Shepperson, "Thomas Chalmers, the Free Church of Scotland, and the South," 517–37; Stouffer, *Light of Nature,* 29–41; Rice, *Scots Abolitionists.*

29. King, "Autobiography," 190–92; Pettinger, "Send Back the Money." Douglass came to Buxton in 1854 and held a public meeting at the Chatham courthouse to apologize for the hard things he had said about King in Edinburgh. Years later, King returned to vindicate his character before an Edinburgh audience in the same hall where he had been covertly criticized. *Edinburgh News,* November 16, 1859.

30. Pettinger, "Send Back the Money," 40.

31. Stouffer, *Light of Nature,* 38.

32. Jamieson, *Friend and Champion,* 73; King, "Autobiography," 217–18; King to Rev. Dr. Cunningham, Toronto, April 6, 1847, King Papers.

33. King, "Autobiography," 206–11; Jamieson, *Friend and Champion,* 74.

34. King, "Autobiography," 210.

35. King to Rev. Dr. Cunningham, Toronto, April 6, 1847, King Papers; James A. Balfour, Secretary of the Colonial Committee, to William King, July 17, 1847, King Papers; Pease and Pease, "William King," 3–10.

36. Stouffer, *Light of Nature,* 39.

37. Ibid., 179–81; Committee of the Free Church Anti-Slavery Society, *Strictures on the Proceedings of the Last General Assembly,* as quoted in Stouffer, *Light of Nature,* 38.

38. Ketcham, "Dictates of Conscience," 48–49.

39. Ibid., 46–62; McGroarty, "Exploration in Mass Emancipation," 208–26.

40. Ketcham, "Dictates of Conscience," 49; Cooper Guasco, "Confronting Democracy," 64.

41. McGroarty, "Exploration in Mass Emancipation," 210.

42. Bagby, "Randolph Slave Saga," ii; McGroarty, "Exploration in Mass Emancipation," 209–11; Schwarz, *Migrants against Slavery,* 122–29. Gist was also an absentee landowner and slaveholder, living in England since before the American Revolution. Like King, therefore, he may have been influenced by the British abolitionist movement.

43. Schwarz, *Migrants against Slavery,* 79–80; Mathias, "John Randolph's Freedmen," 263–72.

44. William King to the Colonial Committee of the Free Church, New Orleans, April 22, 1848, King Papers.

45. King, "Autobiography," 231.

46. Ibid.

47. King, "Autobiography," 227–31; Jamieson, *Friend and Champion,* 72; Minutes of the Presbytery of Toronto, April 28, 1847, National Archives of Canada, Ottawa, Ont.

48. King, "Autobiography," 228–29 (all quotations).

49. Ketcham, "Dictates of Conscience," 58–59, taken from a letter written by Edward Coles to an unknown recipient, April 1844 (all quotations).

50. King, "Autobiography," 234.

51. Ibid., 234–35.

52. Ibid., 235.

53. "Report on Fugitive Slaves," January 18, 1841, *Journal of the House of Representatives of the State of Ohio,* 36 (36th General Assembly), in Middleton, *Black Laws,* 124; Hill, *Freedom Seekers,* 76; Simpson, "Negroes in Ontario," 531.

Chapter 3. An Idea Becomes Reality

1. "Prospectus of a Scheme for the Social and Moral Improvement of the Coloured People of Canada," King Papers; Constitution of the Elgin Association, adopted June 7, 1850, King Papers; Minutes of the Synod of the Presbyterian Church of Canada, June 1847, Presbyterian Church Archives, Toronto.

2. Nore and Norrish, *Edwardsville,* 34; Ketcham, "Dictates of Conscience," 61–62; Cooper Guasco, "Confronting Democracy," 114.

3. William King, "Scheme for Improving the Coloured People of Canada," 1848, King Papers.

4. William King to the Colonial Committee of the Free Church, New Orleans, April 22, 1848, King Papers.

5. Will of Samuel Gist, as printed in McGroarty, "Exploration in Mass Emancipation," 210. Gist's attempt failed largely because of problems with the execution of his will. His slaves were freed, but the money from his estate went to pay off his creditors rather than to purchase land on which the slaves could settle. They were simply dumped in Ohio with no resources or assistance.

6. Trotti, "Freedmen and Enslaved Soil," 459; Pease and Pease, *Black Utopia,* 28–37; *Genius of Universal Emancipation,* October 15, 1825, September 30, 1826.

7. Rice, *Scots Abolitionists,* 124.

8. King, "Autobiography," 168.

9. Watt, *Thomas Chalmers,* 337–39; King, "Autobiography," 168, 174; William King to James Cleveland Hamilton, November 23, 1889, James Cleland Papers.

10. William King to James Cleveland Hamilton, November 23, 1889, James Cleland Papers.

11. Cincinnati's city government granted an extension to allow for the planning of the settlement.

12. Pease and Pease, *Black Utopia,* 6; Chase, *Statutes of Ohio,* 393–94, 555–56; *Cincinnati Advertiser,* March 29, 1828.

13. Pease and Pease, *Black Utopia,* 64, 67; Stouffer, *Light of Nature,* 69–70; Winks, *Blacks in Canada,* 180.

14. William King to John Bonner, October 1849, King Papers.

15. Nore and Norrish, *Edwardsville,* 34; Powell, Kavanaugh, and Christy, "Transplanting Free Negroes," 302–17; McGroarty, "Exploration in Mass Emancipation," 216–17; *Report on the Condition of the Free Colored People of Ohio* (n.p., Beaumont & Wallace, 1835).

16. William King, "Report of the Mission to the Coloured Population," June 1849, King Papers.

17. Ibid.

18. Burton, "Anatomy of an Antebellum Rural Free Black Community," 294–325; Vin-

cent, *Southern Seed, Northern Soil,* 59; William King to Clerk of the Toronto Presbytery, June 21, 1848, King Papers; Pease and Pease, "William King," 7.

19. Gerrit Smith to Charles Ray, November 16, 1848, as quoted in Stauffer, *Black Hearts of Men,* 158.

20. Magdol, *Right to the Land,* 137–73; Cooper Guasco, "Confronting Democracy," 149–51.

21. Cooper Guasco, "Confronting Democracy," 146.

22. Gerrit Smith to Rev. T. S. Wright, C. B. Ray, and Dr. James McCune Smith, November 14, 1846, Gerrit Smith Papers, as quoted in Stauffer, *Black Hearts of Men,* 149.

23. Bagby, "Randolph Slave Saga," 150.

24. Stauffer, *Black Hearts of Men,* 149; Bagby, "Randolph Slave Saga," 94; Cooper, "Elevating the Race," 610.

25. Stouffer, *Light of Nature,* 88–89; King, "Autobiography," 244–47.

26. Stouffer, *Light of Nature,* 185–87; King, "Autobiography," 253–54.

27. *Toronto Globe,* March 21, 1849; *Ecclesiastical and Missionary Record for the Presbyterian Church of Canada,* June 1849; King, "Autobiography," 354; Stouffer, *Light of Nature,* 93–94.

28. "Report of the Mission to the Coloured Population, June 11, 1851," *Ecclesiastical and Missionary Record,* July 1851.

29. Minutes of the Synod of the Presbyterian Church of Canada, June 1847.

30. King, "Scheme for Improving."

31. Minutes of the Synod of the Presbyterian Church of Canada, June 1847.

32. Stouffer, *Light of Nature,* 187; Stouffer, "Michael Willis," 306–7.

33. King, "Autobiography," 249; William King, letter to the editor, *Ecclesiastical and Missionary Record,* March 1850; Petition 3, "R" Bundle 5, 1848–1850, Canada Land Petitions, National Archives of Canada, Ottawa, Ont. (quotation).

34. Petition 3, "R" Bundle 5, Canada Land Petitions, National Archives of Canada.

35. Ibid.

36. Bagby, "Randolph Slave Saga," 154.

37. Mathias, "John Randolph's Freedmen," 263–72; Bagby, "Randolph Slave Saga," 156; Pease and Pease, *Black Utopia,* 26–27.

38. Schwarz, *Migrants against Slavery,* 139.

39. Walton, "Blacks in Buxton and Chatham," 51.

40. William Notman to William King, House of Assembly, Montreal, March 9, 1949, King Papers.

41. Copy of the Petition of the District Council of the Western District to the Legislative Assembly of the Province of Canada, February 19, 1849, King Papers.

42. Memorial to the Presbyterian Synod at Toronto from the Inhabitants of the Township of Raleigh and Vicinity, June 1849, King Papers.

43. Ibid.

44. Ibid.

45. Ibid. (all quotations).

46. *Kent Advertiser,* August 23, 1849.

47. King, "Autobiography," 265.

48. *Kent Advertiser*, August 20, 1849; *Chatham Chronicle*, August 21, 1849; King, "Autobiography," 258–66 (quotation, 265).

49. *Chatham Chronicle*, August 21, 1849.

50. Ibid.

51. King, "Autobiography," 266–67.

52. "Quid to Mr. Editor," *Toronto Globe*, August 25, 1849.

53. Ibid.

54. "Colonization of the Coloured Race in the Settled Townships," *Examiner*, August 29, 1849.

55. Adolphus Judah et al. to Malcolm Cameron, Malcolm Cameron to Adolphus Judah et al., Fred Landon Fonds, the J. J. Talman Regional Collection, University of Western Ontario Archives; Landon, "Records Illustrating the Condition of Refugees," 201–2.

56. *Toronto Globe*, September 13, 1849.

57. *Church*, January 3, 1850.

58. King, "Autobiography," 268.

59. Ibid., 269.

60. Ibid., 270.

61. Ibid.

62. Ibid.

63. *Sandwich Voice of the Fugitive*, September 9, 1852.

64. Ibid.

65. Hill, *Freedom Seekers*, 79.

66. R. Lachlay to Lord Elgin, September 3, 1849, Governor General's Correspondence, vol. 21., RG7 G14, National Archives of Canada, Ottawa, Ont.

67. Ibid.

68. *Chatham Chronicle*, September 4, 1849.

Chapter 4. A Settlement Takes Shape

1. Constitution of the Elgin Association, adopted June 7, 1850, printed at the end of each annual report of the association.

2. King, "Scheme for Improving the Coloured People of Canada," 1848.

3. Solomon Hudson to William Fanning Wickham, November 19, 1849, Wickham Family Papers, as quoted in Trotti, "Freedmen and Enslaved Soil," 472.

4. Trotti, "Freedmen and Enslaved Soil," 469.

5. King, "Scheme for Improving the Coloured People of Canada," 1848.

6. Ibid.

7. Ibid.

8. Blacks who settled on lands adjoining the Elgin tract are sometimes considered part of the Buxton settlement, but for census and tax-assessment matters, only those settlers within the official Elgin tract are considered here.

9. *Chatham Chronicle*, August 21, 1849.

10. Drew, *North-side View of Slavery*, 292–93; Landon, "Buxton Settlement," 360–67; "Colony at Buxton," *National Anti-Slavery Standard*, November 7 and 14, 1857.

11. Faragher, *Sugar Creek*, 54.

12. King, "Scheme for Improving the Coloured People of Canada," 1848.

13. Trotti, "Freedmen and Enslaved Soil," 469. Even today, some descendants of former Gist slaves are struggling to obtain unfettered title to lands their parents, grandparents, and great-grandparents cleared and farmed.

14. David Bailey, Jacob Hadly, et al. to William Fanning Wickham, December 1850, Wickham Family Papers, as quoted in Trotti, "Freedmen and Enslaved Soil," 471.

15. Stauffer, *Black Hearts of Men*, 145; Schwarz, *Migrants against Slavery*, 142–43.

16. Walker, *Free Frank*, 115–16.

17. William Fanning Wickham to David Bailey, Jacob Hadly, et al., January 1, 1851, Wickham Family Papers, as quoted in Trotti, "Freedmen and Enslaved Soil," 469.

18. Canadian Population Census, 1851, 1861, 1871, National Archives of Canada, Ottawa, Ont.

19. First Annual Report of the Elgin Association, 1851.

20. King, "Autobiography," 290.

21. Ibid., 289.

22. Ibid., 295.

23. *Sandwich Voice of the Fugitive*, November 5, 1850; *Detroit Tribune*, Sunday, May 15, 1892.

24. King, "Autobiography," 291–96.

25. Third Annual Report of the Elgin Association, 1852 (Toronto: John Carter, 1853); Trotti, "Freedmen and Enslaved Soil," 467; Walker, *Free Frank*, 110.

26. Samuel J. May, letter to the editor, *Frederick Douglass' Paper*, September 17, 1852.

27. Ibid.

28. Ibid.

29. Ketcham, "Dictates of Conscience," 60, taken from a letter written by Edward Coles to an unknown recipient, April 1844.

30. Ibid.

31. *Chatham Chronicle*, August 21, 1849; *Kent Advertiser*, August 20, 1849; King, "Autobiography," 258–66; Cooper, "Elevating the Race," 622; Blight, "In Search of Learning," 14; Melish, *Disowning Slavery*, 279; Lapsansky, "Since They Got Those Separate Churches," 69.

32. Blight, "In Search of Learning," 10.

33. *Freedmen's Journal*, March 23 and 30, 1827.

34. John Rapier Sr. to John Rapier Jr., September 15, 1856; John Rapier Sr. to John Rapier Jr., June 26, 1857, Rapier Family Papers.

35. Cooper, "Elevating the Race," 624.

36. Ibid., 617; Melish, *Disowning Slavery*, 254.

37. King, "Scheme for Improving the Coloured People of Canada," 1848.

38. Ibid.

39. "Colony at Buxton," *National Anti-Slavery Standard*, November 7 and 14, 1857; Stauffer, *Black Hearts of Men*, 145.

40. Pease and Pease, *Black Utopia*, 51.

41. Ullman, *Look to the North Star*, 125–27; Canadian Population Census, 1861, National Archives of Canada, Ottawa, Ont.

42. Ullman, *Look to the North Star*, 125–27.

43. King, "Autobiography," 241, 244.

44. Torrance, "Noble Friend of Freedmen," *Detroit Tribune*, April 10, 1892.

45. King, "Autobiography," 244.

46. "Prospectus of a Scheme for the Social and Moral Improvement of the Coloured People of Canada," King Papers.

47. Pease and Pease, "Ends, Means, and Attitudes," 117–28; Stewart, *Holy Warriors*, 125.

48. "Philanthropist—Buxton Mission," *Provincial Freeman*, December 16, 1854.

49. Samuel J. May, letter to the editor, *Frederick Douglass' Paper*, September 17, 1852.

50. "Visit to the Elgin Settlement," *Provincial Freeman*, October 6, 1855.

51. Ibid.

52. Ibid.

53. Canadian Population Census, 1861, National Archives of Canada, Ottawa, Ont. The names of the twelve families are Slade, Ryan, Straith, Black, King, Roe, Wood, Broadbent, Thompson, Wallace, Randall, and Lee.

54. James Rapier to John H. Rapier, Buxton, Canada West, January 21, 1853, Rapier Family Papers.

55. Samuel J. May, letter to the editor, *Frederick Douglass' Paper*, September 17, 1852.

56. Ibid.

57. "Visit to the Elgin Settlement," *Provincial Freeman*, October 6, 1855.

58. "Colony at Buxton," *National Anti-Slavery Standard*, November 7 and 14, 1857.

59. Ibid.

60. *Provincial Freeman*, October 20, 1855; *Provincial Freeman*, March 7, 1857; Raleigh Township Assessment Rolls, 1859.

61. Kleinig, *Paternalism*, 66.

Chapter 5. A Community Arises

1. King, "Autobiography," 390–97; Eighth Annual Report of the Elgin Association, 1857.

2. Schwarz, *Migrants against Slavery*, 146.

3. King, "Autobiography," 285.

4. A. R. Abbott to editor, *New York Age*, February 15, 1891; King, "Autobiography," 312–13.

5. "Colony at Buxton," *National Anti-Slavery Standard*, November 7 and 14, 1857.

6. Ibid.

7. Register of Lands entered in Elgin Association, ms., King Papers.

8. Canadian Population Census, 1861, National Archives of Canada, Ottawa, Ont.; Raleigh Township Assessment Rolls, 1880.

9. A. R. Abbott to editor, *New York Age*, February 15, 1894.

10. "Colony at Buxton," *National Anti-Slavery Standard*, November 7 and 14, 1857.

11. Cary, *A Plea for Emigration*, 32.

12. *Sandwich Voice of the Fugitive*, April 8, 1852.

13. Drew, *North-side View of Slavery*, 297.

14. King, "Autobiography," 314.

15. Ibid., 319. ·

16. James Rapier to Brother, Florence, Alabama, September 27, 1859, Rapier Family Papers.

17. Cooper, "Elevating the Race," 614–15.

18. Annual Reports of the Elgin Association, 1851–1861. There is some discrepancy in the population statistics for Buxton. The 1861 Canadian census officially shows 133 families numbering 691 individuals living on the Elgin tract. The difference between King's reports and the census returns occurred because King took into account black families that lived in the vicinity of the Elgin tract as well as those who lived in the actual settlement, whereas the census numbers accounted for only those black individuals living in Raleigh Township between lots six and twelve of concessions A and eight through fourteen, the official boundaries of the Elgin tract.

19. Canadian Population Census, 1861, National Archives of Canada, Ottawa, Ont.

20. Register of Marriages, 1857–1895 for the St. Andrew's Church Congregation.

21. Canadian Population Census, 1861, National Archives of Canada, Ottawa, Ont.

22. Ibid.

23. Walton, "Blacks in Buxton and Chatham," 133.

24. Ibid.; Canadian Population Census, 1851, 1861, National Archives of Canada, Ottawa, Ont.; "Mission to Fugitive Slaves in Canada: Being a Branch of the Operations of the Colonial and Continental Church Society: Report for the Year 1860–61," 43–44.

25. Canadian Population Census, 1861, 1871, National Archives of Canada, Ottawa, Ont.; Raleigh Township Assessment Rolls, 1859, 1873; Raleigh Township Voter's List, 1873.

26. King, "Autobiography," 275.

27. Edward Coles to an unknown recipient, April 1844, in Ketcham, "Dictates of Conscience," 60.

28. Ibid.

29. Cooper Guasco, "Confronting Democracy," 136.

30. Undated map of the Elgin Settlement; Register of Lands entered in Elgin Association, King Papers.

31. Although maps of Buxton show Robert Phares as holding fifty acres, various tax assessment rolls list him as having well under that amount.

32. *Chatham Evening Banner,* January 7, 1895.

33. Register of Marriages, 1857–1895, for the St. Andrew's Church Congregation; Canadian Population Census, 1861, National Archives of Canada, Ottawa, Ont.; Session Book of the Congregation at Buxton; Will of William King, King Papers.

34. Canadian Population Census, 1861, National Archives of Canada, Ottawa, Ont.; Raleigh Township Assessment Rolls, 1873.

35. Robbins, Buxton Settlement maps, 1851–1873; Canadian Population Census, 1861, National Archives of Canada, Ottawa, Ont.; Raleigh Township Assessment Rolls, 1851–1873.

36. Canadian Population Census, 1861, National Archives of Canada, Ottawa, Ont.

37. Ibid.; gravestone in the South Buxton Cemetery.

38. Canadian Population Census, 1861, National Archives of Canada, Ottawa, Ont.; Ullman, *Look to the North Star,* suggests that Sarah was Fanny's child and Peter was Mollie's.

39. "Colony at Buxton," *National Anti-Slavery Standard,* November 7 and 14, 1857.

40. Ezekiel C. Cooper, letter to the editor, *Sandwich Voice of the Fugitive,* July 1, 1852.

41. King, "Autobiography," 330.

42. Canadian Population Census, 1861, National Archives of Canada, Ottawa, Ont.; Ullman, *Look to the North Star,* 232; Robbins, *Legacy to Buxton,* 39.

43. King, "Autobiography," 389.

44. Ibid., 388–90, 331–37.

45. Burgee's arrival in Buxton coincides with Shadrach's disappearance from Boston, although it is impossible to determine definitively whether the two were indeed the same man. Lader, *Bold Brahmins*; William Lloyd Garrison to George Thompson Garrison, Boston, February 18, 1851, in *Letters of William Lloyd Garrison,* 4: 48–49; Canadian Population Census, 1861, National Archives of Canada, Ottawa, Ont.; Robbins, Buxton Settlement maps, 1851–1873; Robbins, *Legacy to Buxton,* 79–80.

46. King, "Autobiography," 338–44.

47. Ibid., 351.

48. Ibid.

49. Ullman, *Look to the North Star,* 157.

50. Schweninger, *James T. Rapier,* 1–14; Schweninger, "Slave Family," 34; Canadian Population Census, 1861, National Archives of Canada, Ottawa, Ont.; H. K. Thomas to John H. Rapier in St. Paul, Buxton, Canada, January 1859, Rapier Family Papers; Erie County court records, land deeds, July 20, 1842.

51. King, "Autobiography," 279–81; Raleigh Township Assessment Rolls, 1859, 1873; Agricultural Census of Canada and Canadian Population Census, 1861, National Archives of Canada, Ottawa, Ont.; *Detroit Tribune,* May 22, 1892.

52. Katz, *Resistance at Christiana,* 262.

53. Parker, "Freedman's Story."

54. Hiram Wilson to "Brother Bibb," May 25, 1852, St. Catharines, published in *Sandwich Voice of the Fugitive,* June 3, 1852; Register of Lands entered in Elgin Association, King Papers.

55. Records of the BME Methodist Church Cemetery; Will of Eliza Parker available from *African American in Lancaster County* at www.lancasterhistory.org.

56. Faragher, *Sugar Creek,* 50.

57. Canadian Population Census, 1861, National Archives of Canada, Ottawa, Ont.; Buxton Settlement Maps; Raleigh Township Assessment Rolls for 1852–1873.

Chapter 6. Family and Community Structure

1. Malone, *Sweet Chariot,* 258.

2. Faragher, *Sugar Creek,* 80.

3. Laslett and Walls, *Household and Family,* 28–31; Malone, *Sweet Chariot,* 7–9; Canadian Population Census, 1861, National Archives of Canada, Ottawa, Ont.

4. Canadian Population Census, 1861, National Archives of Canada, Ottawa, Ont.

5. Ibid.

6. Ibid.

7. Stevenson, *Life in Black and White,* 163, 299–303; Cha-Jua, *America's First Black Town,* 63.

8. Malone, *Sweet Chariot,* 10–14.

9. Canadian Population Census, 1861, National Archives of Canada, Ottawa, Ont.

10. Hodges, *Root and Branch,* 194.

11. Canadian Population Census, 1861, National Archives of Canada, Ottawa, Ont.

12. Ibid.

13. Ibid.

14. "Colony at Buxton," *New York Tribune,* November 7 and 14, 1857.

15. Canadian Population Census, 1861, National Archives of Canada, Ottawa, Ont.; John Rapier Sr. to John Rapier Jr., August 6, 1857, Rapier Family Papers.

16. Canadian Population Census, 1861, National Archives of Canada, Ottawa, Ont.

17. Although Robert was recorded as eleven years old in John Glen's household and sixteen in William Garle's household, the two listings are likely one and the same.

18. Canadian Population Census, 1861, National Archives of Canada, Ottawa, Ont.

19. Ibid.

20. Ibid.; Malone, *Sweet Chariot,* 169–70, 230.

21. Canadian Population Census, 1861, National Archives of Canada, Ottawa, Ont.; King, *Stolen Childhood,* 5; Savitt, *Medicine and Slavery,* 117–19.

22. Franklin and Schweninger, *Runaway Slaves,* 209–21; Curry, *Free Black,* 9.

23. Canadian Population Census, 1861, National Archives of Canada, Ottawa, Ont.

24. Ibid.

25. Ibid.

26. Ibid.

27. Children were susceptible to a wide range of life-threatening ailments: various fevers, intestinal disorders, pneumonia, tuberculosis or consumption, measles, whooping cough, and tetanus. Sickle-cell anemia also took its toll among the black population.

28. Canadian Population Census, 1861, National Archives of Canada, Ottawa, Ont.

29. Ibid.

30. Cody, "There Was No 'Absalom,'" 573; Horton, *Free People of Color,* 155.

31. Canadian Population Census, 1861, National Archives of Canada, Ottawa, Ont.; Buxton Settlement Maps; Assessment Rolls for Raleigh Township, 1852–1873; Register of Marriages, 1857–1895.

32. Canadian Population Census, 1861, National Archives of Canada, Ottawa, Ont.; Buxton Settlement Maps; Assessment Rolls for Raleigh Township, 1852–1873; Register of Marriages, 1857–1895; Cody, "There Was No 'Absalom,'" 575; Inscoe, "Carolina Slave Names," 541.

33. Canadian Population Census, 1861, National Archives of Canada, Ottawa, Ont.

34. Ibid.

35. Ibid., 1861, 1881; Buxton Settlement maps; Assessment Rolls for Raleigh Township, 1852–1873; Register of Marriages, 1857–1895.

36. Canadian Population Census, 1861, 1871, National Archives of Canada, Ottawa, Ont.; Robbins, *Legacy to Buxton,* 80–83; Robbins, Register of Baptisms.

37. Malone, *Sweet Chariot,* 166.

38. Register of Marriages, 1857–1895.

39. Canadian Population Census, 1861, National Archives of Canada, Ottawa, Ont.; Register of Marriages, 1857–1895.

40. Schwarz, *Migrants against Slavery,* 136; Bagby, "Randolph Slave Saga," 6, 196; Vincent, *Southern Seed, Northern Soil,* 30, 40; Faragher, *Sugar Creek,* 56–60.

Chapter 7. Making a Living

1. Constitution of the Elgin Association, adopted June 7, 1850.

2. *New York Age,* February 15, 1895.

3. Murray, "Canada and the Antislavery Movement," 90–91; Stouffer, *Light of Nature,* 70.

4. Fifth Annual Report of the Elgin Association, 1854 (Toronto: Globe Book and Job Office, 1854); King, "Autobiography," 363–68; Harris, *Sketch of the Buxton Mission,* 11.

5. Constitution of the Canada Mill and Mercantile Company, King Papers.

6. *Sandwich Voice of the Fugitive,* April 22, 1852.

7. Ibid.

8. Ibid.

9. Ibid.; Constitution of the Canada Mill and Mercantile Company, King Papers; King, "Autobiography," 364–66.

10. Sixth Annual Report of the Elgin Association, 1855 (Toronto: Globe Book and Job Office, 1855).

11. *New York Age,* February 15, 1894; *Sandwich Voice of the Fugitive,* April 22, 1852; Schweninger, "Fugitive Negro in the Promised Land," 95.

12. King, "Autobiography," 364–66; *New York Age,* February 15, 1894.

13. King, "Autobiography," 367.

14. Ibid., 365–69; Abbott, "Elgin Settlement."

15. James Rapier to John Rapier, Jr., March 3, 1857, Rapier Family Papers.

16. James Rapier to brother, Florence, Alabama, September 27, 1859; James Rapier to John H. Rapier, January 27, 1859; James Rapier to John H. Rapier, Buxton, Canada, March 5, 1859, Rapier Family Papers.

17. Richard Parr to Rev. William King, Chatham, October 5, 1848, King Papers; Canada Land Petitions, Land Book E, National Archives of Canada, Ottawa, Ont.

18. Canadian Population Census, 1861, National Archives of Canada, Ottawa, Ont.; James T. Rapier to John H. Rapier, Buxton, Canada, March 5, 1859, Rapier Family Papers; Session Book of St. Andrew's Church.

19. Ward, *Autobiography of a Fugitive Negro,* 214 (all quotations).

20. *Detroit Tribune,* May 29, 1892; James T. Rapier to John Rapier, Buxton, Canada West, January 27, 1859, Rapier Family Papers.

21. James Rapier to John Rapier Jr., March 3, 1857, Rapier Family Papers.

22. *Antislavery Reporter,* February 1, 1860.

23. Ibid.

24. John Jowitt to Rev. Harrocks Cocks, Leeds, January 7, 1873, King Papers.

25. Arthur Lupton to Rev. Harrocks Cocks, Leeds, January 18, 1873, King Papers.

26. John Jowitt to Rev. Harrocks Cocks, Leeds, January 7, 1873; W. E. Forster to Harrocks Cocks, January 8, 1873; J. G. Barclay to H. Cocks, January 20, 1873—all in King Papers.

27. Richard Parr, Public Land Surveyor, to Rev. William King, Chatham, October 5, 1848, King Papers.

28. Ibid.; a similar description can be found in P. McMullen to James H. Prince, commissioner of Crown Lands, Sandwich, September 12, 1849, Canada Land Petitions, National Archives of Canada, Ottawa, Ont.

29. A. R. Abbott to the editor, *New York Age,* February 8, 1894. A similar description can be found in Abbott, "Elgin Settlement."

30. Petition 4, "R" Bundle 5, 1848–1850, Canada Land Petitions, National Archives of Canada, Ottawa, Ont.

31. Agricultural Census of Canada, 1861, National Archives of Canada, Ottawa, Ont.

32. Strivers, *History of Brown County.*

33. George Carter and David Bailey to William Fanning Wickham, January 18, 1847, Wickham Family Papers, quoted in Trotti, "Freedmen and Enslaved Soil," 467.

34. Stauffer, *Black Hearts of Men,* 139, 149.

35. Vincent, *Southern Seed, Northern Soil,* 40–41.

36. Petition H, "E" Bundle, 1858–1862, Canada Land Petitions, National Archives of Canada, Ottawa, Ont.

37. Ibid.

38. Agricultural Census of Canada, 1861, National Archives of Canada, Ottawa, Ont.

39. Seventh Annual Report of the Elgin Association, 1856 (Toronto: Globe Book and Job Office, 1856).

40. Sarah Thomas to John Rapier, Buxton, Canada West, March 10, 185? Ottawa, Ont.

41. Annual Reports of the Elgin Settlement, 1851–1857; Agricultural Census of Canada, 1861, National Archives of Canada, Ottawa, Ont.

42. Ibid.

43. Agricultural Census of Canada, 1861, National Archives of Canada, Ottawa, Ont.

44. Ibid.; Canadian Population Census, 1861, National Archives of Canada, Ottawa, Ont.

45. Agricultural Census of Canada, 1861, National Archives of Canada, Ottawa, Ont.

46. The 1861 Canadian Census combined the records for hemp and flax under one heading, and so it is impossible to determine exactly which plant was actually grown.

47. Agricultural Census of Canada, 1861, National Archives of Canada, Ottawa, Ont.

48. Ninth Annual Report of the Elgin Association, 1858 (Toronto: John Carter, 1858).

49. Ibid.

50. Agricultural Census of Canada, 1861, National Archives of Canada, Ottawa, Ont.

51. Third Annual Report of the Elgin Association, 1852 (Toronto: John Carter, 1853).

52. Mary Jane Robinson, Buxton, Canada West to Mrs. Sarah Ann Harris, Weeksville, New York, March 23, 1854.

53. Ibid.

54. Agricultural Census of Canada, 1861, National Archives of Canada, Ottawa, Ont.

55. Fourth Annual Report of the Elgin Association, 1853.

56. Agricultural Census of Canada, 1861, National Archives of Canada, Ottawa, Ont.

57. Ibid.

58. Ibid.

59. Ibid.

60. Fifth Annual Report of the Elgin Association, 1854 (Toronto: Globe Book and Job Office, 1854).

61. Map of the Elgin Association Lands, n.d., Copy of Part of the Plan of the Township of Raleigh, Chatham-Kent Museum; King, "Autobiography," 425.

62. Agricultural Census of Canada, 1861, National Archives of Canada, Ottawa, Ont.

63. Sixth Annual Report of the Elgin Association, 1855 (Toronto: Globe Book and Job Office, 1855).

64. Canadian Population Census, 1861, National Archives of Canada, Ottawa, Ont.; Agricultural Census of Canada, 1861, National Archives of Canada, Ottawa, Ont.

65. Agricultural Census of Canada, 1861, National Archives of Canada, Ottawa, Ont.

66. Ibid.

67. Ibid.

68. Ibid.

69. Ibid.

70. Ibid.

Chapter 8. A Spiritual People

1. William King, "Scheme for a Negro Settlement," 1848, King Papers.

2. William King to Rev. John Bonnar, July 15, 18749, King Papers.

3. William King, "Report of the Mission to the Coloured Population," June 1849, King Papers.

4. C. Eric Lincoln, Foreword to William R. Jones, *Is God a White Racist? A Preamble to Black Theology* (Garden City, N.Y.: Anchor, 1973), viii.

5. Litwack, *North of Slavery,* 196.

6. Pease and Pease, *They Who Would Be Free,* 19–20. See also Raboteau, *Slave Religion,* and George, *Segregated Sabbaths.*

7. Horton and Horton, *In Hope of Liberty,* 129–54; Nash, *Forging Freedom,* 192–292.

8. Hill, *Freedom Seekers,* 134; Shreve, *AfriCanadian Church,* 42.

9. Bertley, *Canada and Its People of African Descent,* 152; Shreve, *AfriCanadian Church,* 42–43.

10. Bertley, *Canada and Its People of African Descent,* 152; Shreve, *AfriCanadian Church,* 42–43.

11. Horton and Horton, *In Hope of Liberty,* 138–44; Nash, *Forging Freedom,* 190–95; Bertley, *Canada and Its People of African Descent,* 155; Shreve, *AfriCanadian Church,* 78–83.

12. "Colony at Buxton," *National Anti-Slavery Standard,* November 7 and 14, 1857.

13. Ward, *Autobiography of a Fugitive Negro,* 215.

14. "Seventh Annual Report of the Buxton Mission," Minutes of the Synod of the

Presbyterian Church of Canada, June 1857; King, "Autobiography," 286–88; *Ecclesiastical and Missionary Record,* March 1850.

15. King, "Autobiography," 286–88.

16. William King, "Mission to the Coloured Population," letter to the editor, *Ecclesiastical and Missionary Record,* March 1850. King is referring to the petitions sent to the government in opposition to the establishment of the Buxton settlement.

17. Session Book of the Congregation at Buxton; *Ecclesiastical and Missionary Record,* July 1852; Minutes of the Synod of the Presbyterian Church of Canada, 1860.

18. *Ecclesiastical and Missionary Record,* March 1850 and July 1851; "Report of the Buxton Mission," Minutes of the Synod of the Presbyterian Church of Canada, June 1859.

19. "Sixth Annual Report of the Buxton Mission," Minutes of the Synod of the Presbyterian Church of Canada, June 1856; William King, letter to the editor, *Ecclesiastical and Missionary Record,* March 1852; Statistical Records for the year ending May 1, 1859, Minutes of the Synod of the Presbyterian Church of Canada.

20. "Sixth Annual Report of the Buxton Mission," Minutes of the Synod of the Presbyterian Church of Canada, June 1856.

21. Ibid.; Lord Alfred Churchill, African Aid Society Executive Committee chairman to Rev. William King, March 17, 1861, King Papers.

22. Session Book, St. Andrew's Church, Buxton, 1858–1873.

23. Ibid.; Canadian Population Census, 1861, National Archives of Canada, Ottawa, Ont. ·

24. Nash, *Forging Freedom,* 109–11; Horton and Horton, *In Hope of Liberty,* 142–43.

25. Canadian Population Census, 1861, National Archives of Canada, Ottawa, Ont.; Agricultural Census of Canada, 1861, National Archives of Canada, Ottawa, Ont.

26. Canadian Population Census, 1861, National Archives of Canada, Ottawa, Ont.

27. Ibid.

28. "The Colony at Buxton," *National Anti-Slavery Standard,* November 7 and 14, 1857.

29. "Report of the Buxton Mission," Minutes of the Synod of the Presbyterian Church of Canada, 1859; Canadian Population Census, 1861, National Archives of Canada, Ottawa, Ont.; Agricultural Census of Canada, 1861, National Archives of Canada, Ottawa, Ont.; Walton, "Blacks in Buxton and Chatham," 232; Cha-Jua, *America's First Black Town,* 69–73; Vincent, *Southern Seed, Northern Soil,* 70–73.

30. Amherstburg Baptist Association, MS. Minutes, 1854.

31. *Provincial Freeman,* May 10, 1856.

32. History of the First Baptist Church, Canadian Black Studies Project, University of Western Ontario Archives; Lewis, *Religious Life of Fugitive Slaves,* 153; Shreve, *AfriCanadian Church,* 61–65.

33. History of the First Baptist Church, Canadian Black Studies Project, University of Western Ontario Archives; Robbins, *Legacy to Buxton,* 97, 109; Shreve, *AfriCanadian Church,* 55–58.

34. Robbins, *Legacy to Buxton,* 97.

35. Canadian Anti-Slavery Baptist Association, Minutes, 1854.

36. Canadian Population Census, 1861, National Archives of Canada, Ottawa, Ont.; Robbins, *Legacy to Buxton,* 108; Shreve, *AfriCanadian Church,* 86.

37. Session Book of the Congregation at Buxton, Canada West, 1858–1865.

38. James Rapier to John Rapier Jr., March 6, 1857, Rapier Family Papers.

39. Session Book of the Congregation at Buxton, Canada West, 1858–1865, meeting of October 25, 1860; meeting of February 14, 1864.

40. Walton, "Blacks in Buxton and Chatham," 157.

41. "Colony at Buxton," *National Anti-Slavery Standard,* November 7 and 14, 1857.

42. Session Book of the Congregation at Buxton, 1859.

43. King, "Autobiography," 297–99.

44. "Seventh Annual Report of the Buxton Mission," Minutes of the Synod of the Presbyterian Church, June 1857.

45. James Rapier to John Rapier, Buxton, C.W., April 21, 1857; James Rapier to John Rapier, Jr., September 27, 1858; James Rapier to brother, Florence, Alabama, September 27, 1859, Rapier Family Papers; Bible Society Records, South Buxton 1860–1893.

46. Minutes of the Synod of the Presbyterian Church of Canada, June 1851, 1852, 1853; "Visit to the United States on Behalf of the Raleigh Settlement of Coloured Persons by Dr. Burns and the Rev. W. King," *Ecclesiastical and Missionary Record,* January 1851.

47. Address to William King from the Female Association at Pittsburgh, on behalf of Raleigh, Allegheny City, November 25, 1850, *Ecclesiastical and Missionary Record,* February 1851.

48. King, "Autobiography," 330.

49. "Eighth Annual Report of the Buxton Mission," Minutes of the Synod of the Presbyterian Church of Canada, June 1858.

50. Ibid.

51. "Coloured Mission," *Ecclesiastical and Missionary Record,* November 1849; "Report of the Buxton Mission," Minutes of the Synod of the Presbyterian Church of Canada, June 1859.

52. "Report of Financial Committee of the Buxton Mission," Minutes of the Synod of the Presbyterian Church of Canada, June 1861; Sexsmith, "Some Notes on the Buxton Settlement."

53. Notes of Congregational Meeting, January 19, 1863, obtained privately from Bryan Prince; Deacons' Meeting of May 11, 1863, obtained privately from originals in possession of Bryan Prince (copies also exist at Chatham-Kent Museum, Chatham, Ont.); Minutes of the Synod of the Presbyterian Church of Canada, 1869–1873.

54. Session Book of the Congregation at Buxton, Canada West, 1859.

55. "Report of the Buxton Mission," Minutes of the Synod of the Presbyterian Church of Canada, June 1859.

56. North Buxton Session Book, Meeting of the Deacon's Court, July 12, 1858; North Buxton Session Book, Meeting of the Deacon's Court, January 12, 1859; North Buxton Session Book, Meeting of the Deacon's Court, July 10, 1859; Appendix, Minutes of the Synod of the Presbyterian Church of Canada, Hamilton, June 1869.

57. North Buxton Session Book, Meeting of the Deacon's Court, August 14, 1859, May 31, 1861; Congregational Meeting, January 19, 1863; Deacons' meeting of February 26, 1865, obtained privately from Bryan Prince.

Chapter 9. In Pursuit of an Education

1. Minutes of the Synod of the Presbyterian Church of Canada, June 1857.

2. Vincent, *Southern Seed, Northern Soil*, 78.

3. *Sandwich Voice of the Fugitive,* January 15, 1851.

4. Curry, *Free Black in Urban America,* 168.

5. Blight, "In Search of Learning," 12; Stewart, *Holy Warriors,* 132; Lapsansky, "Since They Got Those Separate Churches," 69; Nash, *Forging Freedom,* 203.

6. *Sandwich Voice of the Fugitive,* January 15, 1851.

7. Silverman and Gillie, "Pursuit of Knowledge," 95.

8. Pease and Pease, *They Who Would Be Free,* 145; Hodges, *Root and Branch,* 218–19.

9. Tanser, *Settlement of Negroes,* 49.

10. Silverman and Gillie, "Pursuit of Knowledge," 97.

11. Stouffer, *Light of Nature,* 104.

12. Silverman and Gillie, "Pursuit of Knowledge," 107; Spencer, "To Nestle in the Mane," 265; Winks, "History of Negro School Segregation," 171; Simpson, "Negroes in Ontario," 236–38.

13. Walker, *History of Blacks in Canada,* 111; Winks, "History of Negro School Segregation," 169–70.

14. Tanser, *Settlement of Negroes,* 47–48.

15. "Report of the Mission to the Coloured Population, June 11, 1851," *Ecclesiastical and Missionary Record,* July 1851, 131–132; King, "Autobiography," 320.

16. Tanser, *Settlement of Negroes,* 49.

17. Ullman, *Look to the North Star,* 117.

18. Tanser, *Settlement of Negroes,* 49.

19. King, "Autobiography," 320.

20. Horton, "Black Education at Oberlin College," 477–99; Lawson and Merrill, "Antebellum 'Talented Thousandth,'" 142–55.

21. "Mission to the Coloured Population," *Ecclesiastical and Missionary Record,* November 1850; William King, letter to the editor, *Ecclesiastical and Missionary Record,* March 1852.

22. Letter from John Jones, E. Weaver, E. Gordon, Alex Smith, and J. H. Baynet to Rev. William King, Chicago, November 25, 1851, *Ecclesiastical and Missionary Record,* February 1852.

23. Minutes of the Synod of the Presbyterian Church of Canada, June 1856.

24. Harris, *Sketch of the Buxton Mission,* 7.

25. "Report of the Mission to the Coloured Population, June 11, 1851," *Ecclesiastical and Missionary Record,* July, 1851.

26. King, "Autobiography," 296; Fuller, *Old Country School,* 162.

27. Minutes of the Synod of the Presbyterian Church of Canada, June 1857.

28. Ibid.; Simpson, "Negroes in Ontario," 541.

29. Walker, *Free Frank,* 136–143; Stouffer, *Light of Nature,* 66.

30. James Rapier to John Rapier Jr., June 26, 1857, Rapier Family Papers.

31. James Rapier to John Rapier Jr., February 28, 1858, Rapier Family Papers.

32. Minutes of the Synod of the Presbyterian Church of Canada, June 1856; King, "Autobiography," 325–26.

33. King, "Autobiography," 303.

34. Minutes of the Synod of the Presbyterian Church of Canada, June 1856; King, "Autobiography," 302–4.

35. *Ecclesiastical and Missionary Record,* December 1852.

36. Drew, *North-side View of Slavery,* 293.

37. Simpson, "Negroes in Ontario," 426–28, 528–29, 555.

38. Schweninger, "Slave Family," 40; Schweninger, "John H. Rapier Sr.," 26.

39. Minutes of the Synod of the Presbyterian Church of Canada, June 1857.

40. Ullman, *Look to the North Star,* 185–87.

41. Eighth Annual Report of the Buxton Mission, Minutes of the Synod of the Presbyterian Church of Canada, June 1858; Ninth Annual Report of the Buxton Mission, Minutes of the Synod of the Presbyterian Church of Canada, June 1859.

42. Hill, *Freedom Seekers,* 84; Robbins, *Legacy to Buxton,* 63; Raleigh Township Assessment Rolls, 1863; Fuller, *Old Country School,* 43.

43. Third Annual Report of the Buxton Mission, Minutes of the Synod of the Presbyterian Church of Canada, June 1852; Walton, "Blacks in Buxton and Chatham," 170; Harris, *Sketch of the Buxton Mission,* 7.

44. Census material provides a substantial data set with which to work, and, although somewhat problematic, it is one of the most comprehensive means to examine school attendance and literacy in Buxton. Despite its richness in raw material, the census returns are not 100 percent accurate, and percentages derived from the census should be taken as relative rather than concrete. As previously mentioned, school attendance and literacy were self-reported and subject to interpretative degrees. In some instances, additional information can be gleaned from other sources. For example, Lorenzo Rann, who was twenty-four in 1861, was not designated illiterate on the census. Yet on his 1890 pension application he made his mark rather than signing his name, signifying illiteracy. Some errors are so blatant that they may be corrected without mention. The 1861 census shows four-year-old Margaret Lightfoot attending school while her seven-year-old brother William did not. Apparently, the census recorder mistakenly marked the wrong line. Other instances raise concerns of accuracy. The Riley family is one such case. The 1861 census shows only thirteen-year-old James Riley attending school. Nineteen-year-old John and seventeen-year-old Jerome had already completed their studies and were preparing for college, while ten-year-old Ann and seven-year-old William were not listed as attending school. The problem with taking this at face value is that the Riley family moved to Buxton in part because of the educational opportunities available there. Both parents, Isaac and Mary Riley, were literate, and it seems unlikely that they would keep their children out of school, thus bringing into question the veracity of the census. Canadian Population Census, 1861, National Archives of Canada, Ottawa, Ont.

45. Canadian Population Census, 1861, National Archives of Canada, Ottawa, Ont.; Vincent, *Southern Seed, Northern Soil,* 74.

46. The Buxton Mission School and Elgin Association reports recorded black and white students who attended the school regardless of where they lived without denoting race. The current analysis includes only black residents living on the Elgin tract.

47. Canadian Population Census, 1861, National Archives of Canada, Ottawa, Ont.

48. Ibid.

49. Ibid.

50. Ibid.

51. Ibid.

52. Ibid.

53. Ibid.

54. Canadian Population Census, 1861, 1871, National Archives of Canada, Ottawa, Ont.

55. Ibid.

56. Minutes of the Synod of the Presbyterian Church of Canada, June 1857; Walton, "Blacks in Buxton and Chatham," 97; Simpson, "Negroes in Ontario," 555–56; Schweninger, "John H. Rapier Sr.," 31n; Robbins, *Legacy to Buxton*, 63; Schweninger, *James T. Rapier*, 110.

57. John Rapier Jr. listed Kingston, Jamaica, as his residence so that, as a foreign student, he would be admitted regardless of his race. Meanwhile, a Detroit resident of mixed racial ancestry was admitted to the school, but when he showed up and it was discovered he was black, he was turned away. John Rapier Jr. to Sarah Thomas, February 7, 1864, Rapier Family Papers.

58. Schweninger, "John H. Rapier Sr.," 27; Robbins, *Legacy to Buxton*, 63.

59. King, "Autobiography," 302–4.

60. William King to Rev. J. Banner, Toronto, July 15, 1849, King Papers.

Chapter 10. A Community Transformed

1. Regimental Service Records, 102d United States Colored Troops, RG 94, National Archives and Records Administration; Pension Records for Solomon King, Elijah Doo, Samuel Lightfoot, and Ezekiel Cooper, RG 15, National Archives and Records Administration.

2. U.S. War Department, *Official Records*, ser. 1, vol. 44 (Washington, D.C.: Government Printing Office, 1880–1901), 434.

3. Ibid., 423–92.

4. Ullman, *Look to the North Star*, 230; Military Records for William Hooper, James Newby, National Archives and Records Administration, RG 94; Medical Officer's File, Records of the Adjutant General's Office, RG 94, National Archives and Records Administration; Ripley, *Black Abolitionist Papers*, vol. 2, 40.

5. Pension Records for Benjamin Matthews, National Archives and Records Administration, RG 15.

6. U.S. War Department, *Official Records*, ser. 1, vol. 44, 423–92; Pension Records for Benjamin Matthews, William Richardson, National Archives and Records Administration, RG 15.

7. Pension Record of Solomon King, National Archives and Records Administration, RG 15.

8. Pension Records for William Hooper, Lorenzo Rann, and James Newby, National Archives and Records Administration, Rb 15.

9. Raleigh Township Assessment Rolls, 1861–1865.

10. Ullman, *Look to the North Star*, 179; King, "Autobiography," 422–46; Robbins, *Legacy to Buxton*, 99–100.

11. Cha-Jua, *America's First Black Town*, 77; Vincent, *Southern Seed, Northern Soil*, 118; Walker, *Free Frank*.

12. Regimental Service Records, 102d United States Colored Troops, RG 94, National Archives and Records Administration; Military Service Records, RG 94, National Archives and Records Administration; Pension Records for Solomon King and James Newby, National Archives and Records Administration, RG 15.

13. Canadian Population Census, 1871, 1881, National Archives of Canada, Ottawa, Ont.; Robbins, *Legacy to Buxton*, 83–87, 106–7.

14. Jane, the family matriarch, had been a slave on a Tennessee plantation. She had had several children by her master, whose feelings for her may have been genuine. He made an arrangement with another of his slaves, Dennis, to marry Jane with the understanding that Dennis would care for the children as if they were his own. Their master then arranged for them to go to Canada and thereby gain their freedom. An additional part of the agreement was that the couple keep the Robbins name. Jane and Dennis first settled at Dawn but later relocated to Buxton. Robbins, *Legacy to Buxton*, 95.

15. King, "Autobiography," 423.

16. Ibid., 422–43; Stouffer, *Light of God*, 102–3; Ullman, *Look to the North Star*, 230.

17. Despite a valiant fight by its residents, the U.S. Supreme Court closed the village in 1882 although continued resistance kept the community open until 1887 when the military finally forced the people to leave. Schildt, "Freedman's Village," 11–21; Reidy, "Coming from the Shadow of the Past," 403–28; Schildt, "Aladdin's Lamp," 6–19.

18. Reidy, "Coming from the Shadow of the Past," 405–6, 409; Schildt, "Freedman's Village," 14–15.

19. *Alabama State Journal*, April 29, 1870.

20. King, "Autobiography," 423–43.

21. Three of the eight black surgeons in the union army during the Civil War had a connection to Buxton: Jerome Riley, Anderson Ruffin Abbott, and John H. Rapier Jr. Riley, Abbott, and another black Canadian, Alexander T. Augusta, helped to establish the Freedmen's Hospital.

22. King, "Autobiography," 457–58.

23. Schweninger, *James T. Rapier*, 110, 113; Pension Records of William Hooper, Kincheon Brooks, William Richardson, Benjamin Brooks, National Archives and Records Administration, RG 15; *Washington Evening Star*, May 19, 1866.

24. *Nashville Daily Press and Times*, August 14, 1865; *Alabama State Journal*, April 29, 1870; Schweninger, "Fugitive Negro in the Promised Land," 92; Schweninger, *James T. Rapier*, 37–54, 86–94, 116, 123, 157–60.

25. Schweninger, *James T. Rapier*, 37–54, 86–94, 116, 123, 157–60.

26. Ibid., 37–54, 86–94, 116, 123, 157–60; Walton, "Blacks in Buxton and Chatham," 166.

27. Canadian Population Census, 1871, 1881, National Archives of Canada, Ottawa, Ont.; Canadian County Atlas Digital Project, 1881 Atlas for Raleigh Township, available at http://digital.library.mcgill.ca/CountyAtlas; Robbins, *Legacy to Buxton*, 81–82; U.S. Census, 1880, Warren County, Miss., Bovina Precinct, Beat no. 4, 561, *Tenth Census of the United States, 1880* (microfilm), National Archives and Records Administration. Henry Thomas died in 1882 and was laid to rest in Bovina, Mississippi.

28. Ullman, *Look to the North Star,* 231–36; Canadian Population Census, 1871, 1881, National Archives of Canada, Ottawa, Ont.

29. King, "Autobiography," 422–43; Canadian Population Census, 1861, 1871, 1881, National Archives of Canada, Ottawa, Ont. Recent scholarship on the black population of Canada has indicated through extensive statistical analysis that there was no mass migration back to the United States in the aftermath of the Civil War, as has typically been alleged. Current evidence suggests that Canada's 1871 black population was approximately 20 percent less than the 1860 population, hardly an exodus. Wayne, "Black Population of Canada," 470–71.

30. Canadian Population Census, 1871, 1881, National Archives of Canada, Ottawa, Ont.; pension records of Lorenzo Rann, Kincheon Brooks, National Archives and Records Administration, RG 15; Register of Marriages, 1857–1895; Robbins, Register of Baptisms at Buxton Presbyterian Church; B.M.E. Methodist Church Cemetery.

31. Register of Marriages, 1857–1895; Robbins, Register of Baptisms at Buxton Presbyterian Church.

32. Register of Marriages, 1857–1895; Robbins, Register of Baptisms at Buxton Presbyterian Church.

33. Raleigh Township Assessment Rolls, 1872.

34. Walton, "Blacks in Buxton and Chatham," 227, 233; Canadian Population Census, 1861, National Archives of Canada, Ottawa, Ont.

35. Canadian Population Census, 1881, National Archives of Canada, Ottawa, Ont.

36. Walton, "Blacks in Buxton and Chatham," 227, 233.

37. At times, Jemima retreated to the King home and refused to leave, finding solace in her piano. During her periods of clarity, she taught music at the settlement. Harriet Rhue was one of the children who received piano lessons from Jemima, becoming quite a talented musician and composer of several songs, including "That Sacred Spot," which was adopted by Canadian troops during World War I as their official marching song.

38. Robbins, *Legacy to Buxton;* Ullman, *Look to the North Star;* Pension record of William Hooper, National Archives and Records Administration, RG 15; Canadian Population Census, 1861, National Archives of Canada, Ottawa, Ont.; U.S. Census, *Tenth Census of the United States, 1880* (microfilm), National Archives and Records Administration.

39. Robbins, *Legacy to Buxton,* 94–97.

40. Ibid., 96, 214.

41. Ibid., 96–102; Raleigh Township Assessment Rolls; Canadian Population Census, 1871, 1881, National Archives of Canada, Ottawa, Ont.

42. Canadian Population Census, 1861, National Archives of Canada, Ottawa, Ont.; Register of Marriages, 1857–1895.

43. John N. Morris is listed as a head of household on the 1871 census.

44. Canadian Population Census, 1861, 1871, 1881, National Archives of Canada, Ottawa, Ont.; List of Voters—Township of Raleigh, 1874, Chatham-Kent Museum.

45. Howe, *Report to the Freedmen's Inquiry Commission,* 70–71.

46. Ibid.

47. King, "Autobiography," 446–47.

48. Howe, *Report to the Freedmen's Inquiry Commission,* 110.

49. King, "Autobiography," 451–52.

50. Samuel May, letter to the editor, *National Anti-Slavery Standard,* August 19, September 2 and 9, 1852.

51. Ibid.

52. Thomas Henning, "Coloured Population in Canada," 271–72.

53. Ibid.

54. Ibid.

55. "Colony at Buxton," *National Anti-Slavery Standard,* November 7 and 14, 1857.

56. Ibid.

57. Ibid.

58. Earl Spencer, John Probyn, and Henry Christy to King, January 19, 1860, *British Anti-Slavery Reporter,* February 1, 1860.

59. King, "Autobiography," 380.

60. Ibid., 382, 388–90; Stouffer, *Light of Nature,* 101.

61. Howe, *Report to the Freedmen's Inquiry Commission,* 59. Of course, the commission may have had an ulterior motive, seeking to discourage the use of federal monies to finance the colonization of American blacks in Africa.

62. Schwarz, *Migrants among Slavery,* 71.

63. Howe, *Report to the Freedmen's Inquiry Commission,* 70–71.

64. Pease and Pease, "William King," 10.

65. Abbott, "Elgin Settlement."

66. Strivers, *The History of Brown County,* as quoted in McGroarty, "Exploration in Mass Emancipation," 225.

67. Vincent, *Southern Seed, Northern Soil,* 150; United States Department of Agriculture, 1997 Census of Agriculture, vol. 1, National, State, and County Tables, available at http://www.nass.usda.gov/census/census97/volume1/vol1pubs.htm.

68. Robbins, *Legacy to Buxton,* 115–16.

69. Ibid., 145–51.

70. Ibid., 157–58, 185–90.

71. Ibid., 193.

72. Harris, *Sketch of the Buxton Mission,* 5.

73. Ibid.

74. Ibid., 5; Ullman, *Look to the North Star,* 213; Gregg, "African in North America." Whether Stowe's book was truly based on King's life may be best judged by individuals themselves. King and Stowe were acquainted, and she was familiar with his work at Buxton. Stowe included a footnote in the first edition of *Dred:* "These statements are all true of the Elgin Settlement, founded by Mr. King, a gentleman who removed and settled his slaves in the south of Canada." Stowe, *Dred,* 330–31.

Bibliography

Archival and Artifactual Sources

Abbott, Anderson Ruffin. "The Elgin Settlement." Abbott Papers, Toronto Metropolitan Reference Library. Toronto, Ont.

Agricultural Census of Canada, 1861, National Archives of Canada, Ottawa, Ont.

Amherstburg Baptist Association. MS. Minutes, 1854. Canadian Baptist Historical Collection, McMaster Divinity College, Hamilton, Ont.

B.M.E. Methodist Church Cemetery, North Buxton, Ont. Chatham-Kent Museum, Chatham, Ont. Transcribed on Behalf of the Kent County Branch of the Ontario Genealogical Society.

· Bible Society Records, South Buxton, 1860–1893. J. J. Talman Regional Collection, University of Western Ontario Archives, London, Ont.

Canada Land Petitions. RG1, L3, National Archives of Canada, Ottawa, Ont.

Canadian Anti-Slavery Baptist Association, Minutes, 1854. Canadian Institute for Historical Microreproductions, Ottawa, Ont. Microfiche.

Canadian Black Studies Project, University of Western Ontario Archives, London, Ont.

Canadian Population Census, 1861, 1871, 1881. National Archives of Canada, Ottawa, Ont.

Cleland, James (1836–1907). Papers. MG 29 C51, National Archives of Canada, Ottawa, Ont.

Early Elgin Settlers and Land Owners. Buxton National Historic Site and Museum, Buxton, Ont.

Elgin Association Annual Reports, 1851–1859. Toronto Metropolitan Reference Library, Toronto, Ont.

Erie County court records. Land deeds. County Hall, Buffalo, N.Y.

Fred Landon Fonds. J. J. Talman Regional Collection, University of Western Ontario Archives, London, Ont.

Gregg, William R. "The African in North America, Their Welfare after Freedom As Effected and Influenced by the Life of William King." File #1873–5004–1–5, William Gregg Family fonds at the Presbyterian Church in Canada Archives.

Jamieson, Annie Straith. Papers. J. J. Talman Regional Collection, University of Western Ontario Archives, London, Ont.

Kent County Directory, 1880. J. J. Talman Regional Collection, University of Western Ontario Archives, London, Ont.

King, Rev. William. "Autobiography of Rev. Wm. King Written During the Last Three Years of His Life, January 6, 1892." Typed copy at the Presbyterian Church Archives, Knox College, Toronto. The original is part of the King Papers at the National Archives of Canada, Ottawa, Ont.

King, Rev. William, Papers. MG 24, J 14, National Archives of Canada, Ottawa, Ont.

Map of the Elgin Association Lands, n.d., Copy of Part of the Plan of the Township of Raleigh. Chatham-Kent Museum, Chatham, Ont.

Memorial Baptist Cemetery, North Buxton, Concession 8. Chatham-Kent Museum, Chatham, Ont. Transcribed on Behalf of the Kent County Branch of the Ontario Genealogical Society.

Minute Book. Presbytery of Toronto, 1844–1861. United Church Archives, Toronto, Ont.

Minutes and Proceedings of the First Annual Convention of the People of Colour, Philadelphia, 1831.

Minutes and Proceedings of the Second Annual Convention for the Improvement of the Free People of Colour in These United States, Philadelphia, 1832.

Minutes of Chatham Common Schools. J. J. Talman Regional Collection, University of Western Ontario Archives, London, Ont.

Minutes of the Synod of the Presbyterian Church of Canada, 1848–1875. Presbyterian Church Archives, Toronto, Ont.

"Mission to Fugitive Slaves in Canada: Being a Branch of the Operations of the Colonial and Continental Church Society: Report for the Year 1860–61," King Papers.

North Buxton Session Book (Deacon's Court). June 12, 1858–July 27, 1880. MS, Chatham-Kent Museum, Chatham, Ont.

U.S. Army Pension Records. RG 15. National Archives and Records Administration, Washington, D.C.

U.S. Military Records, Rb 94. National Archives and Records Administration, Washington, D.C.

"Prospectus for the Oberlin Collegiate Institute," 1833, Oberlin College Archives, Oberlin, Ohio.

Raleigh Township abandoned cemetery records, Lot 8, Concession A, Chatham-Kent Museum, Chatham, Ont. Transcribed on Behalf of the Kent County Branch of the Ontario Genealogical Society.

Raleigh Township Assessment Rolls. Raleigh Township Records. J. J. Talman Regional Collection, University of Western Ontario Archives, London, Ont.

Raleigh Township Voter's List, 1874. Chatham-Kent Museum, Chatham, Ont.

Rapier Papers. Moorland-Spingarn Research Center, Howard University, Washington, D.C.

Records of St. Andrew's United Church, South Buxton, 1857–1939. J. J. Talman Regional Collection, University of Western Ont.

Regimental Service Records, 102d United States Colored Troops, RG 94, National Archives and Records Administration, College Park, Md.

Register of Marriages, 1857–1895, for the St. Andrew's Church Congregation at Buxton, Canada West, microfilm, J. J. Talman Regional Collection, University of Western Ontario Archives, London, Ont.

Robbins, Arlie C., compiler. Maps of the Elgin Settlement, 1851–1873. Buxton National Historic Site and Museum, Buxton, Ont.

———. Register of Baptisms, Buxton Presbyterian Church, 1859–1903. Buxton National Historic Site and Museum, Buxton, Ont.

Session Book of the Congregation at Buxton, Canada West, 1858–1865. J. J. Talman Regional Collection, University of Western Ontario Archives, London, Ont.

Seward, William Henry. Papers. MG 24 B 105, National Archives of Canada, Ottawa, Ont.

Shadd Family Papers and Account Books. J. J. Talman Regional Collection, University of Western Ontario Archives, London, Ont.

South Buxton Cemetery, Lot 8, Concession Eleven, Raleigh Township. Chatham-Kent Museum, Chatham, Ont. Transcribed on Behalf of the Kent County Branch of the Ontario Genealogical Society.

Wickham Family Papers, Virginia Historical Society, Richmond, Virginia.

Published Sources

Angle, Paul M., ed. *The Complete Lincoln-Douglas Debates of 1858.* Chicago: University of Chicago Press, 1958.

Aptheker, Herbert. *American Negro Slave Revolts.* New York: International Publishers, 1974.

Bagby, Ross Frederick. "The Randolph Slave Saga: Communities in Collision." Ph.D. diss., Ohio State University, 1998.

Bearden, Jim, and Linda Jean Butler. *Shadd: The Life and Times of Mary Shadd Cary.* Toronto: NC Press, 1977.

Bell, Howard H. "Free Negroes of the North, 1830–1835: A Study in National Cooperation." *Journal of Negro Education* 26 (1957): 447–55.

———, ed. *Minutes of the Proceedings of the National Negro Conventions, 1830–1864.* New York: Arno Press, 1969.

Berlin, Ira. *Many Thousands Gone: The First Two Centuries of Slavery in North America.* Cambridge, Mass.: Harvard University Press, 1998.

Bertley, Leo W. *Canada and Its People of African Descent.* Pierrefonds, QC: Bilongo, 1977.

Berwanger, Eugene. *The Frontier against Slavery: Western Anti-Negro Prejudice and the Slavery Extension Controversy.* Urbana: University of Illinois Press, 1967.

Blassingame, John W., ed. *Slave Testimony: Two Centuries of Letters, Speeches, Interviews, and Autobiographies.* Baton Rouge: Louisiana University Press, 1977.

Blassingame, John W., and Mae H. Henderson, eds. *Antislavery Newspapers and Periodicals.* 5 vols. Boston: G. K. Hall, 1980–84.

Blight, David W. "In Search of Learning, Liberty, and Self-Definition: James McCune

Smith and the Ordeal of the American Black Intellectual." *Afro-Americans in New York Life and History* 9 (July 1985): 7–25.

Bogger, Tommy L. *Free Blacks in Norfolk, Virginia, 1790–1860.* Charlottesville, Va.: University Press of Virginia, 1997.

Brown, Lloyd W. "Beneath the North Star: The Canadian Image in Black Literature." *Dalhousie Review* (1970): 317–29.

Brown, Stewart J. *Thomas Chalmers and the Godly Commonwealth in Scotland.* New York: Oxford University Press, 1982.

Burns, Robert F., ed. *The Life and Times of the Rev. Robert Burns, Including an Unfinished Autobiography.* Toronto: J. Campbell & Son, 1872.

Burton, Orville Vernon. "Anatomy of an Antebellum Rural Free Black Community: Social Structure and Social Interaction in Edgefield District, South Carolina, 1850–1860." *Southern Studies* 21, no. 3 (1982): 294–325.

Campbell, Stanley W. *The Slave Catchers: Enforcement of the Fugitive Slave Law 1850–1860.* Chapel Hill: University of North Carolina Press, 1970.

Carlton, Sylvia. "Egerton Ryerson and Education in Ontario, 1844–1877." Ph.D. diss., University of Pennsylvania, 1950.

Cary, Mary Ann Shadd. "A Plea for Emigration; or, Notes on Canada West for the Information of Coloured Immigrants." Detroit, 1852.

Catterall, Helen Tunnicliff, ed. *Judicial Cases Concerning American Slavery and the Negro.* 5 vols. Washington, D.C.: Carnegie Institute of Washington, 1926–1937.

Caven, William. "The Rev. Michael Willis, D.D., L.L.D." *Knox College Monthly* 3 (Jan. 1886): 97–101.

Cha-Jua, Sundiata Keita. *America's First Black Town: Brooklyn, Illinois, 1830–1915.* Urbana: University of Illinois Press, 2000.

Chase, Salmon P., ed. *The Statutes of Ohio and of the Northwest Territory.* 3 vols. Cincinnati, Ohio: Corey & Fairbank, 1833.

Cobb, W. Montague. "Alexander Thomas Augusta." *Journal of the National Medical Association* 44, no. 4 (1952): 327–29.

Cody, Cheryll Ann. "There Was No 'Absalom' on the Ball Plantations: Slave-Naming Practices in the South Carolina Low Country, 1720–1865." *American Historical Review* 92, no. 3 (June 1987): 563–96.

Coffin, Levi. *Reminiscences of an Abolitionist.* Cincinnati: Western Tract Society, 1876.

Cooper, Frederick. "Elevating the Race: The Social Thought of Black Leaders, 1827–1850." *American Quarterly* 25 (1972): 604–25.

Cooper Guasco, Suzanne D. "Confronting Democracy: Edward Coles and the Cultivation of Authority in the Young Nation." Ph.D. diss., College of William and Mary, 2004.

Creighton, Donald. *A History of Canada: Dominion of the North.* Boston: Houghton Mifflin, 1958.

Curry, Leonard P. *The Free Black in Urban America: 1800–1850.* Chicago: University of Chicago Press, 1981.

Dillon, Merton L. *The Abolitionists: The Growth of a Dissenting Minority.* DeKalb: Northern Illinois University Press, 1974.

————. *Benjamin Lundy and the Struggle for Negro Freedom*. Urbana: University of Illinois Press, 1966.

Dorn, A. E. "A History of the Antislavery Movement in Rochester and Vicinity." M.A. thesis, University of Buffalo, 1932.

Doughty, Sir Arthur G., ed. *The Elgin-Grey Papers, 1846–1852*. 4 vols. Ottawa, Ont.: J. O. Patenaude, 1937.

Douglass, Frederick. *Life and Times of Frederick Douglass: His Early Life As a Slave, His Escape from Bondage, and His Complete History*. Hartford, Conn.: Park, 1881; reprint, New York: Macmillan, 1962.

Drew, Benjamin. *A North-side View of Slavery*. Boston: J. P. Jewett, 1856; reprint, New York: Negro Universities Press, 1968.

Du Bois, W. E. B. *The Souls of Black Folk*. New York: Dover, 1994.

Faragher, John Mack. *Sugar Creek: Life on the Illinois Prairie*. New Haven, Conn.: Yale University Press, 1986.

Farrell, John K. A. "The History of the Negro Community in Chatham, Ontario, 1787–1865." Ph.D. diss., University of Ottawa, 1955.

Feldman, Eugene. "James T. Rapier, Negro Congressman from Alabama." *Phylon* 19 (1958): 417–23.

Finkelman, Paul. *An Imperfect Union: Slavery, Federalism, and Comity*. Chapel Hill: University of North Carolina Press, 1981.

Franklin, John Hope, and Loren Schweninger. *Runaway Slaves: Rebels on the Plantation*. New York: Oxford University Press, 1999.

Fuller, Wayne E. *The Old Country School: The Story of Rural Education in the Middle West*. Chicago: University of Chicago Press, 1982.

Garrison, William L., ed. *Thought on African Colonization*. Boston: Garrison & Knapp, 1832.

George, Carol V. R. *Segregated Sabbaths: Richard Allen and the Emergence of Independent Black Churches, 1760–1840*. New York: Oxford University Press, 1973.

Hamilton, J. C. "The African in Canada: The Reverend William King and the Elgin Association." *Knox College Monthly and Presbyterian Magazine* 11 (1889): 30–37.

Harris, A. M. *A Sketch of the Buxton Mission and the Elgin Settlement*. Raleigh, Can.: J. S. Wilson, 1866.

Henning, Thomas. "The Coloured Population in Canada." *British and Foreign Anti-Slavery Reporter* 3 (Dec. 1855), 271–72.

Henning, Thomas, and William Reid. "Report of the Elgin Association," March 18, 1873. *Ontario Legislature Sessional Papers*, 36 Victoria [1873].

Hershberg, Theodore. "Free Blacks in Antebellum Philadelphia: A Study of Ex-Slaves, Freeborn, and Socioeconomic Decline." *Journal of Social History* 5 (1971): 183–209.

Hill, Daniel G. *The Freedom-Seekers: Blacks in Early Canada*. Agincourt, Ont.: Book Society of Canada, 1981.

Hodges, Graham Russell. *Root and Branch: African Americans in New York and East Jersey, 1613–1863*. Chapel Hill: University of North Carolina Press, 1999.

Horton, James Oliver. "Black Education at Oberlin College: A Controversial Commitment." *Journal of Negro Education* 54 (1985): 477–99.

———. *Free People of Color: Inside the African American Community.* Washington, D.C.: Smithsonian Institution Press, 1993.

Horton, James Oliver, and Lois E. Horton. *Black Bostonians: Family Life and Community Struggle in the Ante-Bellum North.* New York: Homes & Meier, 1979.

———. *In Hope of Liberty: Culture, Community, and Protest among Northern Free Blacks, 1700–1860.* New York: Oxford University Press, 1997.

Howe, S. G. *Report to the Freedmen's Inquiry Commission 1864: The Refugees from Slavery in Canada West.* Boston: Wright & Potter, 1864; reprint, New York: Arno Press, 1969.

Inscoe, John C. "Carolina Slave Names: An Index to Acculturation" *Journal of Southern History* 49, no. 4 (1983): 527–54.

Jamieson, Annie Straith. *William King: Friend and Champion of the Slaves.* Toronto: Missions of Evangelism, 1925; reprint, New York: Negro Universities Press, 1969.

Jones, Thomas H. *The Experience of Thomas Jones, Who Was a Slave for Forty Three Years.* Springfield, Mass.: H. S. Taylor, 1954.

Jones, William R. *Is God a White Racist? A Preamble to Black Theology.* Garden City, N.Y.: Anchor, 1973.

Katz, Jonathan. *Resistance at Christiana: The Fugitive Slave Rebellion, Christiana, Pennsylvania, September 11, 1851.* New York: Thomas Y. Crowell, 1974.

Ketcham, Ralph L. "The Dictates of Conscience: Edward Coles and Slavery." *Virginia Quarterly Review* 36 (1960): 46–62.

King, Rev. William. *History of the King Family Who Settled in the Woods Near Where the Village of Delta, Ohio, Now Stands in the Year 1834.* Delta, Ohio: n.p., 1893.

King, William, and Robert Burns. "Fugitive Slaves in Canada, Elgin Settlement." N.p., 1860.

King, Wilma. *Stolen Childhood, Slave Youth in Nineteenth Century America.* Bloomington: University of Indiana Press, 1995.

Kleinig, John. *Paternalism.* Totowa, N.J.: Rowman & Littlefield, 1984.

Knight, Claudette. "Black Parents Speak: Education in Mid-Nineteenth Century Canada West." *Ontario History* 89 (1997): 269–84.

Kusmer, Kenneth. "The Black Urban Experience in American History." In *The State of Afro-American History: Past, Present, and Future,* edited by Darlene Clark Hine, 91–122. Baton Rouge: Louisiana State University Press, 1986.

Lader, Lawrence. *The Bold Brahmins: New England's War against Slavery, 1831–1863.* New York: Dutton, 1961.

Landon, Fred. "Agriculture among the Negro Refugees in Upper Canada." *Journal of Negro History* 21 (1936): 304–12.

———. "The Buxton Settlement in Canada." *Journal of Negro History* 3 (1918): 360–67.

———. "The Negro Migration to Canada after the Passing of the Fugitive Slave Act." *Journal of Negro History* 5 (1920): 22–36.

———. "Records Illustrating the Condition of Refugees from Slavery in Upper Canada before 1860." *Journal of Negro History* 13 (1928): 201–2.

Lapsansky, Emma Jones. "'Since They Got Those Separate Churches': Afro-Americans and Racism in Jacksonian Philadelphia." *American Quarterly* 32 (1980): 54–78.

Laslett, Peter, and Richard Walls, eds. *Household and Family in Past Time.* Cambridge, U.K.: Cambridge University Press, 1972.

Law, Howard. "Self-Reliance Is the True Road to Independence: Ideology and the Ex-Slaves in Buxton and Chatham." *Ontario History* 77 (1985): 107–21.

Lawson, Ellen N., and Marlene Merrill. "The Antebellum 'Talented Thousandth': Black College Students at Oberlin before the Civil War." *Journal of Negro Education* 52 (1983): 142–55.

Lewis, James K. *Religious Life of Fugitive Slaves and Rise of Coloured Baptist Churches, 1820–1865, in What Is Now Known As Ontario.* New York: Arno Press, 1980.

———. "Religious Nature of the Early Negro Migration to Canada and the Amherstburg Baptist Association." *Ontario History* 58 (1966): 117–33.

Litwack, Leon F. *North of Slavery: The Negro in the Free States, 1790–1860.* Chicago: University of Chicago Press, 1961.

Loguen, J. W. *The Rev. J. W. Loguen, As a Slave and As a Freeman.* Syracuse, N.Y.: J. G. K. Thair, 1859.

Lundy, Benjamin. *The Life, Travels, and Opinions of Benjamin Lundy.* Philadelphia: W. D. Parrish, 1847.

Magdol, Edward. *A Right to the Land: Essays on the Freedmen's Community.* Westport., Conn.: Greenwood Press, 1977.

Mahoney, Olivia. "Black Abolitionist." *Chicago History* 20 (1991): 22–37.

Malone, Ann Patton. *Sweet Chariot: Slave Family and Household Structure in Nineteenth Century Louisiana.* Chapel Hill: University of North Carolina Press, 1992.

Manning, William R. *Diplomatic Correspondence of the United States Canadian Relations, 1784–1860.* Millwood, N.Y.: Kraus Reprint, 1975 rprnt.

Mathias, Frank F. "John Randolph's Freedmen: The Thwarting of a Will." *Journal of Southern History* 39, no. 2 (May 1973): 263–72.

McDonnell, Michael. "Other Loyalists: A Reconsideration of the Black Loyalist Experience in the American Revolutionary Era." *Southern Historian* 16 (1995): 9–18.

McGroarty, William Buckner. "Exploration in Mass Emancipation." *William and Mary Quarterly* 21, no. 3 (July 1941): 208–26.

Melish, Joanne Pope. *Disowning Slavery: Gradual Emancipation and "Race" in New England, 1780–1860.* Ithaca, N.Y.: Cornell University Press, 1998.

Middleton, Stephen, ed. *The Black Laws in the Old Northwest: A Documentary History.* Westport, Conn.: Greenwood Press, 1993.

Miles, Edwin A. "The Mississippi Slave Insurrection Scare of 1835." *Journal of Negro History* 32 (1957): 48–60.

Miller, Floyd J. *The Search for a Black Nationality: Black Emigration and Colonization 1787–1863.* Urbana: University of Illinois Press, 1975.

Morgan, Philip D. *Slave Counterpoint: Black Culture in the Eighteenth-Century Chesapeake and Lowcountry.* Chapel Hill: University of North Carolina Press, 1998.

Murray, Alexander L. "Canada and the Anglo-American Anti-Slavery Movement: A Study in International Philanthropy." Ph.D. diss., University of Pennsylvania, 1960.

———. "Extradition of Fugitive Slaves from Canada." *Canadian Historical Review* 43 (1962): 98–314.

Nash, Gary B. *Forging Freedom: The Formation of Philadelphia's Black Community, 1720–1840.* Cambridge, Mass.: Harvard University Press, 1988.

Nash, Roderick W. "William Parker and the Christiana Riot." *Journal of Negro History* 46 (1961): 24–31.

Nore, Ellen, and Dick Norrish. *Edwardsville: An Illustrated History.* St. Louis: B. Bradley, 1996.

Ohio Antislavery Society. *Condition of the People of Color in the State of Ohio.* Boston: I. Knapp, 1839.

Parker, William. "The Freedman's Story." *Atlantic Monthly,* February 1866, 152–66, and March 1866, 276–95.

Pease, William H., and Jane H. Pease. *Black Utopia: Negro Communal Experiments in America.* Madison: University of Wisconsin Press, 1963.

———. "Ends, Means, and Attitudes: Black-White Conflict in the Antislavery Movement." *Civil War History* 18 (June 1972): 117–28.

———. "Opposition to the Founding of the Elgin Settlement." *Canadian Historical Review* 38 (1957): 202–18.

———. "Organized Negro Communities: A North American Experiment." *Journal of Negro History* 47 (1962): 19–34.

———. *They Who Would Be Free: Blacks' Search for Freedom.* New York: Atheneum, 1974.

———. "William King: From Master to Servant." *Renssalaer Review of Graduate Studies* 16 (1959): 3–10.

Pettinger, Alasdair. "'Send Back the Money': Douglass and the Free Church of Scotland." In *Liberating Sojourn: Frederick Douglass and Transatlantic Reform,* edited by Alan J. Rice and Martin Crawford, 31–55. Athens: University of Georgia Press, 1999.

Powell, C. A., B. T. Kavanaugh, and David Christy. "Transplanting Free Negroes to Ohio from 1815 to 1858." *Journal of Negro History* 1, no. 3 (1916): 302–17.

Quarles, Benjamin. *The Negro in the American Revolution.* Chapel Hill: University of North Carolina Press, 1961.

Raboteau, Albert J. *Slave Religion: The "Invisible Institution" in the Antebellum South.* New York: Oxford University Press, 1978.

Reidy, Joseph P. "Coming from the Shadow of the Past: The Transition from Slavery to Freedom at Freedmen's Village, 1863–1869." *Virginia Magazine of History and Biography* 95 (Oct. 1987): 403–28.

Report on the Condition of the Free Colored People of Ohio. N.p., Beaumont & Wallace, 1835.

Rice, C. Duncan. *The Scots Abolitionists, 1833–1861.* Baton Rouge: Louisiana State University Press, 1981.

Riendeau, Roger. *An Enduring Heritage: Black Contributions to Early Ontario.* Toronto: Dundurn Press, 1984.

Ripley, C. Peter, ed. *The Black Abolitionist Papers.* 5 vols. Chapel Hill: University of North Carolina Press, 1986–92.

Robbins, Arlie C. *Legacy to Buxton.* Chatham, Ont.: Ideal, 1983.

Robinson, Armstead L. "The Difference Freedom Made: The Emancipation of Afro-Americans." In *The State of Afro-American History: Past, Present, and Future,* edited by Darlene Clark Hine, 51–74. Baton Rouge: Louisiana State University Press, 1986.

Ruchames, Louis, and Walter Merrill, eds. *The Letters of William Lloyd Garrison,* 6 vols. (Cambridge, Mass.: Harvard University Press, 1971–1981).

Savitt, Todd L. *Medicine and Slavery: The Diseases and Health Care of Blacks in Antebellum Virginia.* Chicago: University of Chicago Press, 1978.

Schildt, Roberta. "Aladdin's Lamp: Education in Freedman's Village." *Arlington Historical Magazine* 10 (Oct. 1995): 6–19.

———. "Freedman's Village: Arlington, Virginia, 1863–1900." *Arlington Historical Magazine* 7 (Oct. 1984): 11–21.

Schwarz, Philip J. *Migrants against Slavery: Virginians and the Nation.* Charlottesville: University Press of Virginia, 2001.

Schweninger, Loren. *Black Property Owners in the South, 1790–1915.* Chicago: University of Illinois Press, 1990.

———. "A Fugitive Negro in the Promised Land: James Rapier in Canada, 1856–1864." *Ontario History* 67 (1975): 91–104.

———. *James T. Rapier and Reconstruction.* Chicago: University of Chicago Press, 1978.

———. "John H. Rapier Sr.: A Slave and Freedman in the Ante-Bellum South." *Civil War History* 20 (1974): 23–34.

———. "A Slave Family in the Ante Bellum South." *Journal of Negro History* 60 (1975): 29–44.

Sexsmith, W. N. "Some Notes on the Buxton Settlement, Raleigh, Kent County." *Kent Historical Society,* Papers and Addresses, Chatham, Ont., 1914.

Shepperson, George. "The Free Church and American Slavery." *Scottish Historical Review* 30 (1951): 126–43.

———. "Thomas Chalmers, the Free Church of Scotland, and the South." *Journal of Southern History* 17 (1951): 517–37.

Shore, Laurence. "Making Mississippi Safe for Slavery: The Insurrectionary Panic of 1835." *Class, Conflict, and Consensus: Antebellum Southern Community Studies,* edited by Orville Burton and Robert McMath Jr., 96–127. Westport, Conn.: Greenwood Press, 1982.

Shreve, Dorothy Shadd. *The AfriCanadian Church: A Stabilizer.* Jordan Station, Ont.: Paideia Press, 1983.

Silverman, Jason H. *Unwelcome Guests: Canada West's Response to American Fugitive Slaves, 1800–1865.* Millwood, N.Y.: Associated Faculty Press, 1985.

Silverman, Jason H., and Donna J. Gillie. "The Pursuit of Knowledge under Difficulties: Education and the Fugitive Slaves in Canada." *Ontario History* 74 (1982): 95–112.

Simpson, Donald. "Negroes in Ontario from Early Times to 1870." Ph.D. diss., University of Western Ontario, 1971.

Smith, H. Shelton. *In His Image, But . . . Racism in Southern Religion, 1780–1910.* Durham, N.C.: Duke University Press, 1972.

Spencer, H. H. "To Nestle in the Mane of the British Lion: A History of Canadian Black Education: 1820–1870." Ph.D. diss., Northwestern University, 1970.

Stauffer, John. *The Black Hearts of Men: Radical Abolitionists and the Transformation of Race.* Cambridge, Mass.: Harvard University Press, 2002.

Stevenson, Brenda E. *Life in Black and White: Family Community in the Slave South.* New York: Oxford University Press, 1996.

Steward, Austin. *Twenty-Two Years a Slave and Forty Years a Freeman.* Rochester, N.Y.: W. Alling, 1857; reprint, New York: Negro Universities Press, 1968.

Stewart, James Brewer. *Holy Warriors: The Abolitionists and Slavery.* New York: Hill & Wang, 1976.

———. "The Emergence of Racial Modernity and the Rise of the White North, 1790–1849." *Journal of the Early Republic* 18 (1998): 191–217.

Stouffer, Allen P. *The Light of Nature and the Law of God: Antislavery in Ontario, 1833–1877.* Baton Rouge: Louisiana State University Press, 1992.

———. "Michael Willis and the British Roots of Canadian Antislavery." *Slavery and Abolition* 8 (1987): 294–312.

Strivers, E. B. *The History of Brown County, Ohio.* Chicago: W. H. Beer, 1883.

Tanser, H. A. *Settlement of Negroes in Kent County.* Chatham, Ont.: Shephard, 1939.

Tise, Larry E. *Proslavery: A History of the Defense of Slavery in America, 1701–1840.* Athens: University Press of Georgia, 1987.

Torrey, Jesse. *A Portraiture of Domestic Slavery in the United States.* Ballston Spa, N.Y.: Author, 1818.

Trotti, Michael. "Freedmen and Enslaved Soil: A Case Study in Manumission, Migration, and Land," *Virginia Magazine of History and Biography* 104 (1996): 455–80.

Ullman, Victor. *Look to the North Star: A Life of William King.* Boston: Beacon Press, 1969.

U.S. War Department. *The War of the Rebellion: A Compilation of the Official Records of the Union and Confederate Armies.* 128 vols. Washington: Government Printing Office, 1880–1902.

Vincent, Stephen A. *Southern Seed, Northern Soil: African American Farm Communities in the Midwest, 1765–1900.* Bloomington: Indiana University Press, 1999.

Wade, Richard C. "The Negro in Cincinnati, 1800–30." *Journal of Negro History* 39 (1954): 9–51.

Walker, David. "Appeal to the Colored Citizens of the World." In *One Continual Cry,* edited by Herbert Aptheker. New York: Humanities Press, 1965.

Walker, James W. *A History of Blacks in Canada.* Quebec, Que.: Minister of State Multiculturalism, 1980.

Walker, Juliet E. K. *Free Frank: A Black Pioneer on the Antebellum Frontier.* Lexington: University Press of Kentucky, 1983.

Walton, Jonathan. "Blacks in Buxton and Chatham, Ontario 1830–1890." Ph.D. diss., Princeton University, 1979.

Ward, Samuel Ringgold. *Autobiography of a Fugitive Negro.* London, J. Snow, 1855; reprint, New York: Arno Press, 1968.

Watt, Hugh. *Thomas Chalmers and the Disruption.* New York: Nelson & Sons, 1943.

Wayne, Michael. "The Black Population of Canada West on the Eve of the Civil War." *Social History* 28 (1996): 465–85.

Williams, George. *History of Twelfth Baptist Church, Boston Massachusetts, from 1840–1874.* Boston: Twelfth Baptist Church, 1874.

Wilson, Carol. *Freedom at Risk: The Kidnapping of Free Blacks in America, 1780–1865.* Lexington: University Press of Kentucky, 1994.

Winks, Robin W. *The Blacks in Canada: A History.* New Haven, Conn.: Yale University Press, 1971.

———. *Canada and the United States: The Civil War Years.* Baltimore: Johns Hopkins University Press, 1960.

———. "The Canadian Negro: A Historical Assessment." *Journal of Negro History* 53, no. 3 (1968): 283–300.

———. "A History of Negro School Segregation in Nova Scotia and Ontario." *Canadian Historical Review* 52, no. 2 (1969): 164–91.

Yee, Shirley J. "Finding a Place: Mary Ann Shadd Cary and the Dilemmas of Black Migration to Canada, 1850–1870." *Frontiers* 18, no. 3 (1997): 1–16.

Zorn, Roman J. "Criminal Extradition Menaces the Canadian Haven for Fugitive Slaves, 1841–1861." *Canadian Historical Review* 38 (1957): 284–94.

Newspapers

British Anti-Slavery Reporter. London, England.

Chatham (Ont.) *Chronicle.*

Chatham (Ont.) *Evening Banner.*

Church.

Cincinnati Advertiser.

Cincinnati Gazette.

Coloured American. New York.

Detroit Tribune.

Ecclesiastical and Missionary Record. Toronto, Ont.

Examiner. Toronto, Ont.

Frederick Douglass' Paper. Rochester, N.Y.

Freedmen's Journal. New York.

Genius of Universal Emancipation. Mount Pleasant, Ohio.

Kent Advertiser. Chatham, Ont.

Liberator. Boston, Mass.

London Anti-Slavery Reporter.

National Anti-Slavery Standard. New York.

New York Age.

New York Tribune.

Pennsylvania Freeman. Philadelphia.

Pennsylvania Telegraph. Harrisburg.

Provincial Freeman. Windsor, Ont. [1853–1854]; Toronto, Ont. [1854–1855]; Chatham, Ont. [1855–1857].

Toronto Globe.

Voice of the Fugitive. Sandwich [now Windsor] (Ont.).

Index

SHARON A. ROGER HEPBURN is a professor of history at Radford University, Virginia. She has published articles in the *Michigan Historical Review* and the *American Nineteenth Century History* in addition to several reference books, including the *New Dictionary of National Biography* and the *Historical Encyclopedia of World Slavery*.

The University of Illinois Press
is a founding member of the
Association of American University Presses.

Composed in 10.5/13 Adobe Minion
with Meta display
by Celia Shapland
at the University of Illinois Press
Designed by Paula Newcomb
Manufactured by Thomson-Shore, Inc.

University of Illinois Press
1325 South Oak Street
Champaign, IL 61820-6903
www.press.uillinois.edu